ESSENTIAL ESSEX

ESSENTIAL ESSEX

CAROL TWINCH

First published in Great Britain in 2009 by The Breedon Books Publishing Company Limited, Breedon House, 3 The Parker Centre, Derby, DE21 4SZ.

This paperback edition published in Great Britain in 2013 by DB Publishing, an imprint of JMD Media Ltd

© Carol Twinch, 2009

All Rights Reserved. No part of this publication may be reproduced, stored in a retrieval system, or transmitted in any form, or by any means, electronic, mechanical, photocopying, recording or otherwise without the prior permission in writing of the copyright holders, nor be otherwise circulated in any form or binding or cover other than in which it is published and without a similar condition being imposed on the subsequent publisher.

A catalogue record for this book is available from the British Library.

ISBN 978-1-78091-389-6

Printed and bound in the UK by Copytech (UK) Ltd Peterborough

Contents

	INTRODUCTION	7
ONE	THIS AND THAT	9
TWO	COASTAL ESSEX	26
THREE	PARTICULAR TO ESSEX	45
FOUR	ARTISTIC ESSEX	70
FIVE	WHY IS IT CALLED THAT?	95
SIX	ESSEX PEOPLE	112
SEVEN	CHAPELS AND CHURCHES	133
EIGHT	EPITAPHS AND MEMORIALS	155
NINE	CUSTOMS AND CURIOSITIES	173
TEN	MISCELLANY	194
	BIBLIOGRAPHY	219

INTRODUCTION

The county of Essex has been described as a 'parallelogram of contrast' and 'a square, with a protuberance on the north east to the east of Colchester'. Thomas Wright wrote that 'the county of Essex is large, populous and fertile' and John Betjeman thought of it as 'a large square with two sides water, [with] a stronger contrast of beauty and ugliness than any southern English county'. Whichever way you look at it, Essex is renowned for its extremes, both of terrain and culture, from the industrial south-east border with London, to the intensive agriculture of the north, and the wild, mysterious and often treacherous coastline along its jigsaw encounter with the North Sea.

The beauty must be its coastline and countryside, but where is the ugliness? Such concepts are subjective. London Stansted, for example, is Britain's third busiest airport with 22.8 million passengers a year through its doors. Stansted is, at the very least, controversial and is somehow symptomatic of the conundrum of the proximity of Essex to London. Some regard it with pride and others with dismay: it all depends on where you are standing. The same goes for the industrial south, which provides names of international standing, such as Ford, Yardley, Courtauld, Crittall and Marconi. Some of its historic towns and villages hark back to pre-history, while others, like Harlow and Basildon, were created in answer to London's post-war housing needs. All have a place in the Essex story.

Essex has an overwhelming depth of history and almost every village has a story to tell. While some will rue the (obvious to them) many omissions, *Essential Essex* is intended as just that, a personal collection of things that reflect the county. Happily, Essex has such a wide diversity of people and culture that you do not need to have been born here to have an affiliation to the county or affection for it.

Since the five London boroughs of Barking and Dagenham, Havering, Newham, Redbridge and Waltham Forest were part of Essex until 1965, their history belongs to Essex and is therefore included.

Grateful thanks are extended to those who helped with local knowledge, especially John Barrow (for information relating to Bradfield Church), Pat Carver (of Burnham-on-Crouch), Colchester and Ipswich Museum Services, Jeffrey Deung, Essex Libraries, Joe Firman (Essex Moth Group), Greg Lansdowne (Essex Cricket Board), Susanne J. McClelland, Alan Mackley, Robert and Pearl Simper (for advice on traditional craft), Pat and Martin Spiro and Jill Goodwin. Thanks also to all my Essex cousins, my son for his recollections of his time at Writtle College and my daughter, who lived for a time in Walthamstow.

ONE
THIS AND THAT

The county of **Essex** is located north-east of London, bordered by Suffolk to the north with a small area adjacent to Cambridgeshire on the north-west edge, and Hertfordshire and Middlesex to the west. The southern boundary is the River Thames and Greater London, and eastward is the coastline with the North Sea. Its inland boundaries are marked by the rivers **Stour**, **Lea** and **Stort**. It has a defined border with Kent in the centre of the River **Thames**.

* The border with Suffolk runs down the centre of the River **Stour**, but dips south to touch the coast at **Mistley**.

* **Great Chishill** is on the stream called **Cumberton Brook**, which formed the ancient boundary between the old kingdoms of Mercia and Essex.

* The county covers an area of almost 1,500 square miles.

* The highest point in Essex is **Chrishall Common** at 482ft (147m) on the Cambridgeshire border.

* The highest church in Essex is St John the Baptist **Danbury**. It is sometimes called the Mariner's Beacon.

* The **triple point** (where the three geographical regions of Cambridgeshire, Essex and Hertfordshire meet) is close to Chrishall Common about a mile south of Great Chishill (in Cambridgeshire).

✸ The kingdom of **Essex** was formed in the sixth century by Saxon settlers whose rulers claimed descent from an obscure Saxon deity, **Seaxneat**.

✸ **Essex** takes its name from the Old English *East Seaxe* which referred to the land of the East Saxons. Traditionally, the kingdom was formed by **Aeswine** in AD 527 and occupied roughly the area it does today, together with parts of Hertfordshire and Middlesex. In the seventh century, London was included in the kingdom of Essex and was Aeswine's capital.

✸ The village of **Rickling** is said to mean 'Ricola's people' and to have been named for **Ricola of Kent**, one of the sixth-century founders of the kingdom of Essex. Palaeolithic and Neolithic remains have been found at **Quendon** and Rickling, suggesting that people having been living there for thousands of years.

✸ Ring ditches and banks to the south of Reed Island at **Lawford** are the remnants of a Neolithic religious site. Flint implements and Neolithic pottery have been found there.

✸ The county's coat of arms was granted on 15 July 1932 and consists of three **Saxon seaxe daggers** placed fessewise on a red background. The seaxe is a type of single-edged knife used as both tool and weapon and resembles the form of a scimitar. The same device is also used as the official logo of Essex County Council and appears on the county's road signs.

✸ **Clacton (Great Clacton**, **Clacton-on-Sea** and **Little Clacton**) is one of the earliest known occupied sites in Britain. Clactonian man arrived there at the beginning of the second glaciations, 475–450,000 years ago. Archaeological investigation points to Clacton having been an important and very early flint-working centre. As well as evidence of human activity, remains have been found of straight-tusked elephants, rhinoceros, the cave lion, horse, pig, bison, giant beaver and numerous smaller animals. Recent erosion along the Clacton channel at Cudmore Grove, **East**

Mersea revealed a range of fossil plants and animals from the Hoxnian age together with a collection of small vertebrates said to be the richest ever found in Britain.

※ **Prittlewell** is an area of **Southend-on-Sea**, and was originally settled some 10,000 years ago, during the Stone Age. Southend is at the south end of Prittlewell.

※ The largest **Iron Age** hill fort in Essex was found at Uphall Camp, **Ilford**.

※ Pre-historic, Iron Age and Roman material has been found at **West Bergholt**, indicating that the area has been continuously inhabited for thousands of years.

※ Several **Bronze Age** barrows occur in Essex, especially in the **Stour valley** and **Tendring**.

※ Late **Bronze Age** axe heads were found at **Dovercourt**.

※ During the 1980s an **Iron Age** funerary site at **Stanway** was found to contain the remains of eminent people interred around AD 43 in the final days of Iron Age Camulodunum (later Colchester), which was colonised by the invading Romans at around that time. The graves are those of a high-ranking or royal household, which contain artefacts that prove a contemporary trade with continental Europe on a massive scale. Originally discovered in the 1930s, archaeological excavations only began in earnest in 1987.

※ In 1996 a number of spectacular chambered burial sites were discovered at Stanway including the **Warrior's Grave** and the **Doctor's Grave**, which contained a remarkable gaming board (with glass counters set out as though a game was about to commence), a tea strainer containing Artemisia (a herbal remedy), rods likely to have been used for divining water, and a unique set of surgical instruments. The medical sets included scalpels, a surgical saw, needles, forceps and other 'basic sets of surgical tools' and turned out to be among the oldest surviving from anywhere in the ancient world.

✻ In 2008 a member of the excavation team from **Colchester Archaeological Trust** made the astounding announcement that archaeologists were considering the possibility that the Doctor's Grave was, in fact, that of an **Iron Age Druid**. A member of the **Colchester Archaeological Trust** said that it was hard to avoid the conclusion that the 'doctor' belonged 'to the stratum of late Iron Age society that comprised druids, diviners and healers'.

The Druids were members of an esoteric Celtic priesthood with a reputation for natural philosophy, healing and astronomy. Their opposition to Roman rule resulted in their very existence being terminated with ruthless ferocity by order of Emperor Claudius (AD 41–54). The grave of the Essex Druid is the only one of its kind ever found and reinforces the belief that the area known as Camulodunum was an important estate inhabited and farmed by members of the native **Catuvellaunian tribe**, the pre-Roman ruling class. The powerful Catuvellaunian tribe (whose lands extended into western Essex) and the **Trinovantes tribe** (who occupied most of present-day Essex and South Suffolk) were primarily farmers and lived in self-contained communities of varying sizes dotted throughout the countryside. Until the Romans built towns, public meeting places were restricted to fairs, markets, festival days or other public gatherings and there were no urban centres.

✻ **Camulodunum** took its name from *Camulos,* the Celtic god of war.

✻ There were two main areas of pre-Roman Camulodunum, **Sheepen** (where commerce and trade took place) and **Gosbecks** (which is thought to have been a high-status estate, possibly royal).

✻ The **Trinovantes tribe** were the first to enter into a treaty with Julius Caesar during his first invasion of Britain in 54 BC. It was thought that a treaty with Rome would ensure a certain degree of protection for the tribe, but it was not enough to prevent the **Catuvellaunian tribe** from moving eastwards in AD 10 to colonise Trinovantian land and effectively unite the two tribes. Julius Caesar gave jurisdiction to the Catuvellaunian king **Cunobelin** (died AD 40).

King Cunobelin (*Cymbeline* in Shakespeare's eponymous play) set up his court at **Camulodunum** (modern Colchester) and presided over a golden period of trade and progress lasting around 30 years. His kingdom stretched across the lands of both tribes and included an area south of Norfolk (home of the **Iceni tribe**). However, only three years after the death of Cunobelin the Roman Emperor **Claudius** (AD 41–54) marched on Camulodunum and made it the new Roman capital of Britain.

❋ Legend has it that **King Cunobelin** (or Coel) was the model for the nursery rhyme **Old King Cole** and that when he called for his pipe it was not to smoke (tobacco not reach England until 1585) but to play, it being a musical instrument with which to accompany 'the fiddlers three'.

❋ There is a **Cymbeline Way** and a **Cunobelin Way** in **Colchester**.

❋ A Roman gravel quarry in **Colchester** is still named 'King Cole's Kitchen'.

❋ A descendant of **King Cunobelin** was **Coel the Magnificent of Colchester** (died between AD 262 and 280) who was the father of **St Helen** (AD 230–320), Patron Saint of **Colchester**. Helen married the Roman General Constantius Chlorus in AD 270, but when he became emperor in 292 he divorced her. Her son, however, became Constantine the Great, the first Christian Emperor, and greatly honoured and respected her.

❋ **St Helen** is reputed to have journeyed to the Holy Land, where she discovered and divided the True Cross on which Christ was crucified. Her journey is immortalised in Colchester's mediaeval coat of arms, a copy of which can be seen in stained glass at the Old Library in the Town Hall. 'St Helena' is also found in stained glass next to Boadicea in the Town Hall in **Colchester**.

※ **The New Camulodunum**
When the Roman Emperor Claudius entered **Camulodunum** in AD 43, only three years after the death of **King Cunobelin**, it marked the end of the Celtic era in Essex. The presiding **Catuvellaunian tribe** were defeated and, although Claudius himself was only in Britain for 16 days, he established a Roman *colonia* at Camulodunum which was intended as the capital for the new province of Britain. He returned to Rome in triumph and bestowed the title *Britannicus* on his son.

Immediately the Romans set about establishing a legionary fortress close to the site of the old Celtic settlement. Towns were a new concept to the indigenous Britons, who lived on farms and in small rural communities, and the surviving Celts must have looked on in astonishment as a conglomerate of hostelries, shops and entertainment, along with public buildings, were built along streets that dissected one another. What was also alien was the imposing **Temple of Claudius**, started around AD 54. It was one of the most important and symbolic buildings in the *colonia* and the seat of the imperial cult and *concilium provinciae* (provincial council) for all Britain. The idea was to 'civilize' and subjugate the Britons, not only with military superiority, but also with Roman urbanity and by the means of efficient administration.

To demonstrate the status of the *colonia* town walls were also constructed, part of which can still be seen near the **Balkerne Gate**. The wall had six gates and between 12 and 24 towers. It took many years to complete and cost a great deal of money.

※ The **Colchester** town wall is the oldest in the country.

※ The **Colchester Vase** is one of the finest examples of Roman pottery found in Britain and can be seen at **Colchester Castle Museum** along with a magnificent Roman bronze statue of Mercury, gold coins of King Cunobelin and the **Colchester Sphinx**, which once formed part of an elaborate Roman tomb.

※ **The Boudiccan Revolt**
While the Trinovantian and Catuvellaunian tribes had perforce thrown their lot in with the Romans, the **Iceni tribe** of Suffolk and south Norfolk

still entertained the notion that the Romans could, and should, be driven out of Britain. In the winter of AD 60 a few Trinovantian rebels joined forces with the new queen of the Iceni, **Boudicca**, whose husband **King Prasutagas** had kept the Romans at bay by becoming a 'client king'.

In AD 54 Emperor Claudius died and the mood throughout the Empire changed under the tyrannical new emperor Nero, ripples of which were felt in the new British colony. When in AD 60 King Prasutagas died the Romans decided to incorporate the Iceni territory into the new province. The tribal lands were seized by the invaders and claimed as *agri captivi* (captured territory) and new taxes imposed. When she objected, Boudicca was publicly flogged and her two daughters raped. It was fight or surrender and the Iceni chose to fight.

Boudicca and her daughters began amassing an army from dissident tribesmen and marched south to the Roman *colonia*, enlisting disaffected Britons as they went. The *colonia* was only lightly defended that winter, Legion XX having been sent west to subdue the Welsh Druids.

After a two-day siege the Boudiccan troops burst into the town, manoeuvring the Romans into the Temple of Claudius, which they then tore down, slaughtering those within it, smashing pottery and setting fire to anything that would burn. They ransacked the shops and all but razed the *colonia* to the ground. Even today archaeologists are finding more evidence of the 'Boudiccan layer' of scorched earth and destruction.

The victorious sacking of the Temple complete, Boudicca set out to destroy the other Roman colonies at Londinium (London) and Verulamium (St Albans). But it was not to be. On hearing that Camulodunum had fallen, the Romans brought their campaign in Wales to an abrupt halt and, in the spring of AD 61, met and defeated the Iceni warriors. It was barely a contest: on one side was a disciplined Roman legion and on the other a ragtag army of native Britons, disorganised and with no war strategy beyond rebellion.

It is said that Boudicca and her daughters took poison rather than suffer further indignities at Roman hands, but their graves have never been discovered. The most popular theory is that they lie under platform eight at King's Cross railway station in London.

It was the end of tribal life for the native Britons. Roman rule was to endure until AD 450.

※ **City of Victory**
For many years after the Boudiccan revolt relations between the Romans and the native population were soured. Camulodunum became known as *Colonia Victricensis* (City of Victory), but never recovered its status and its importance began to slip away. Although it was in a good position strategically, on the River **Colne**, *Colonia Victricensis* did not have the advantages of the mighty River Thames. The Colne is lined with salt marsh and mud flats and is unsuitable for large ships. Goods had to be offloaded at **Fingringhoe** and taken upriver in smaller craft. Londinium gradually supplanted Colchester as the new capital of Britain.

Nevertheless, the Romans built a theatre at **Gosbecks** that could hold up to 5,000 people and was the largest in Britain. It was only discovered in 1950 and was excavated in 1967.

※ The Romans called **Chelmsford** *Caesaromagus*, the only British town with an imperial prefix.

※ **Chelmsford** has been the county town since at least the 13th century. It stands at the confluence of the rivers Chelmer and Can and derives its modern name from the former. Although it is in the heart of Essex, it is only 30 miles from London.

※ Boudicca, in her Victorian incarnation as **Boadicea**, appears in stained glass at the **Colchester Town Hall**. A modern aluminium sculpture of **Boudicca** by Jonathan Clarke (1999) can be seen on the roundabout near **North Station**.

※ **The King of Bling**
The only fully intact tomb of the early seventh century to be found in Britain is that at **Prittlewell**, just to the east of **Prittle Brook** in what was the original site of **Southend-on-Sea**. In October 2003 a piece of land lying between a railway line and a busy road was needed for a road-widening scheme. Archaeologists were called in to evaluate it as the nearby Prittlewell site had been known for more than 70 years and had yielded many treasures, including warrior graves containing spears and shields and several *seaxe*, the curved sword displayed on

the county's coat of arms. Evidence of settlement going back 10,000 years had been previously discovered, but no one was prepared for what the archaeologists uncovered in 2003. A wooden burial chamber was unearthed and found to contain an undisturbed tomb with a lavish collection of grave goods, obviously belonging to a Saxon nobleman or king. So much gold, silver and precious objects were revealed that he was immediately named **The King of Bling**. He had been laid to rest wearing a belt with a solid gold buckle, a gold-fringed tunic and gold coins from Paris. There were bronze vessels, a flagon and silver spoon from Byzantium (Constantinople), rare glass jars, a Coptic bowl from the eastern Mediterranean, and a folding stool associated with only kings and emperors. Artefacts from across the known world show that this was the burial place of a powerful ruler with links far beyond Prittlewell. Even the wooden bowls had beautifully decorated gilded mounts.

The status of the burial shows that the internee was a king or prince of early Christianity: there were several religious artefacts and gold, Latin-styled crosses. It is thought that the burial took place between AD 600 and 650 and it is the richest Anglo-Saxon find since the Sutton Hoo ship burial (1939). The Prittlewell tomb gives new and exciting insight into what was happening in Essex in the seventh century and shed light on what was previously known as the Dark Ages. Analysis of the finds will help historians understand the Saxon burial process and show how Christianity eventually emerged as the universal religion. Could the King of Bling be **King Sigeberht** (c.AD 630–40), said by the historian and theologian the Venerable Bede (673–735) to have brought Christianity back to Essex after a pagan lapse? Or is it **Saebert, King of the Saxons**, who was converted to Christianity in AD 604 and ruled until his death in 616?

The Prittlewell burial is an internationally significant discovery, not least because it would appear that all the objects remained where they had been placed on the day of the funeral.

❈ A Micro Anglo-Saxon Kingdom

The **Rodings** (or Roothings) is a cluster of eight parishes lying between **Ongar** and **Dunmow** and is the largest group of parishes in England to bear the same name. Roding is said to derive from 'the people of Hrotha', a Saxon ruler who settled the parishes before Christianity. They are: **Abbess** (held by the Abbess of **Barking**), **Aythorpe, Barwick, Beauchamp, Berners, High, Leaden, Margaret** and **White**. St Margaret takes its name from the church dedication and Leaden Roding was the first among the Rodings to be roofed with lead. White Roding gets its name from the colour of the church.

In the Domesday Book (1086) the eight parishes contained 16 manors. Until 1848 there was also **Murrell Roding**, a hamlet (now lost) with an ancient chapel that was converted into a pigeon house but demolished in 1870. A Roman road (and part of the B184) runs through the Rodings.

❋ Osyth, Saxon Queen and Saint

The Saxon nunnery founded by Osyth, wife of **King Sighere of the East Saxons** (*c.*664–83), is no longer visible but the name of its founder lives on in **St Osyth** (originally called Chich, meaning 'creek', and pronounced 'Tosey' by the locals). Only a 15th-century gatehouse of flint and stone flushwork, described by Norman Scarfe as 'probably the finest of the surviving monastic gatehouses of Essex and East Anglia', survives to mark the site of the 12th-century building.

Osyth came from the lost West Saxon tribe of the Hwiccas and her father betrothed her to Sighere in an effort to consolidate Christianity in Essex. She complied with her family's wishes and she and Sighere had a son, Offa, who became king of the East Saxons. Osyth, however, did not take kindly to married life and, having persuaded her husband to give her land at Chich, she set out to found a nunnery there and devote herself entirely to prayer. Unfortunately for Osyth, the nunnery was attacked by pirates, who beheaded her when she refused to commit idolatry or to renounce Christianity. Her legend is that she carried her severed head after death to a church some miles away, where she was buried. She was declared a saint and her body brought back to Chich for reinterment, where a shrine was dedicated to her.

Several stories are attributed to the cult of St Osyth, including reports of her haunting Nun's Wood, carrying her head under her arm. One of her emblems in religious art is a white stag. The story goes that at her wedding feast her husband Sighere caught sight of a white stag passing the window. Without a thought for his bride he called his men and rushed off in pursuit. Osyth, not unreasonably, decided that hunting was more important to Sighere than his marriage and vowed that she would retire to a nunnery.

❋ There are numerous representations of St Osyth in Essex churches including that at St Michael's **Kirby-le-Soken** in 1950s glass. There are two memorial windows at St Peter and St Paul, St Osyth. The Roman Catholic church at **Clacton-on-Sea** is dedicated to Our Lady of Light and St Osyth.

❋ **Edmund Ironside**

The year 1016 is an important date in Essex and English history as the **Battle of Assandun** took place at **Ashingdon-on-the-Crouch** on 18 October, the outcome of which sealed the fate of **Edmund Ironside** (980–1016) the last English king. The victorious Dane, **Cnut** (died 1035), was the youngest son of the King of Denmark, Sweyn Forkbeard, who had forced Edmund's father (King Ethelred the Unready) into exile. The two sons were left to fight for the English crown, Edmund defending the Saxon kingdom.

Edmund was only in his early twenties when forced to take command of the English forces resisting the Danish incursions along the East Coast. Before the final battle, the Danish troops were camped at **Canewdon** and it is recorded in the *Anglo-Saxon Chronicle* that Edmund was betrayed by Ealdorman Eadric who, at a critical moment, lost his nerve and fled the field. Edmund was defeated and, although there was a power-sharing agreement with Cnut, he died a few months later and his children were sent into exile in Hungary. Cnut was crowned King of England and ruled for some twenty years, ironically bringing a period of peace and prosperity to the nation that he and his father had so ruthlessly pillaged.

As might be expected, there have over the years been various challenges to the facts surrounding identification of the Assandun site (**Ashdon** is another contender) but none has, so far, offered incontrovertible evidence of an alternative location.

❋ There is a public house named **King Canute** on **Canvey Island**.

❋ **Anglo-Saxon Door**

In 2005 an extremely battered and ancient storeroom door at **Westminster Abbey** was identified as the oldest known door in Britain, dating from the 1050s. It is the country's only surviving **Anglo-Saxon door** and dendrochronological tests revealed ring patterns in the oak indicating that it was felled in the extensive woodland owned by the Abbey in Essex. A spokesman for Westminster Abbey said that the door belonged to the great abbey 'constructed by Edward the Confessor'. A single tree, felled between 1032 and 1064, was used for the door's five vertical planks.

❋ The Conquest

Because of its proximity to London and the coast, Essex was of prime importance to the Norman conquerors when, in 1066, **William of Normandy** (1027–1087) invaded England and claimed the throne. The famous encounter at the **Battle of Hastings** (1066) left **Harold Godwinson** (1022–66) dead and the Norman invaders victorious. Harold, son of the powerful Earl Godwin of Wessex, had a particular affection for **Waltham** and the Abbey Church of **Waltham Holy Cross**, which he had previously rebuilt on a magnificent scale, founding a college of secular canons there to serve in the church. Passing through Essex after his triumph at the Battle of Stamford Bridge he visited Waltham. He prayed at the altar and before leaving 'remained for some time prone on his face before the miraculous cross or Holy Crucifix there enshrined'. It was said that Harold had been given a sign by the Holy Rood not to engage the Normans in battle but he ignored it, just as he dismissed the soothsayers who prophesied the appearance of a comet in the skies as a bad omen.

Harold fell in battle, famously shot in the eye, and died soon afterwards. Folklore has it that he was brought back to Waltham and buried behind the Great Altar, though some think that William would not have allowed the body to be returned to Essex. Legends abound as to the fate of Harold's body, some saying that his mother offered William 'its weight in gold' and then ordered it to be buried in Sussex. Others suspect that Harold's mistress, and mother of his several children, identified the body on the battlefield and brought it back to Waltham Abbey.

- ❋ **Waltham Abbey** was the last abbey to be dissolved by Henry VIII. In 1540 most of the fabric was pulled down and only the nave left to serve as a parish church. A stone marks the supposed site of Harold's burial.

- ❋ The victorious William was extremely thorough in removing the previous ruling elite and Norman nobles quickly established themselves on land granted by the new king in return for their past allegiance. Over 90 landowners in Essex were dispossessed, their assets confiscated and lands and manors redistributed.

* One of the most ruthless and avaricious of the new Norman overlords was **Turold of Rochester**, the trusted ally of **Odo, Bishop of Bayeux** (the troublesome half-brother of William the Conqueror, who was dubbed 'the mitred plunderer'). He held lands for Bishop Odo all over England but was awarded Rochester as his base and ransacked much of Essex to pay for it. Odo commandeered 43 estates in Essex and Turold held sway over many of them. He acted as under-tenant at **Vange** and seized properties at **Barking Abbey**, **Fobbing** and **Thorrington**. Since it was Bishop Odo who commissioned and paid for the Bayeux Tapestry, it is likely that he intervened personally to make sure that his trusted Turold was one of the few on the Tapestry to be mentioned by name. Turold has been called the greatest land-grabber in Essex history, and is immortalised on the Tapestry holding a sword in one hand and an arrow in the other. That the Tapestry was begun in 1067, only one year after the invasion, shows a remarkable confidence in a lasting victory and a strong desire to commit the events to posterity as rapidly as possible. On the Tapestry, Bishop Odo is seen brandishing a club rather than a sword: it was acceptable for a priest to bludgeon someone to death but not to spear them, thereby spilling blood.

* Author, farmer and colour dye expert **Jill Goodwin** (born 1917) of **Kelvedon** provided dyed wool samples and plants for the restoration of the **Bayeux Tapestry**. Jill is author of *A Dyer's Manual* (1981) and was a founder member of the mid-Essex **Guild of Weavers, Spinners and Dyers**. She is a renowned authority on the use of woad and the eight other plants which yielded the original colours of the tapestry. In 1983–88, Jill produced 560 samples for what was a long-term restoration project.

* The Normans threw up motte and bailey castles quickly and cheaply to overawe the indigenous population. Among those remaining (often only in ruins or as mounds) are **Great Canfield**, **Pleshey**, **Ongar**, **Clavering**,

Walden, **Hadleigh** and **Rayleigh**. William gave **Colchester** 'and all its appurtenances' to Eudo Dapifer, a man with considerable holdings in Normandy who eventually owned around 65 manors in Eastern England. By the time Eudo died (1120) he had rebuilt Colchester Castle using bricks and dressed stone from the ruins of Roman Camulodunum, which has the largest Norman keep in Europe.

* **Barking** has a special place in Anglo-Norman history as it was in **Barking Abbey** that **William the Conqueror** lived while his own house – the Tower of London – was being built. It was to the Abbey, founded for Benedictine nuns in 675, that William brought the nucleus of kingship from both London and France and here the king held sway as the vanquished Saxons came to swear fealty to their new overlord.

* Having established himself as king, William wanted to know the extent and value of his new kingdom and sent his clerks out to make an inventory. Essex appears as **Exsessa** in Volume Two of the ***Little Domesday Book*** (LDB) which consists of 450 folios relating to Essex, Suffolk and Norfolk and is preserved at the Public Record Office at Kew. The entries for Essex are more detailed and unabridged than most of the other counties, but they are written more untidily and the assessments are given in 'hides' (one hide of land could measure between 60 and 100 acres), a system used for taxation outside the Danelaw areas of Norfolk and Suffolk. The *Victoria History of the County of Essex* (1903) suggests that this separates Essex 'from the historic kingdom of East Anglia and links it with the rest of Saxon England'.

* The LDB scribes began their survey in about 1085, at a time when Essex was a county of small villages and hamlets (around 440 are named) and there were only two towns – **Colchester** and **Maldon**. The Survey for Essex was written by more than one scribe on either side of leaves (or folios) of sheepskin (parchment).

* The LDB shows that there was a great interest in grape-growing among the Normans, with vineyards at **Ashdon**, **Belchamp**, **Debden**, **Great**

Waltham, Hedingham, Mundon, Rayleigh, Stambourne and Toppesfield (counted as one) and **Stebbing**. There is some dispute among historians as to whether, or not, the Normans introduced viticulture to England. One faction suggests that the vineyards were already there at the Conquest, having been planted in the time of Edward the Confessor, while another suggests that 'the culture of the vine' was a Norman import. However, the LDB was compiled only 20 years into the Norman occupation, making it more a portrait of Anglo-Saxon England than Anglo-Norman.

* Names of the new Norman landowners in the Essex LDB include Robert the Perverted (also known as Robert the Lascivious), Ralph the Haunted, Godwin Weakfeet, Roger God-save-Ladies and Humphrey Goldenbollocks.

* During excavations to restore **Rayleigh Mount** some rabbit bones were uncovered, now thought to date from around 1070 when **Sweyn of Essex** (who came over with the Norman invasion in 1066) built the castle. Could these be the oldest rabbit bones to have been found in Essex?

* The area of Norman Essex in the LDB roughly translates to the old county boundaries (before the 1832 and 1965 changes), with a few overlaps between parishes on the Essex-Suffolk border. **Toppesfield**, for instance, had some of its land surveyed in the Suffolk folios, but it subsequently remained in Essex. Although **Ballingdon** and **Brundon** appear in the LDB, both were moved to Suffolk as part of the Reform Act of 1832. They were then merged to become **Ballingdon-cum-Brundon**.

* **Chishill** (Great and Little) was in Essex until 1895 when it was moved to Cambridgeshire, and this may account for the variant spelling **Chrishall**. The church, however, remains in the **Diocese of Chelmsford**.

* **Heydon** was also in Essex until moved to Cambridgeshire in 1895 and **Haverhill** and **Kedlington** tipped into Suffolk.

❋ Magna Carta

The Essex Barons were among those who forced **King John** (1199–1216) to sign the **Magna Carta** (or Great Charter) in 1215, led by **Robert Fitzwalter**, 3rd Lord of **Little Dunmow** (died 1235), **Geoffrey de Mandeville**, Earl of Essex and Gloucester and **Robert de Vere**, Lord of **Hedingham** and Earl of Oxford. They were supported by **Richard de Mountfitchet** of **Stansted Mountfitchet** (whose sister was a former mistress of the king). Under pretext of pilgrimage, Cardinal Langton and the 25 Barons met at Bury St Edmunds (Suffolk) on St Edmund's Feast day, 20 November 1214, and swore at St Edmund's Altar that they would obtain from King John the ratification of the Magna Carta. The king signed the Magna Carta on 15 June 1215 at Runnymede.

Robert Fitzwalter was the son of **Walter Fitz Robert** of **Woodham Walter** (Fitz meaning son of) and had an eventful, if not entirely successful, military career and joined the Fifth Crusade (1217–21). It is thought that the famous clause in the Magna Carta prohibiting sentences of exile, except as the result of a lawful trial, refers directly to Fitzwalter, who was outlawed after being implicated in baronial insurrections.

❋ Myths and legends have grown up around Robert Fitzwalter's daughter **Matilda Fitzwalter,** who is reputed to have become Robin Hood's female companion, 'Maid Marian'.

❋ The Eve of Armada

It was in 1588 at **Tilbury** that Elizabeth I (1558–1603) made her rallying speech to the troops as they assembled to defend against the threatened invasion of the Spanish Armada (though it is now thought that the most likely place for the troops to assemble was **West Tilbury**). Her **Eve of Armada** address was made close to the ramparts looking out across the River Thames at the Artillery Fort built by her father, Henry VIII. 'By your concord in the camp' she said 'and your valour in the field, we shall shortly have a famous victory over those enemies of my God, of my Kingdom and of my People.'

The most apocryphal yet famous part of her address remains: 'Let tyrants fear…I know I have the body of a weak, feeble woman, but I have the heart of a king, and a king of England, too, and think foul scorn that any prince of Europe should dare to invade the borders of my realm.'

The Armada sent by Philip II of Spain comprised 138 vessels containing around 7,000 seamen and 17,000 soldiers. The English forces had 34 royal warships and 170 privately-owned ships, many drawn from Essex and Kent. The English won the day, aided, it is now thought, by their superior and more accurate guns.

TWO
COASTAL ESSEX

Few places in Essex are very far from water, be it the North Sea or one of the county's many rivers. The estuaries of the rivers Colne, Crouch, Blackwater and Thames, together with numerous creeks and friths, break up what is already a ragged, constantly changing meeting of land and water. Famously, the fretted shoreline is not one long glorious stretch of golden sand, as anyone who has witnessed the annual Maldon Mud Race can attest. The rivers are bordered by sticky mud that restricts navigation and challenges even the shallowest keel. An outgoing tide can reduce some of the river channels to little more than a trickle and even the most experienced sailors run aground on Essex mud.

Of course there are sandy beaches, like those at **Jaywick**, **Clacton**, **Leigh-on-Sea** and **Southend**, which have been attracting holidaymakers since the Victorian day-trippers began the fashion in the 1830s. Without them there would be no piers. 'The Pier is Southend, Southend is the Pier' wrote Sir John Betjeman.

The port of **Harwich** occupies a special place in the maritime history of the East Coast and has supplied men for English ships since Anglo-Saxon days. Being in the forefront of any European attack, its strategic importance was recognised by Henry VIII, while in the Elizabethan era Harwich men showed themselves to be exceptional nautical pioneers, venturing across the Atlantic to the New World.

In 1724 Daniel Defoe claimed Harwich harbour to be 'one of the best and securest in England' and 'able to receive the biggest ships'. He recalled that 'in the old Dutch War, great use has been made of the harbour and I have known there to have been 100 sail of Men of War and their attendants, and between three and four hundred sail of collier ships, all in this harbour at a time'. The moated **Harwich Redoubt Fort** was built in 1808 to defend Essex against a possible Napoleonic invasion.

Life along coastal Essex is a large proportion of what makes up the county's persona and such words as creek, reach, peninsula, channel, fleet, inlet and island are familiar in the county vernacular. It has been written about endlessly, notably by Sabine Baring Gould, Hervey Benham, Charles Dickens and Arthur Ransome. Comparing the Blackwater to other east coast rivers, Arnold Bennett said 'It is a noble stream, a true arm of the sea. Its moods are more various, its bank wilder (and) its atmospheric effects much grander'.

- The Essex seaboard is more than 300 miles long and comprises eight per cent of England's coastline.

- Over 80 per cent of the Essex coast is designated as a series of Sites of Special Scientific Interest (SSSI).

- **Mersea Island** is the most easterly permanently inhabited island in Great Britain. It covers an area of approximately five square miles. In *History of Essex* (1836) it was described as having 'a bold commanding coast towards the German ocean, but on the north-west and south it is low and flat, with a great extent of salt marshes'.

- **The Strood** is the only surviving **Anglo-Saxon** causeway in England and was built in the seventh century. It is half a mile long and links **Mersea Island** to mainland Essex as part of the B1025 Colchester Road. At high spring tides the road is liable to flooding and the island is cut off from the mainland for over an hour.

- **Samphire Island** (also known as Sunken Island) consists of 70 acres but is half submerged at high tide. It is mentioned in the Domesday Book (1086) and takes its name from the edible sea asparagus that grows there. In the 17th and 18th centuries the island was a popular haunt of smugglers, who used flat-bottomed boats to bring contraband ashore in the tiny creeks and inlets.

✳ Seahorses set up home in Dagenham

Early in 2008 it was discovered that a threatened and elusive species of seahorse (*Hippocampus hippocampus*) had been found in **Dagenham**, where the tides maintain the brackish water essential to their survival. Previously, the Zoological Society had only anecdotal evidence that seahorses had been found in estuary waters off **Southend** and regarded the return of the seahorse to the River Thames as a further sign of improvement in the Thames's water quality.

Seahorses had not been seen in the Thames since 1976 and as of April 2008 they were given legal protection against being killed or caught. Due to their use in traditional medicine, and because they are extremely difficult to breed in captivity, their initial discovery was kept secret for fear that they would be hunted by collectors.

✳ Subsequently a fishing trawler brought up a short-snouted seahorse at **Leigh-on-Sea**, which was handed over to the **Sealife Adventure Centre** at **Southend**-on-Sea and put in a 60-litre tank with two hermit crabs.

✳ Admiral in the 'Cups'

Admiral Horatio Nelson (1758–1805) stayed at the Three Cups inn (known as the 'Cups') when at **Harwich** and, on at least one occasion, with Lady Hamilton. It is no longer a hostelry but a plaque was erected on its former wall fronting Church Street by **The Harwich Society**.

In 1801 Nelson got into difficulties off Harwich when the wind made it impossible for his flagship HMS *Medusa* to take the usual channel. He remembered a certain Graham Spence, whom he knew to be a Marine Surveyor of the coastal waters off **Harwich**, and requested him to pilot the ship south. Spence duly piloted the *Medusa* safely through the deeper water. The new navigation channel was originally named the Nelson Channel, but Nelson himself said he wished it to be known as the **Medusa Channel**, by which name it is known today. The present **Medusa Buoy** is south of the channel, just off the **Naze Ledge**.

❉ Oldest Motor Lifeboat

The Maritime Museum at The Old Lifeboat House, **Walton-on-the-Naze**, is home to one of the oldest surviving motor lifeboats in the world, the *James Stevens No.14*.

❉ The Lost Arts of Seamanship

Hervey Benham (1910–87) was author of many well-known books on the Essex coast and sailed on the East Coast for most of his life. He also worked on local Essex newspapers for over 40 years and was Editor-in-Chief of Essex County Newspapers and editor of the *Essex County Standard*. He is most fondly remembered for his knowledge of, and affection for, the ships and seamen of the East Coast. He lived in **West Mersea**. In *Last Stronghold of Sail* (1986) he wrote 'ever since he had a rag to his back and an idea in his head, man must have been sailing about the Essex rivers for one purpose or another'. He documented the lost arts of seamanship, and chronicled stories of smacks and barges, which he felt strongly should be recorded before they were gone and forgotten. The sailing ship, in all guises whether for pleasure or for work, has stood 'pre-eminent in beauty among man's achievements, and here I include the humble little craft just as much as the deep-sea windjammers'.

Hervey Benham rued the decline of craft such as the Colchester cutter and the Thames Estuary sailing barges and wrote evocatively of them, dismissive of their memory 'queasily enshrined in a thousand calendars and Christmas cards'. Instead he enshrined in his writing what would otherwise have been lost, such as the story of *Exact*, the only barge ever built at **Colchester**. She was built on beer barrels in a field (which became part of Francis and Gilders' yard) and after her launch she would not go under Hythe Bridge 'so they cut an inch and a half off her stemhead, shoved her under, and with that unerring deftness of humour that is an Essex characteristic, named her *Exact*'.

Of the **Brightlingsea** smacks he recalled that most were built by Aldous, the most productive of all the builders of the Colchester fishing boats, 'every one, when built, was provided with a Bible and had a box to hold it built into the cabin'.

* The **Albert Sloman Library** at the **University of Essex** holds the **Hervey Benham Sound Archive** that comprises 1,400 tape cassettes covering many aspects of **Colchester** and Essex life.

* The late **Jane Benham MBE**, daughter of Hervey Benham, was instrumental in forming the **East Coast Sail Trust**, which owned and operated two school ships – the 200-ton *Sir Alan Herbert* (previously *Lady Jean)* and the ketch-rigged *Thalatta* (built 1908), which is currently undergoing a major refit at **St Osyth**. Jane Benham was an artist of some repute, painting the varying scenes and moods of the Essex coast in oils, acrylic and watercolours. She was awarded the MBE for her work with the East Coast Sail Trust. The *Sir Alan Herbert* was named in honour of a successful London barrister who had a special affection for Thames barges. However, when the Trust sold *Sir Alan Herbert* her new owner reinstated the original name, *Lady Jean*.

* Sir Alan Herbert was better known as A.P. Herbert (1890–1971), novelist, humorist, lyricist and law reform activist. He wrote eight novels, including *The Water Gypsies* (1930), which footnoted the author's fight for freedom of the Thames to non-commercial craft. *The Thames* (1966) explored the workings of the river in all its aspects.

* **Unexploded Bombs**

There are still hundreds of unexploded World War Two bombs (UXBs) scattered across Essex, many of them in coastal waters. For two years a team of researchers from site investigators Zetica trawled through Ministry of Defence papers and in 2008 compiled a 'bomb map'. Additional data was drawn from the Public Records Office and the German Luftwaffe. Because the Essex and Suffolk coastlines had been easy targets for German bombing raids a considerable number of UXBs remain undetected. Around 10 per cent of those known to have been dropped are likely 'not to have detonated'. The report pointed out that 'UXBs often entered the ground unnoticed at high velocity and penetrated to a depth of several metres'. Bombs were also dropped by German planes that ditched their loads before they reached the English Channel to save fuel on the return trip.

In the **Frinton** and **Walton** area alone there are estimated to be 229 UXBs, in the **Chelmsford** district 313 and around **Hornchurch** an estimated 1,272 devices lie undetected. Other areas affected are **Burnham on Crouch**, **Billericay**, **Brentwood**, **Canvey Island**, **Southend** and **Thurrock**.

- In May 2008 a UXB was found close to **Burnham on Crouch**. It was discovered about four miles out to sea by the crew of a small fishing boat, who lowered it back onto the seabed (as is the usual procedure) and notified the Royal Navy explosive ordnance disposal team. On 15 May a Royal Navy diver successfully detonated it. A spokesman for the Thames Coastguard said 'there were no problems and no casualties, except perhaps for some dead fish'.

- In March 2009 a World War Two parachute mine was exploded off St Peter's Flats, **Bradwell-on-Sea**. It was picked up off the seabed by a fisherman and its location marked. The area was cordoned off by the Essex Marine police and the device blown up by the Royal Navy.

- **'One of the most heart-warming movies ever made'**
The Snow Goose (1971), directed by Patrick Garland, was filmed on 'The Great Marsh' and other locations along the Essex coast. Starring Richard Harris (as the artist, Philip Rhayadar) and Jenny Agutter (as Fritha), the film won a Golden Globe award and nine other nominations. *The Snow Goose* was originally a short story written by Paul Gallico in 1940 and expanded into a novella entitled *The Snow Goose: A Story of Dunkirk* the following year. 'Philip Rhayadar' lives in an old lighthouse on the Essex marshes and cares for wild birds, including an injured snow goose. It was filmed for BBC television in 1971 and billed as 'one of the most heart-warming movies ever made'.

- **The Mistley Swans**
The swan colony of **Baltic Wharf** at **Mistley** is said to number around 5,000 birds, most of them White Mute although a few pairs of Black Swans add to the number. They can be found at different times of the day along the coast

between Mistley and **Manningtree** and were originally attracted to the spilt grain and waste malt on the quaysides when Mistley was a prosperous port and brewing centre. The colony is now maintained (controversially it must be said) by swan enthusiasts.

❋ Harwich Ferry Disaster

In April 1807 over 90 people died in the **Harwich Ferry Disaster** that took place off the beach at **Landguard Fort**. The regular ferry was too small to take all the waiting passengers and a local boat owner offered to take the whole party. As the boat left the beach it was hit by a strong gust of wind that caught the sails and capsized the vessel. Thomas Wright recorded that they had been put 'in a crazy vessel called a bug…she upset with 115 persons on board…on this melancholy occasion were drowned Captain Dawson and 73 soldiers, 13 women, 8 children and 3 soldiers'.

The Times reported that many who drowned were soldiers from a detachment of the 79th Highland Regiment on temporary duty at the Fort, then a small army encampment. The men had previously distinguished themselves in action in the British Egyptian Campaign (1801) under Sir Ralph Abercromby.

❋ The Naze Landmark

The **Naze Tower** at **Walton-on-the-Naze** is an 86-foot high octagonal unlit sea mark and was built in 1720 by the Elder Brothers of Trinity House. It is thought to be the only one of its kind in existence. Although unlit, the tower probably once had a beacon used as a marker for ships approaching **Harwich** at night or in fog. When it was built it was 500 yards from the cliff edge, but erosion has shrunk the distance to less than 200 yards.

During World War Two the Tower was requisitioned and a large radar scanner sited at the top.

❋ The First Non-sinkable Lifeboat

To the outside world, the inventor of the first non-sinkable lifeboat is a forgotten hero, but he is still celebrated in Essex. **Lionel Lukin** (1742–1834) of **Great Dunmow** had the idea for a shell-shaped boat with air bags round the gunwales and an additional steel keel. He called it the 'unimmergible' lifeboat. In 1742 he made a series of models and tried them out on the **Doctor's Pond** in Dunmow. Unfortunately for Lionel Lukin his original full-scale model was stolen and never retrieved. He died at Hythe in Kent an unsung hero.

✳ Oldest Fishery

The two hamlets of **East End** and **Church End**, now known as **Paglesham**, at the mouth of the River **Roach**, form one of Essex's oldest fishing villages. The Romans and the Normans were here, as were many native tribes before them. It was once famed for its oyster production and in the 18th and 19th centuries was the centre of extensive smuggling operations – both aspects represented on the Millennium village sign. It is now part of the **Roach Valley Conservation Zone**.

✳ Regina vs Dudley and Stephens

One of the most famous naval law cases of Victorian England concerned the yacht *Mignonette*, a 52ft cruiser built at **Brightlingsea** in 1867. In 1883 the *Mignonette* underwent a refit and became what was known in the trade as a 'bodge job'. Almost three tons of her ballast was carried externally on her keel and much of the woodwork was rotten. However, she was purchased by an Australian lawyer, John Henry Want, who arranged for a crew to sail her the 15,000 miles to Sydney. Tom Dudley was captain and he received £100 on commission with another £100 due on arrival in Australia. Dudley took on three crew – Edwin Stephens, Edmund Brooks and **Richard Parker** (an inexperienced cabin boy), the last two from Brightlingsea.

The *Mignonette* set sail in May 1884, intending to approach the Cape of Good Hope via Madeira and the Cape Verde islands. The voyage was difficult and the *Mignonette* did not ride the rough seas with anything like ease. They crossed the Equator on 17 June, the weather still unrelenting and the yacht barely able to maintain her course. On 5 July a gale blew up around 1,600 miles north-west of the Cape, causing a huge wave to break over the *Mignonette*. Captain Tom Dudley realised that the yacht was doomed and ordered the crew into the lifeboat. Unfortunately the lifeboat was in just as poor a state as the yacht and they had only a short time to make it seaworthy before abandoning ship. Within minutes of being struck the yacht *Mignonette* sank. The crew managed to salvage a few navigational instruments, some tins of food and a water cask.

Cast adrift, they realised that they had lost the water cask and they had only two tins of food (which turned out to be turnips). On the first night they had to fight off a shark with their oars, but a few days later they managed to haul a turtle on board, which kept them going for several days. However, there was no rain and they dared not drink the seawater, knowing it to be fatal. On or about the 23 July, Captain Dudley and his crew were in a poor state and young Richard Parker was delirious, having succumbed to drinking seawater. In such circumstances it was natural that they should consider invoking the Custom of the Sea, which concerned survival cannibalism. Stranded sailors would draw lots to see who would be killed and eaten so that the rest could live. Dudley and Stephens reasoned that since the cabin boy was almost dead, he should be sacrificed. By mutual consent they slit the cabin boy's throat and drank his blood and then fed on his body.

Miraculously, they were eventually sighted by a German sailing barque and taken to Falmouth (Cornwall). The three assumed that what they had done was legal and that they were therefore protected by 'common law'. In their depositions they made no secret of how Richard Parker had died. The police, however, took a different view and all three were arrested for 'murder on the high seas'. Confident that the judge would dismiss the charges, the men were not unduly concerned and they pleaded 'not guilty'. The press delighted in the proceedings and, as the months dragged on, and the case became more and more convoluted, it became a *cause célèbre* in Victorian England. After a sensational trial Captain Dudley and Edwin Stephens (Edmund Brooks was held not to have been implicated) were convicted and sentenced to death, later commuted to six months' imprisonment.

* In *Down Tops'l*, Hervey Benham records hearing from Jim Frost of **Brightlingsea** who considered himself lucky, since he and his brother were originally to have sailed on the *Mignonette* as crew. However, Jim's brother was not able to go so '[Jim] also was prevented, and his place was taken by a nineteen-year-old lad named Richard Parker'.

✳ Wild Mignonette (*Reseda lutea*) grows in the creeks near **Brightlingsea**.

✳ Overthrown by the Sea
On a prebendal stall in St Paul's Cathedral **London** is a reminder of the coastal erosion that has been affecting the Essex coast for hundreds of years. Estates of **Old Walton** that once belonged to the Cathedral were washed into the sea in the 18th century and instead of the customary name of the manor over the stall are found the Latin words *Prebenda Consumpta per Mare* (property overthrown or consumed by the sea).

✳ Named for Cathedral
The parish of **Belchamp St Paul** is so called because the manor was granted in 930 to the Dean and Chapter of St Paul's Cathedral who, Pevsner notes, 'ensured that the church was of some consequence'.

✳ Robotic Fish
In 2009 **Essex University** announced a £2.5 million share in the development of a robotic fish, equipped with chemical sensors and capable of analysing pollution. The autonomous robot will be a tool in the armoury of port authorities in their bid to increase their monitoring of ship-source pollution and other types of 'harmful contaminants and pollutants from underwater pipelines'. The Essex team is being led by Professor Huosheng Hu from the university's School of Computer Science and Electronic Engineering. The research, named the 'SHOAL' project, is a world first and is backed by the European Union. It is hoped that a 'team' of robotic fish will search and analyse chemicals on the surface of the water (for example, oil) plus others that have dissolved in deeper water.

✳ The Yantlet Line
An obelisk on the mud off **Westcliff-on-Sea** is known as the **Crowstone** and is an ancient boundary with London. It was erected in 1834 to replace the original and smaller stone of 1755, which was moved to Priory Park, **Southend**. The line between the Crowstone and the London Stone at Yantlet Creek marked the end of the City of London's authority over the Thames and is known as the **Yantlet Line**.

❋ The Essex Piers

There are four piers off the Essex coast at **Clacton-on-Sea**, **Harwich**, **Southend-on-Sea** and **Walton-on-the-Naze**.

Clacton Pier was built originally in 1871 and designed as a landing pier first for goods and then passengers. No one envisaged that once the railways were built Clacton would become a popular destination for London day-trippers. They did not approach the pier from the water, but from the town, and they quickly discovered the joys of strolling along the pier for its own sake in what became a quintessentially Victorian fashion of 'taking the air' for its reputedly therapeutic effects.

In 1893 the old wooden pier was extended, with a pitch pine pier head and a Regency-style pavilion that offered entertainment and refreshment. Over the years other additions and improvements were made, including a roller coaster and the Crystal Casino. During World War Two, however, the pier was out of bounds and some of its amusements were demolished. After the war it resumed its old life until the public changed its holiday habits and trips to Spain took over from a stroll along Clacton Pier. In the 1970s it sustained both fire and storm damage, but it has lately enjoyed a renaissance and once more attracts day-trippers and holidaymakers.

The **Ha'penny Pier** at **Harwich** was once twice as long and was opened in July 1845. It was so named as an old ha'penny (or halfpenny) was the amount of levy per person payable to the Harwich Company. The Victorian ticket office still stands in front of the Ha'penny Pier Hotel.

The longest pier on the Thames, and indeed the longest pleasure pier in the world, is **Southend Pier**, 7,080ft (2,158m) long. The original wooden pier was built in 1830 and passengers were transported along it by a horse shod with leather shoes and carriages for two or three passengers.

In 1889 it was bought by the Council for £10,000. They renovated it and replaced the wood with iron, in response to the increasing number of visitors. Further extensions in 1929 gave the pier its present record-breaking length. Trains have long since replaced the horse carriages and run every 30 minutes. Dreadful fire damage has been caused to the pier during the 20th century, first in 1959 (when the pavilion was destroyed), again in 1976, and in the mid-1990s the ten-pin bowling alley went up in smoke. In 1986 a freighter cut clean through the pier and wrecked the RNLI station.

At 2,600ft (792m) in length, **Walton-on-the-Naze** is the third-longest pier in the British Isles after Southend and Southport (Lancashire). Built in 1830, it began with only 330ft, but a new pier was constructed in 1895 to cope with its extended usage and day-trippers. Walton pier still provides year-round family entertainment in the tradition of English seaside piers over the last 200 years. With over 30 different rides it is the largest undercover funfair in East Anglia.

※ **Lost Light Railway**
A few remains of **Tollesbury Pier** can still be seen on the edge of the River **Blackwater**. Only a few wooden piles survive from the pier, opened in 1907 at a time when it was hoped that Tollesbury would emulate **Clacton-on-Sea** in terms of day-trippers who would arrive on the Kelvedon, Tiptree & Tollesbury Light Railway (of which only a small section of the tracks can still be found).

※ **Shoebury Lookout**
Shoeburyness has two beaches, **East Beach** and **Shoebury Common Beach** (sometimes known as West Beach). The Common Beach is famous for its array of **beach huts** strung along the promenade and the beach.

※ The **Shoebury Coastguard Tower** is operated by the Maritime and Coastguard Agency and stands at the eastern end of **Common Beach**. The Tower monitors shipping traffic in the **Yantlet Channel** and keeps an ear out for distress calls in what is one of the busiest estuaries in the world.

※ Between 1894 and 1933 **Shoeburyness** was an urban district of Essex. In 1933 it became part of the county borough of **Southend-on-Sea**.

※ **'Spirit of the Age'**
In *Last Stronghold of Sail* (1986), Hervey Benham called the **Chelmer and Blackwater Navigation Canal** the 'epitome of the commercial spirit of the age'. Designed by John Rennie between 1793 and 1797, it links **Chelmsford** with the River Blackwater at the **Heybridge Basin**. The canal cost £50,000 and stretches 14 miles from Springfield Wharf to Heybridge with 12 locks

on the way. 'Within the locks all is as tranquil as a lady's boudoir, the unruffled water the mirror' wrote Hervey Benham poetically in 1986. Huge tonnages of coal and other goods were transported along the canal, although its heyday was not as long as was envisaged or predicted. In common with many such schemes it suffered commercially from the introduction of the railways in the 1850s. However, freight was carried right up until 1972 and it is now used by pleasure craft. Although maintained by Essex Waterways, it is still owned by the original company of the Proprietors of the Chelmer and Blackwater Navigation Limited.

❋ Siberian Visitors

Each autumn some 4,500 Brent Geese travel 2,500 miles from Siberia to feed on the eel grass found in the mudflats of **Leigh-on-Sea**.

❋ Essex Islands

Essex has more islands within its boundary than any other English county – 30 or 40 depending on the definition and the tide! The three largest are **Canvey**, **Foulness** and **Mersea**, followed closely by **Wallasea**. Foulness is the largest of them all and is the fourth largest island by area off the English coast. Canvey is the fourth most highly populated island in English waters.

Offshore islands include **Bridgemarsh**, **Cobmarsh**, **Havengore**, **Horsey**, **Lower Horse**, **Osea**, **Pitsea Hall**, **Skippers** and **Two Tree**.

❋ The Dickens Connection

One of England's most famous novelists, **Charles Dickens** (1812–70) spent much of his time in Essex and set many of his best-known works along the coast. The weatherboarded Lobster Smack Inn (known locally as the Lobby) on **Canvey Island** is mentioned in *Great Expectations* (1860–61) as Sluice House. It is the oldest building on the island and was also once known as the World's End. In the novel, Pip knows the sluice well and can find his way about the marshes on the darkest night. He is told 'if you are not afraid to come to the old marshes tonight or tomorrow night at nine, and to come to the little sluice-house by the limekiln'.

Dickens wrote about Canvey Island in *Dictionary of the Thames from Oxford to the Nore* (1880) and would have known **Holehaven Creek**, which once offered shelter for vessels as a stopping-off point. It was just below here that Pip rowed against the tide so that 'we should then be well in those long reaches below Gravesend, between Kent and Essex, where the river is broad and solitary, where the water-side inhabitants are very few, and where lone public-houses are scattered here and there'.

❋ The BBC adaptation of *Great Expectations* was filmed at **Cricksea Place Manor**.

❋ Bare Knuckle Fight

The Lobster Smack Inn on **Canvey Island** (known locally as the Lobby) saw many bare-knuckle fights in the 1850s, but few as dramatic as that between Tom 'The Brighton Boy' Sayers (1826–65) and Aaron Jones on 6 January 1857. The fight lasted for three hours and 65 rounds, and was finally declared a draw when it became too dark to see. Sayers won at the rematch a month later in London.

Sometimes the matches were between local families, the best known being that between champion Ben Court and Nat Langham. The fight arose from a family feud and Court took Langham to 60 rounds in September 1853. Langham was knocked down 59 times during the match and due, it is said, to his sportsmanship Court agreed to settle their differences with a handshake.

❋ Dutch Cottage Museum

Two small octagonal thatched Dutch Cottages on **Canvey Island** are a reminder of the 17th century when water engineer **Joas Croppenburgh**, a Dutchman with a haberdashery company in London, agreed to finance the famous drainage engineer, **Sir Cornelius Vermuyden** (1590–1677) to reclaim 3,600 acres of land on the island. One of the cottages is now the **Dutch Cottage Museum**.

A commission to repair the sea wall at **Dagenham** was the first that Vermuyden undertook in England, but he and Croppenburgh later agreed the massive reclamation project with the island's chief landowner, Sir Henry Appleton, in 1623. Croppenburgh undertook to do the drainage at his own expense in return for a third of the reclaimed land. He brought over a crew of Dutch workers and a small wooden chapel was built for their use.

However, it was ironically destroyed by part of the Dutch fleet in 1667 when England and Holland were at war. A raiding party came up the Thames and burnt it to the ground.

* A foundation school on **Canvey Island** is named the **Cornelius Vermuyden School and Arts College**.

* The motto on the **Canvey Island** coat of arms is *Ex Mare Dei Gratia* (From the sea by the grace of God).

* In 1690 there was severe flooding at **Vange** (south of **Basildon**) and another Dutch merchant and water engineer, **Cornelius Vandenanker**, was called in to manage the excess water. Vandenanker began his task by transporting tons of chalk from quarries at **Grays** and constructed three walls built inside one another for extra strength. Vandenanker's wife died in 1692 and was buried in **Downham Church**.

* **According to Tide**
Osea Island has a letter box where the 'Time of Next Collection' is indicated as 'According to Tide'.

* *Mi Amigo* **Runs Aground**
On 20 January 1966 a Force 8 storm caused the Radio Caroline MV *Mi Amigo* to break free from the swivel rope controlling the three anchors. Unknown to the crew and 'pirate' broadcasters, who had closed down for the night, the ship began to drift towards the Essex coast. It was snowing but the **Walton Coastguard** saw her adrift and attempted to contact the ship, without success. By the time help arrived *Mi Amigo* had run aground at **Holland Haven** (off **Frinton-on-Sea**). The last man hoisted to safety was the DJ Tony Blackburn, who was winched off by the Thames coastguard with the use of a breeches buoy. Everyone was rescued unharmed, but as day broke it became obvious how lucky the ship was, having gone aground between two groynes.

The following day a tug tried to pull her free but after the lines broke the tug's Captain decided to try a technique known as 'kedging', which proved successful, and the *Mi Amigo* was secured offshore. She was taken to Holland for repairs, during which time *Cheeta II* took over the Caroline South transmission. *Mi Amigo* returned in April to continue transmission.

Radio Caroline began broadcasting on Easter Sunday 1964 from the MV *Fredericia* anchored in international waters off the Essex-Suffolk coast. Radio Caroline was the sole 'pirate' to defy the Marine Broadcasting Offences Act (1967), which made it illegal to advertise or supply offshore radio from the United Kingdom. Eventually the *Fredericia* went to the Isle of Man and became Radio Caroline North and the *Mi Amigo* became Radio Caroline South. Both ships were forced off the air in 1968, though Radio Caroline was relaunched in 1972 anchored off the Dutch coast. It was estimated that, during the 1970s, 25 million people listened to pirate radio stations daily. In the early days of Radio Caroline car drivers lined up at Frinton and Clacton seafronts, flashing their headlights out to sea in support of the broadcasters.

❋ The present Radio Caroline ship, the *Ross Revenge*, is currently operating from **Tilbury Docks**.

❋ Captain Newport

In 1607 three English ships anchored off Chesapeake Bay bringing the first settlers of what became Jamestown (named for James I) in the Virginia Colony. It became the first permanent English settlement in North America. In overall command was **Captain Christopher Newport** (1561–1618) of **Harwich**. His vessel was the *Susan Constant*, the others being *Godspeed* and *Discovery*.

Born into the Elizabethan age of maritime and navigational advancement, Captain Newport was a highly successful sailor and an adventurer worthy of the name. He sailed in his youth with Sir Francis Drake on the attack on the Spanish fleet at Cadiz and took part in the defeat of the Spanish Armada (1588). After some years as a privateer, raiding Spanish ships in the Caribbean, he took command of the *Susan Constant* and spent the next few years sailing the Atlantic. He made five trips to America, taking supplies and passengers, and in 1609 became Captain of a new ship, *Sea Venture*. The *Sea Venture* lost its caulking in a hurricane off

Bermuda and sank with the loss of many crew and passengers. Using reclaimed timbers from the stricken ship, together with some local wood, Captain Newport and the survivors managed to build two ships that eventually took them to Jamestown.

Captain Newport's last voyage to Jamestown was in 1611, after which he began sailing for the British East India Company. He died in Java in 1618.

✻ Captain of the *Mayflower*

Ship owner and mariner **Captain Christopher Jones** (1570–1622, also of **Harwich**, has a unique place in 17th-century maritime history and has, perhaps, stolen the thunder of earlier trans-Atlantic mariners. Captain Jones was Master and part-owner of the *Mayflower,* the sailing ship that transported the English separatists on the **Mayflower Expedition (1620–1621)** to establish the Plymouth Colony in the New World. Captain Jones lived in Kings Head Street in Harwich and inherited a part share in his father's ship, *Mary Fortune*. He married his first wife at St Nicholas's church in 1593, but when she died in 1603 he married Josian (née Thompson) Gray, widow of Richard Gray of **Great Oakley**. The late Mr Gray had had considerable shipping interests, his family having been sailors in the Armada fleet and some reputed to have been treasure hunters in the Indies. Thus Captain and Mrs Jones between them were prominent members of Harwich society and had interests far beyond Essex.

Captain Jones prospered and used some of the profits from trading with Europe to build his own ships, one of which was named *Josian* after his wife. It is thought that his first connection with the *Mayflower* was confirmed in 1611 when he was involved in a salvage claim and is identified as 'Captain Jones of Harwich, Master of the *Mayflower* of the same place'. In the same year he, Josian and their children moved to Rotherhithe (Kent).

When the *Mayflower* set sail from Plymouth in September 1620 there were 102 passengers on board, 41 religious pilgrims and 61 adventurers. Among them were several from Essex including Richard Gardiner and John Alden from Harwich (a cooper by trade who was allegedly the first to step ashore), John Crakston and his son from **Colchester**, and Solomon Prower from **Billericay**. Christopher and Marie Martin from **Great Burstead** joined the ship at **Leigh**.

The voyage was successful, *Mayflower* arriving at what is now known as Provincetown Harbour in November 1620. But the settlers were to endure a series of mishaps, due to heavy rains and attacks by native Indians, before attempts could be made to establish a new colony. It was not until March 1621 that Captain Jones was able to land the last of the passengers. Many died during the first winter and several of the crew became ill. However, on 5 April the *Mayflower* set sail for England. Unlike the outward journey the return was storm-free and they took only a month to return to England. Captain Jones died the following year and was buried at St Mary's Rotherhithe. The *Mayflower*, it is believed, ended her days in a breaker's yard a few years later.

❈ The home of Captain Jones's first wife, **Sarah Twitt** (died 1603), became the Alma Inn, Kings Head Street, **Harwich**.

❈ **Secret Water**
Walton Backwaters, **Hamford Water** and **Walton-on-the-Naze** are among the parts of the Essex coast immortalised in the books of **Arthur Ransome** (1884–1967). Ransome's books are widely recognised as classics among children's seafaring literature. Having made his name with *Swallows and Amazons* (1930), set in the Lake District, he and his wife Evgenia moved to East Anglia in the hope that the sea air would improve Arthur's health. They spent much of their time sailing the waterways of Essex and Suffolk and set *Secret Water*, the sequel to *We Didn't Mean to Go to Sea*, in Hamford Water.

❈ **Cowes of the East Coast**
At the end of August **Burnham-on-Crouch** becomes the 'Cowes of the East Coast' when craft converge there for **Burnham Week**, arguably the longest-running annual yacht regatta on mainland Britain. Burnham Week used to be considered the last date in the sailing calendar, yachts having made their way to Burnham at the end of the season for winter 'laying up'. It started in 1893 and benefited hugely from the advent of a branch railway line in 1889, which brought visitors to Burnham as never before. The line later escaped closure because of its usefulness in supplying the nearby **Bradwell** nuclear power station. It was electrified in the 1980s and still has a direct service to London Liverpool Street.

- The permanent population of Burnham is 8,000, but there are nine public houses and over 20 eating establishments, which cater for the swell of summer visitors.

- There are four sailing clubs in Burnham – the Burnham Sailing Club, the Crouch Yacht Club, the Royal Burnham Yacht Club and the Royal Corinthian Yacht Club. The Princess Royal is patron of the Royal Corinthian YC, while the Duke of Edinburgh is patron of the Royal Burnham YC.

- The **Royal Corinthian Yacht Club** is a fine example of 1930s architecture and is a distinctively broad, white building with long bands of windows constructed so that it juts out over the shoreline. The end windows are stair lights and are set at a 45-degree angle. It was built by Joseph Emberton and in 1931 won the Architecture Medal awarded by the Royal Institute of British Architects (RIBA). It is regarded as an early example of what became known as International Modernism, of which Emberton was an exponent.

THREE
PARTICULAR TO ESSEX

All manner of people, events and geographical aspects have, over the centuries, made Essex what it is today. Yet even now, when the same national department stores are on all the high streets, and there is a universality to everyday life, some things are still special to the county. The flower named Bardfield Oxlip is unique, as is the Fyfield Pea. The Essex terret is the county's own version of the corn dolly, and where else would you find candied eringo? There is even a butterfly called the Essex Skipper and a moth named the Essex Emerald. Nowhere else has Bronze Age red hills, together with its own pig, apples and an internationally renowned jam factory. Here is a glimpse of a few things that remain particular to Essex.

✻ The Essex Pig

The **Essex Pig** is officially extinct and is so rare that it is not even recognised by the Rare Breeds Trust. However, it is currently making something of a comeback which, if successful, will be the first time a breed has been reintroduced after being classed as extinct. The pig has a black head and neck with a clearly defined belt of white round the shoulders, extending down to the front legs. The rest of the body is black except for the tip of the tail.

It is believed that the ancestors of the 'Essex' once foraged the huge Anglo-Saxon woodlands of Essex, including **Epping Forest**. In the 1840s, when there was a fashion for English stock breeders to improve and refine the native breeds, **Lord Western of Rivenhall** brought some Neapolitan pigs from Italy to Essex for just such a purpose. One of his tenants, William Fisher Hobbs of **Boxted Lodge**, eventually bred the Improved Essex to great success. In 1840, a boar and sow from the Fisher Hobbs herd both won first prize in their respective classes and he began exporting the Essex Pig to America.

The breed continued to flourish until the 1950s when it lost ground to the more popular white breeds and was combined with the Wessex Saddleback to form the British Saddleback. By 1967 the Essex Pig was believed to have died out, until it was discovered that one farmer, John Crowshaw, still had a herd of pure-bred Essex. A small band of enthusiasts set about reviving the old breed. In 1997, 30 years after it had been officially declared extinct, the Essex Pig Society was formed and a breeding programme began.

* When **Jimmy Doherty**, of television's ***Jimmy's Farm***, began farming he took an interest in the Essex Pig and acquired some stock from John Crowshaw. Jimmy's Farm, on the Essex-Suffolk border, is now the home of the Essex Pig Company.

* Early in 2008 an Essex sow named Suzy arrived at **Colchester Zoo** from Jimmy's Farm and gave birth to nine piglets. Suzy returned to Jimmy's Farm, but the zoo now has two gilts (young females) on show. The zoo is helping to educate visitors about the importance of saving domestic species and spreading the word about the plight of the Essex pig.

* **The County Flower**

The traditional county flower of Essex is the **cowslip** (*Primula veris*), known locally as the Paigle or Peggle. It is mentioned in the writings of Samuel Bensusan, C.H. Warren and Culpeper, who says that cowslips 'strengthen the brain and nerves, and remedy palsies'.

The cowslip is also known as Herb Peter, St Peter having dropped the keys to the Gates of Heaven wherever the cowslip (said to resemble a bunch of keys) grows.

* The **cowslip** is depicted on the Millennium village sign at **Paglesham**.

* **The Bardfield Oxlip**

At a place where Essex, Suffolk and Cambridgeshire meet the **Bardfield Oxlip** (*Primula elatior*) is found in the meadowlands of **Great Bardfield**.

Here they once grew in profusion 'by thousands in the meadows…in one instance a meadow of about two acres is entirely covered by them, being a very mass of yellow bloom'. After a decline in numbers a community planting scheme of 3,000 oxlip plants took place in 2008 at **Piper's Meadow** in Great Bardfield next to the River **Pant**. The plants were grown by **Writtle College** from seeds taken from the few remaining plants found in the village in 2007. The Bardfield Oxlip has long been prized as a local treasure: it appears in the village coat of arms and on a plaque at the Town Hall.

❋ The Essex Sun Dawg

A **sun dawg** (dog) is the Essex name for a rarely seen weather phenomenon resembling the end of a rainbow appearing near the sun. In *Last Stronghold of Sail*, Hervey Benham writes that 'much of the coast's weather lore has become understood by the scientists and "met men" but today the oldest hand gives up pacing his decks looking for "sun dawgs" in order to go below and turn on the BBC forecast'.

❋ An Old Essex Word

Harve is an old Essex word for an allotment, or small enclosed piece of land near the house. The antiquary Thomas Wright (1810–1877), in his *Dictionary of Obsolete and Provincial English* (1857) gave an additional meaning as 'haw' (fruit of the hawthorn hedge). Thomas Wright wrote extensively about the history and topography of Essex and *A Glossary of the Essex Dialect* says it is used only in north Essex.

❋ So who's a grockle, then?

A **grockle** is an Essex word for a modern tourist. Although it is not found historically in any part of the county, it does occur in other parts of contemporary Britain and is said to mean 'a person who visits the British seaside', 'holiday maker' or just a visitor from 'out of town'. The word was popularised in the film *The System* (1962), which was filmed in Devon where the word is also found.

❋ The Essex Emerald

The **Essex Emerald moth** is now considered to be extinct as a British species. Joe Firmin, chairman of the **Essex Lepidoptera Panel**, writes that 'it was confined to salt marsh areas on the Essex coast, mainly on the estuaries of the rivers **Crouch** and **Thames** with a long-time colony along the north Kent coast'.

The Essex Emerald is a beautiful pale green moth and is the only moth to bear the Essex prefix. An attempt was made to save it in the 1990s with a captive breeding programme from the last surviving wild moths, but it failed due to genetic weaknesses caused by in-breeding. It suffers from the increasing rarity of its main food plant, the sea wormwood. The species is known in Europe, where there has also been a serious dip in numbers. Mr Firman thinks that it is just possible that some Essex Emeralds may have survived in remote creeks 'as it is difficult to check every part of this vast area of tidal creeks and mosaic of marshes'.

❋ **Essex Skipper**
Having been first recorded in Germany in 1808, this small butterfly, the **Essex Skipper** (*Thymelicus lineola*), turned up at **St Osyth** in 1889. It is distinguished by the glossy black undersides at the ends of the antennae, described as if 'the tips have been pressed into a black ink pad to take their prints'. It is closely related to the Small Skipper, which flies at the same time (in July and August) and shares the same grassy habitat. It has the distinction of showing a greater increase in breeding range than any other species of butterfly. It is now found over a wide area of south-east England in grassy places, its larvae feeding on various species of grasses.

❋ **Skipper's Island** is home to the Essex Skipper and was once owned by the late Fred Williams, a well-known naturalist and an authority on butterflies and moths. He first acquired it in the mid-1950s and encouraged members of the **Essex Field Club** (founded 1880) to carry out wildlife surveys. Mr Williams gave the 219-acre island to the **Essex Wildlife Trust**.

❋ **Watch over Essex**
The kestrel was adopted as the symbol of the **Essex Naturalists' Trust**, whose motto 'Watch over Essex' is intended as a reminder that the Trust also acts as a watchdog, seeking out and challenging threats to the county's wildlife.

❋ The Essex Terret

The making of corn dollies is associated with the end of harvest and the need to provide a resting place for the corn spirit during the winter months. The idea of the corn spirit is ancient; corn dollies have been found in Egyptian tomb paintings. Almost everyone from the Druids to the Victorians had a custom of preserving the corn spirit: as the last wheat sheaf (or other cereal crop) was gathered, farmers wove a few wisps of straw into a 'dolly' and hung it safely in the farmhouse. The following spring the dollies were thrown into the first plough furrow of the new season so that the spirit could again inhabit the growing corn. The custom died out after World War Two when mechanical harvesters replaced the horse-drawn binders, which in their turn had replaced the reapers with their sickles.

It became popular for counties to have their own particular dolly and in Essex it is a group of the **Essex Terret** (including the Ring and Bar Terret), known as the **Collar Terret**, consisting of straw woven into rings or loops like those on a horse's harness pad through which the driving reins pass. There is also a more complicated design beloved of the craft movement called the **Essex Bell**.

The word 'dolly' is thought to be a corruption of the Greek word *eidololatria*, meaning the worship of an idol or image – in this case the corn spirit.

❋ The **Great Bardfield Cottage Museum** has a special interest in the corn dolly. Exhibits of Straw Plaiting and Corn Dolly Making are made by members of the Guild of Straw Craftsmen.

❋ **Straw plaiting** was an extensive industry in Essex, introduced at **Gosfield** in 1790 by George Grenville, the first Marquis of Buckingham (1753–1813) to give employment to the rural poor. Essex being an arable county, there was plenty of straw and this was purchased from the farmers in bundles (a bundle being as much as a person could conveniently carry). The plaiters prepared the straw for it to be woven into straw hats by Essex and London hatters. Both the Marquis and his Marchioness did their bit by wearing straw hats to church, the Marchioness decorating hers with ribbons and the Marquis placing his in a prominent position in full sight of the congregation.

The fashion took off and straw plaiting spread to the **Hedinghams**, the **Maplesteads**, the **Yeldhams**, the **Bardfields**, **Pebmarsh**, **Braintree** and **Bocking**. In 1806 it was reported that in Gosfield, which had a population of 453, the sum of £1,700 had been earned by straw plaiting in a single year and the 1871 census records the number of persons engaged in straw plaiting as 2,889. However, towards the end of the 19th-century cheap imports put many plaiters out of business and after World War One fashions changed, with straw hats out of vogue. By then there were almost no straw plaiters left in Essex.

❋ David Essex

Born David Cook (in 1947) the actor, pop star and composer **David Essex** needed a stage name when he first embarked on a solo career in the music business. In his autobiography *A Charmed Life*, he wrote that when he applied to join Equity (the actor's union) he found there was already a member called David Cook, so he had to think of a new name. His manager rang and suggested David Essex 'as I was now living in Essex'. He was afterwards glad that he had not been living in Middlesex!

❋ Essex Huffers

Triangular-shaped bread rolls found originally in the **Maldon** and **Great Dunmow** areas were called **huffers**. However, nowadays almost any bread roll or bap can be called a huffer. No one is entirely sure how they came to be so called, but one theory is that they were originally baked by people who lived on or near a hill. The root 'huff' (or 'hough' as it appears in modern spelling) is Old English for 'spur of a hill'.

Alternatively, the word 'huffler' was given to the man who ferried goods from ships' chandlers ashore to the ships at anchor.

❋ The Red Flowering Fyfield Pea

The crimson-flowered clambering perennial, the **Fyfield Pea** (*Lathyrus tuberosus*), was first recorded in 1859 by the botanist and pharmaceutical chemist **Octavius Corder** (1828–1910), tenant farmer of **Fyfield Hall**. Octavius and his brother, Thomas Corder (also a naturalist and Fellow of the Linnean Society), noted that it was 'so abundant as to damage the corn'. It is one of the few wild flowers to take its name from the parish in which it was first identified. In the 19th century it was believed to have inhabited the **Fyfield** and **High Ongar** cornfields and hedges exclusively, but it was later discovered to have flourished in surrounding areas, though not in such profusion as at Fyfield.

The Fyfield Pea is also known as the 'tuberous pea' or 'earth-nut pea', the latter because its tubers taste like fresh, raw hazelnuts. Although it is now rare it is not extinct and in 2007 some plants were identified in its eponymous home.

❋ Somewhere to Tie up the Horse

Tye (or tie) is an Essex place name meaning a strip of pasture, or green, usually belonging to a parish, and occurs chiefly in a small area of Essex and the Suffolk border. There is also **Staple Tye** in the west of the county, near **Harlow**, and **Matching Tye** and **Matching Green**.

There are also several areas called Tye Green (two near **Broxted**, one near **Cressing** and another just outside **Braintree**). Others include **Bulmer Tye**, **Honey Tye** and **Margaretting Tye**.

In *A Glossary of the Essex Dialect*, Richard Stephen Charnock suggests that the tyes were usually near a crossroads. They were grassed – or green – public spaces and had a post in the centre 'to where horses are directed to be tied up by parties coming from a distance, and having to proceed further, riding so far and sending their first steeds back'.

❋ Essex Jam

In 1860 the **Wilkin** family started fruit growing at **Tiptree** and in 1885 **Arthur Charles Wilkin** (died 1913) started a jam-making business using family recipes formulated by his wife, Mary. The Wilkins stipulated that the jam must be free of glucose, preservatives and colouring. They called it the **Britannia Fruit Preserving Company** and by 1900 employed over 200 full-time workers, almost 800 seasonal pickers, and had 8,000 customers. In 1905 it was renamed Wilkin & Sons (to distinguish it from the multitude of other 'Britannia' companies of the time) and in 1923 an order arrived for some tiny Wilkin's jam jars for Queen Mary's dolls' house.

After World War One the burgeoning urban middle classes took to Wilkin's jam in a big way. By 1920 annual sales exceeded £100,000 and there were over

200,000 customers on the books. Ten years later business was still increasing and the number of summer part-time workers had risen to over 1,000.

Wilkin's jam and Tiptree are now synonymous and visitors come from far and wide to visit the tea room and museum and students take advantage of the working holiday opportunities. There is now an annual **Strawberry Race**, a charity fundraiser in which the field workers compete for a trophy awarded to the fastest pickers in the allotted hour.

* Part of the Tiptree estate is **Tiptree Farm**, once the seat and famous experimental farm of **Alderman John Joseph Mechi** (1802–80). Mechi constructed a model farm at Tiptree and his various experiments became the subject of many publications, including *How to Farm Profitably* (1857). One of his inventions was a mechanical device that could irrigate the field with liquid manure that ran straight off the cattle yards. However, he encountered severe opposition from the locals, who resented the fact that such a 'farming novice' from London could presume to know anything about agriculture. They disapproved wholeheartedly of his new-fangled ways and prophesied that it was 'a mere will o' the wisp leading its dupes into bogs of bankruptcy'. However, Mechi improved his yields considerably and the great agriculturists of the day beat a path to Tiptree Farm. He died at Tiptree and was buried in the local churchyard.

* The Red Hills of Essex

The science of **salt making** has been practised on a 12 square mile area of the Essex coast since the Bronze Age (3,500 years ago) and flourished in both the Iron Age and the early part of the Roman occupation. Conditions are ideal – strong winds, low rainfall, bright sunshine and low-lying marshes that produce salty water. Relics of the salt pans are the red hills, a series of low mounds which vary in height from two to five feet. The 300 or so mounds are composed of burnt earth and many have been found to contain coarse pottery and broken brick. Underneath the mounds the remains of hearths and salt water settling tanks have been discovered.

As salt water was reduced to brine the surrounding earth was heated and reheated until over the centuries the burnt soil debris built up into 'hills'. As the saline solution evaporated bacteria produced red deposits and turned the salt pans red. The strain *Serratia Marcescens* is found in modern salt pans where the ancient methods are still used.

The earliest known site for salt production is **Fenn Creek** near **South Woodham Ferrers** with similarly early activity at **Mucking** and **Canewdon**, where remains of wooden platforms (thought to be landing stages) date from around 900 BC.

Salt was essential for a variety of processes, chiefly the preserving of meat, curing fish, cheese making, medicine and food seasoning, but towards the end of the first century AD the salt pans mysteriously fell into disuse. It is likely the Romans found other, better sources of salt, possibly in Lincolnshire, and the improved road network meant it was easier to transport it than pan for it. Later in the Roman period the salt pan marshlands were used for sheep grazing, not for meat but for wool. In the 18th century many hills were removed for agricultural purposes when it was discovered that the earth was useful for dressing clay soils. By then salt was obtained from Droitwich and Nantwich (Cheshire), where deep brine salt pits had been in use since the Middle Ages.

※ In the ***Little Domesday Book*** (1086) the 22 salt-making villages were restricted to the three hundreds of **Tendring**, **Winstree** and **Thurstable**. There was one solitary pan at **Wanstead** in the south-west corner of Essex.

※ One of the few survivors of the ancient salt industry is the **Maldon Crystal Salt Company**, which stands on what is believed to be the site of an ancient salt works. They still rely on the favourable conditions that gave rise to the centuries-old industry, and 'water for processing is taken after a period of dry weather on the fortnightly highs, commonly known as *spring tides* when the salt content is invariably at its maximum'. The water is transferred to holding tanks and after settling is filtered and pumped to storage tanks, where it can be drawn off to fill the salt pans. The company uses the traditional method of 'harvesting' the salt known as 'drawing the pans'.

※ **Patron Saint of Essex**
St Cedd (died 664), bishop of the East Saxons, is the **Patron Saint of Essex**, which is one of only 11 English counties with a Patron Saint. Most of what

is known about St Cedd comes from the writings of the Venerable Bede (673–735), biblical scholar and first English historian. **Sigeberht, king of the East Saxons**, was converted to Christianity and invited Cedd to evangelise Essex, where he founded monasteries at **Bradwell-on-Sea** and **Tilbury**. St Peter's Chapel at Bradwell-on-Sea is Britain's oldest Saxon church, built using stone from a former Roman fort on the same site. (See also Chapter Seven, Chapels and Churches.)

* In addition to that at Bradwell Chapel there are representations of St Cedd across the county, including one in a niche at St Mary the Virgin **Saffron Walden**, and stained glass at **Kirby-le-Soken**. At St Mary the Virgin **Great Bardfield** there is a Chapel to St Cedd and two stained-glass windows, and St Cedd's Well at **North Ockendon**.

* The Cathedral for the **Diocese of Chelmsford** is dedicated to St Mary, St Peter and St Cedd. The Celtic Cross of St Cedd has been adopted by the Cathedral as its symbol as it comprises two Christian symbols: firstly the cross (because Jesus died on a cross) and secondly a circle (to represent the concept of never-ending life). Celtic Christians are believed to have used the cross and circle together to show that they believed in the Resurrection.

* **Chadwell St Mary** is named for St Chad (died 672), the first bishop of Mercia. Chad was the brother of St Cedd and is said to have baptised his converts into Christianity there and built a church between Chadwell St Mary and **West Tilbury**.

* **The Earls of Essex**
The history of the Earldom of Essex is among the most complicated in the annals of ancestry and has been held by several families in nine separate creations of the title. It began with the post of earldom created by King Stephen (1135–1154) in 1140, which he conferred on **Geoffrey de Mandeville, 1st Earl of Essex** (died 1144) of **Pleshey**, who was also made justice, sheriff and escheator of the county. Several times the title became extinct, and was then re-created, until its last and ninth creation in 1661

when **Arthur Capell** (1631–1683) of **Raynes Hall** became the 1st Earl of Essex. His father, **Arthur Capell, 1st Baron Capell** (1604–1649) had been part of the Royalist scheme to rescue Charles I from the Isle of Wight, but suffered the same fate as his king shortly after the plot failed.

At various times the families of **Bourchier**, **de Bohun**, **Cromwell**, **Capell**, **Parr** and **de Vere** held the title with the properties and privileges accruing from the Earldom of Essex.

Almost all the earls of Essex played significant roles on the national political stage, but the best known of all was **Robert Devereaux, 2nd Earl of Essex** (1566–1601), soldier and politician, who became a favourite with Elizabeth I (1558–1603) late in her reign. He distinguished himself on the battlefield and was a familiar, if controversial, figure at court, making enemies through his close relationship with the Queen. In 1599 he was appointed Lord Lieutenant of Ireland and led an army against the Irish rebels in Ulster. The campaign was unsuccessful and Essex made an unauthorized truce with the rebels. Elizabeth forbade him to return to court but, thinking he was sufficiently in her favour, he defied her and entered the City of London with a body of supporters (this is known as the **Essex Rebellion**). He was duly arrested, tried for treason and executed on Tower Green in 1601. Although Essex had sent his ring to the Queen, a ring she had once given to him only to be returned to her if he had dire need of her support, it failed to reach her in time. She was said to have grieved constantly for him during the remaining two years of her life.

The Earl's career and relations with Elizabeth I have been ideal subjects for literary, operatic and cinematic portrayals of his dashing endeavour and political ambition. He has been portrayed on the screen by Charlton Heston, Robin Ellis, Hugh Dancy and Joseph Fiennes, among others.

❋ **Viscount Maldon** is the courtesy title used by the Heir Apparent to the earldom.

❋ **The Real Shakespeare?**
Rumours persist that there was no such person as William Shakespeare and that the bulk of his work can be attributed to **Edward de Vere, 17th Earl of Oxford** (1550–1604), whose ancestral home, **Hedingham Castle**, is still

owned by his descendants. As an Elizabethan courtier, playwright, poet, sportsman and sponsor of at least two acting companies, Edward de Vere is eminently qualified to 'be Shakespeare', but nothing has ever been proved.

❋ The Essex Peculiars

The **Peculiar People of Essex** was a religious sect founded at **Rochford** in 1838 by James Banyard (born 1800). Banyard was a ploughman and for the first 30 years of his life led a rough and disreputable life, being frequently drunk and lawless. Somehow his wife persuaded him to attend a service at the Wesleyan Chapel where he experienced a 'rebirth' and immediately set out to become a preacher.

He quickly acquired a following, known as Banyanites, and left the Wesleyans to found a sect of the Peculiars (similar to the Plumstead Peculiars founded by James Bridges). Within 10 years the Peculiars had established chapels throughout the **Dengie Peninsula** and beyond, but not everyone approved of this new puritanical group. John Hibbs in *The Country Chapel* (1988) records that at **Great Wakering** when Banyard stood up to preach 'the door opened [and] stones and brickbats were hurled in, but they never hit him, and the more they came the more the little man's eyes sparkled and shone'. The fact that the stones never hit him was taken by Banyard to mean that God was on his side.

The Peculiars took their authority from the Bible and chose their name from four texts including the first book of Peter, which begins 'you are a chosen generation, a royal priesthood, a holy nation, a **peculiar people**'. They interpreted 'peculiar' to mean 'chosen' and 'pure' in all its aspects; as a main tenet of their faith they rejected all medical advice, relying only on prayer (faith-healing) and anointing with oil to cure their ills.

Although they gained a reputation for hard work and clean living, they became increasingly isolated by the closeness of their society, set apart by their strict black clothing and puritanical form of evangelism, considering themselves bound by the literal interpretation of the King James Bible. During World War One the Peculiars registered as conscientious objectors and consequently suffered at the hands of the law.

A crisis occurred in 1910 when diphtheria swept through Essex and the Peculiar People refused treatment for their children, in spite of attempts to force medical attention on them through the courts. The Irish dramatist, George Bernard Shaw (1856–1950) expressed sympathy for one of the Peculiars, imprisoned for his belief, and wrote that nothing had been proved against him 'except that his child died without the interference of a doctor as effectually as many of the hundreds of children who die every day of the same disease in the doctor's care'.

After the diphtheria troubles the sect split into the Old Peculiars (who still refused medicine) and the New Peculiars (who allowed it on occasions). The split was healed in 1931, the New Peculiars prevailing. At the height of their popularity the Peculiars had 30 chapels across Essex including one at **Hadleigh**, which was the third chapel to be built.

James Banyard is buried in the churchyard of St Andrew's **Rochford**.

In 1956 the remaining Essex Peculiars joined the Union of Evangelical Churches.

※ The Peculiars' Chapel at **Steeple** was the first to be built by the sect in 1877. It ceased to be used as a chapel in the 1950s and has been converted into a house.

※ A Chapel of the Peculiar People at **Tillingham** was one of four traditions of religion in the village including the parish church, the Congregational chapel and the meeting house of the Peculiars. A split in the Peculiar movement saw the establishment of a second chapel that was called the Original Peculiar People's Chapel (disused after 1913 when the split was healed).

※ **Bernard Cornwell** (born 1944), the creator of the fictional hero Richard Sharpe, was a 'war baby', his father a Canadian airman and his mother a member of the Women's Auxiliary Air Force. He was one of five children adopted by an Essex couple who were members of the **Peculiar People** and was brought up in strict adherence to the sect's principles, where the only book allowed was the Bible. To recall his days living on the Essex marshes he set the novel *Sharpe's Regiment* (1986) on the **Dengie Peninsula** along the banks of the **Crouch**. Sharpe is sent home to raise soldiers for his regiment (the 'South Essex') and once in England runs into a Colonel of the South Essex, an old enemy.

The fictional 'South Essex Regiment' depicted in the Sharpe novels has yellow coat facings like the real **44th (East Essex) Regiment of Foot**, an infantry regiment in the British Army. The 1st Battalion saw service during the Napoleonic Wars (1792–1815) and the 2nd Battalion (formed in 1803) served in the Peninsular War and the Waterloo Campaign.

❈ Eringo

Throughout the 17th and 18th centuries the delicacy **candied Eringo** was a sweetmeat for which **Colchester** was celebrated. Eringo (*eryngium maritimum*), also known as **Sea Holly**, grew profusely along the sandy parts of the Essex coast and was easily harvested. The thick white roots sometimes penetrate the sand or shingle to a depth of 3ft and were used in both folkloric medicine and candied confectionary. The leaves are hard with sharp prickles.

The process of candying, recorded the *Little Guide* (1909), 'was somewhat elaborate and laborious' with much boiling and straining. Recipes existed for it from as long ago as the 16th century and it became so popular with the Colchester Corporation that they presented packets of it to distinguished visitors. In 1621, four pounds of Eringo was presented to the chancellor of the Bishop of London, its value being then four shillings per pound.

In 1795, George III's wife **Queen Charlotte** was presented with a box of it as she passed through Colchester.

Eringo appears in *Culpeper's Complete Herbal* (1649), in which it is said to possess any number of curative properties. Nicholas Culpeper (1616–54) was an apothecary who published a collection of herbal remedies for the first time, thus making such medicines available to the poor, who could not afford doctors' fees. Culpeper recommended a decoction of the root in wine as it was 'effectual to open obstructions of the spleen and liver, and helps yellow jaundice, dropsy, pains of the loins, wind colic, provokes urine, expels the stone, and procures women's courses'. The roots bruised and applied outwardly helped 'the kernels of the throat, commonly called the king's-evil' and, if taken inwardly, healed a sting or bite 'by any serpent'. It was also very good against earache, too.

Pickled, the roots enjoyed a reputation as an aphrodisiac, especially during Elizabethan times. In Shakespeare's *Merry Wives of Windsor* the greedy and lustful Sir John Falstaff says 'Let the sky rain potatoes; let it thunder to the tune of *Green Sleeves*; hail kissing-comfits, and snow eringoes.'

❉ In 1835, Wright's *Essex* advertised the gathering of Eringo as one of the pleasures of visiting **Walton-on-the-Naze**.

❉ **Essex Calves and Lions**

The explanation for the saying '**Essex Calf**' or calves, involves a story about a prize calf that got its head jammed tightly in a five-barred gate, unable to free itself. A group steadily gathered to consider the situation until a boy announced that he had thought of a way. The calf was indeed freed, but the boy had struck off the calf's head with an axe, and since then the nickname 'Essex Calf' has referred to impulsive youths.

The name Essex Calf is also said to derive from the time when the county was famous for rearing beef cattle, which were sold in London's Smithfield meat markets. The beasts were prized for both size and stamina and became known as **Essex Lions**.

❉ *The Brewer Dictionary of Phrase and Fable* (1870) quotes the old adage '**Valiant as an Essex lion**' as being said ironically of a timid person.

❉ **The County Bird**

There is no official county bird for Essex, but over the years a special affection has arisen for the **Lapwing** (*Vanellus*), a type of plover whose distinctive cry is heard across the Essex saltings, giving it the local name 'Peewit'.

There are three Essex islands which bear the name Peewit, or similar, but Ian Yearsley in *Islands of Essex* (2000) writes that the one north of **Hamford Water** 'almost certainly owes its name to the call of the peewit bird. There is an old story that the annual arrival of these birds on the island always took place on St George's Day – quite why is unclear!'

❉ **The D'Arcy Spice**

Essex has around 15 different varieties of apple but its most famous is the **D'Arcy Spice**, a late Russet dessert apple that is picked in November and will keep until the following May. It needs a hot summer to achieve the spicy flavour for which it was named.

The D'Arcy Spice originated in 1785 in the gardens of the hall at **Tolleshunt D'Arcy** and is included in the National Fruit Trials. It was introduced as a variety for cultivation in 1848 by nurseryman John Harris. Synonyms for the D'Arcy Spice include Baddow Pippin, Essex Spice and Pepin de Baddow.

* It was the Darcy family who gave **Tolleshunt D'Arcy** its name and they lived thereabouts during the 15th and 16th century.

* Other varieties of Essex apples are George Cave, Braintree Seedling, Chelmsford Wonder, Maldon Wonder, Edith Hopwood and Waltham Abbey.

* **Essex Eagles**

Essex is renowned as a sporting county and nowhere is that more apparent than at **Chelmsford**, where the **Essex County Cricket Club** – known as **Essex Eagles** – has a strong following. The county ground has been at New Writtle Street since 1966.

Essex was granted first-class status by the MCC in 1894, in its Classification of Counties, and a faithful and loyal following for the county team has grown up over the years. The Club was formed in 1876 at **Brentwood**, but its county headquarters was moved to **Leyton** as Brentwood was then considered too remote from London. Essex CCC is one of 18 major county clubs that make up the English cricketing structure.

A number of famous cricketing names have been associated with Essex CCC over the years, but none more so than **Graham Alan Gooch OBE** (born 1953 in **Leytonstone**) who captained Essex and England (34 times) and is one of the most successful batsmen of his generation. When he retired in 1997 he had scored a total of 8,900 runs and 20 centuries.

* In 2006 the **Peter Edwards Museum and Library** was opened at the Chelmsford's Ford County Ground to house a permanent collection of Essex cricketing history over more than 130 years. Peter Edwards

(1936–2000) was Secretary and General Manager of Essex County Cricket Club from 1979 until his death in 2000. This was a period of great success for the Club, during which it won six County Championship titles and numerous one-day competitions.

❋ The degree of importance given to Essex cricket by **BBC Radio Essex** is reflected in the four-strong team that works on cricket matches during the season, providing ball-by-ball commentary under the direction of Glenn Speller and the Sports Team.

❋ **The Salamanca Eagle**
The **Essex County Cricket Club** takes its name **Essex Eagles** from the heroic adventures of the 2nd Battalion of the **44th Essex Regiment of Foot** which fought in the Waterloo Campaign, notably at the Siege of Badajoz (1812), the Battle of Salamanca (1812) and the Battle of Waterloo (1815). It was at Salamanca that the 2nd Battalion won glory when it captured the French Imperial Eagle (the equivalent of a British Regimental Colour) from the French 62nd Regiment, thereafter called the **Salamanca Eagle.** The tradition of bearing the Eagle on parade was carried on by the 2nd and 3rd Battalion and continued after it was transferred to the Essex Regiment in 1881. It is maintained by its successor, the 1st Battalion of the **Royal Anglian Regiment**.

The history of the Regiment from 1741, when it was named **James Long's Regiment of Foot**, to the present day (including the Salamanca Eagle) can be seen at the **Essex Regiment Museum** in **Chelmsford.**

❋ **A Rickling Good Score!**
The cricket pitch overlooked by the Cricketers Arms at **Rickling Green** has been in use since 1850 and was the venue for one of the most phenomenal scores in the history of English cricket. The two-day match was played in August 1882 – Rickling Green versus Orleans Club. The home team opened the batting but were all out for 94 runs. The Orleans Club did rather better – they batted into the second day and scored 920 runs.

Cricket is still played on the green and the Cricketers Arms has memorabilia of the 1882 match and a full account of the event.

❋ Castle Park

In 1968 the *Essex County Standard* reported that a bomb disposal team from the Royal Engineers' depot in Felixstowe (Suffolk) had been summoned to **Colchester Castle Park** cricket ground after a groundsman had found an unexploded hand grenade on the pitch. Sappers removed the grenade and detonated it safely. Police later said they thought the device had been left in the park by someone who could not be bothered to take advantage of the prevailing arms amnesty. Castle Park is considered one of the most picturesque cricket grounds in Eastern England and celebrated its centenary in 2008. Originally the ground was rented to **Colchester Cricket Club** (formed in 1862, now Colchester and East Essex Cricket Club) for their first match of 1908 (on 9 May), an inter-club game between the Captain's XI and the Honorary Secretary's XI, and it has remained their ground ever since. It was first used for a County Championship match in 1914 – Essex versus Worcestershire. Essex won by 193 runs.

❋ The Gentlemen of Maldon

According to the farmer and miller **John Crozier** (1753–88), the Gentlemen of **Maldon** were 'associated into a cricket club' in 1786. Not all members were keen on playing, however, and many remained in the Ship public house smoking their pipes and playing cards while the 'regular set' played cricket. John Crozier kept a famous diary of his times now in the **Essex Record Office**. He was buried at **Woodham Walter**.

❋ Ringers' Jars

One 17th-century curiosity, found only in the Eastern counties and specially favoured in Essex, was **ringers' jars**. These were red earthenware jars that could hold between three and four gallons of liquid, which was usually a mixture of beer, wine and spirits and sometimes known as 'hot pot'. The jars had two handles and were black glazed, sometimes decorated, and fitted at the base with a hole for a spigot. Jars were taken from house to house by bellringers on New Year's Eve, and alcoholic contributions of all kinds were invited. The jar was then taken to the church and placed on a block in the centre of the belfry, where the ringers could draw on it during the session. The most famous example is the **Braintree Ringers' Jar** that was made at

Stock in 1658 (and kept at **Colchester Museum**), but it is hardly surprising that very few ringers' jars survived!

❋ Essex Man
Essex Girl and **Essex Man** were terms coined in the 1980s as belonging to the county that was home to the 'upwardly-mobile children of the Thatcher generation'. Furthermore, the Ford Escort came to represent the 'carnal Essex Man'. Parodied by the Harry Enfield character 'Loadsa Money', the 'Essex' tag became something of a mixed blessing for those attempting to promote the county.

Essex resident **Germaine Greer**, the Australian-born academic, writer and journalist, wrote in 2001 that 'the Essex girl is becoming more difficult to spot these days' although 'when she and her mates descend upon Southend for a rave, even the bouncers grow pale'.

❋ Professor Greer was made an Honorary Graduate of the University of Essex in 2003.

❋ Birds of a Feather
A BBC television series transmitted between 1989 and 1998, ***Birds of a Feather***, starring Pauline Quirke, Linda Robson and Lesley Joseph, was based in **Chigwell**, although it was also filmed at other locations across Essex.

❋ Essex Wives
The ITV television documentary ***Essex Wives*** (2002) portrayed women living in Essex. It featured Jodie Marsh and led to her career and subsequent fame as a topless model. The press dubbed the area of **Chigwell**, **Buckhurst Hill** and **Loughton** 'The Golden Triangle'. The programme did not meet with universal approval, with some Essex people resenting the sort of stereotyping reflected in the ITV fictional drama *Footballers' Wives* (2002–06).

❋ The Essex Rose
The **Essex Rose** (varietal name *Poulnoz*) is a ground cover rose, medium pink in colour. It was introduced in 1988 and has a fragrance level of 3–5 medium.

❋ There is a 16th-century tea room called the Essex Rose Tea House at **Dedham**. It operated under various names until Miss Mary Loe named it the Essex Rose in 1959 and in 1964 it was renamed the Essex Rose Tea House. It is now owned by Wilkin & Sons of **Tiptree**.

❋ **Cants of Colchester** claims to be the oldest recorded rose grower in the United Kingdom and began trading in 1765. The company is run by direct descendants of the founder, Benjamin R. Cant. One of their roses is named **Colchester Castle**.

❋ **The Mills of Essex**
Although there is no mill design particular to Essex, windmills have been part of the Essex landscape for many hundreds of years. The first windmills were designed in the 12th century when someone had the idea of harnessing wind to grind cereals in the same way that water had been used in watermills. In the 18th century there were at least 285 working windmills in Essex, of which 43 survive in one form or another – some as private houses and others restored or in the process of restoration. The first mill to be actively preserved was that at **Bocking** in 1929. A decline in wind and water mills started in around 1850 when the railways took over the supply of flour from large roller-mills, which were more efficient at grinding and rolling whole cereals.

The three types of windmill common in England (all of which can still be found in Essex) are the post mill, tower mill and smock mill.

Essex County Council was the first local authority in England to take mills into guardianship. It now maintains windmills across Essex including those at **Aythorpe Roding**, **Sible Hedingham**, **Beeleigh Steam Mill** (near **Maldon**), **Mountnessing**, **Stock** and **Finchingfield** (Duck End Mill) together with **Thorrington Tide Mill**, one of only a handful of tide mills in England still in working order.

❋ The earliest windmill mentioned in any known manuscript is that at **Henham**, which existed in 1202. Another at **Purleigh** dates from around the same time.

❋ One of the last mills to be built in Essex was a black tower mill at **Toppesfield** in 1869.

* Among the surviving 15th-century stained glass in St Mary and St Clement's **Clavering** can be seen a white windmill sail, said to be a 'common sail'.

* Windmills were invariably built on raised circular mounds. Old windmill sites are often mistaken for crop circles. One of these ancient mill sites was excavated at **Mucking** and found to be mid-15th century.

* The post mill of **Finchingfield** is the smallest windmill in Essex. Although the present mill dates from the 1750s, it stands on the site of much older mills going back to mediaeval times. There were once eight or nine mills in the village.

* The late 18th-century smock windmill at **Terling** was the last working mill in Essex. The sweeps measure 56ft across and could drive three pairs of stones plus an oat crusher. The mill once stood at **Cressing** (about 1770) but was taken down in 1818 and reassembled at Terling. It was originally white, but during World War One the government instructed that because of the risk from Zeppelin airships mills should either be demolished or painted black. Happily, Terling mill was painted.

* The octagonal smock mill at **Upminster** was built by a local farmer named James Noakes in 1803 and was bought by Essex County Council in 1937. Originally it was the intention of the Council to demolish it, but **Hornchurch Urban District Council** launched a fundraising campaign to save it. The opening of the mill to the public in 2009 was overseen by the **Friends of Upminster Windmill**, an offshoot of the **Hornchurch and District Historical Society**.

* A 16th-century watermill at **Bourne Mill** at **Old Heath** (Colchester) still has a working waterwheel (now run by the National Trust). It is thought to have been built on the site of ponds that once belonged to the mediaeval Abbey of St John's, which was converted to a fishing lodge in 1591 by Thomas Lucas. During the 17th century it was used as a cloth mill by Dutch refugees, but was transformed into a corn mill in the 19th century.

❋ Colchester Natives

Essex is renowned for its oysters, but one in particular is considered unique. In 2008 application was made to the European Union for Protected Geographical Indication (PGI) to be given to the **Colchester Native Oyster** (*Ostrea Edulis*), which would mean that, like Champagne and Parma ham, its name would be protected. The application is currently being considered by the Department of the Environment, Farming and Rural Affairs (DEFRA) and the European Commission. The native oyster is found in the Colne Estuary and is particularly associated with **Mersea Island**. Oysters have been cultivated there since before Roman times and, indeed, the Romans found them so good that they exported them back home.

❋ The law prohibits the sale of oysters during the breeding season, hence the expression 'Oysters should only be eaten when there is an R in the month'.

❋ When Celia Fiennes visited **Colchester** in 1698 she was very keen to try the 'exceedingly good oysters', but found it more expensive than she had anticipated, complaining that 'to grattifye my curiosity to eat them…I paid dear'.

❋ In Charles Dickens's time, however, oysters were seen as a food for the poor. In *The Pickwick Papers* (1836–37) Sam Weller remarks that 'oysters and poverty always seem to go together'.

❋ **Daniel Defoe** (1660–1731) was a great admirer of Essex oysters and thought them 'the best and nicest, though not the largest, oysters in England'. In 1724 he wrote that the chief place where oysters could be found was in **Wivenhoe** 'and the shore adjacent whither they are brought by the fishermen, who take them at the mouth of, that they call, Colchester Water…they are laid in beds or pits on the shore to feed…and then being barrelled up and carried to Colchester, which is but three miles off, they are sent to London by land and are, from thence, called Colchester oysters.'

❋ University of Essex

Since the **University of Essex** opened in October 1964 over 50,000 students have graduated, the first degrees being awarded in 1967. The 200-acre main campus is at **Wivenhoe Park** with other campuses at **Southend** and **Loughton**. The University motto is 'Thought the harder, heart the keener', adapted from the Anglo-Saxon poem commemorating the **Battle of Maldon**.

The University has 19 academic departments that span humanities and comparative studies, law, science and engineering. It is one of Britain's most international universities, with students from over 135 countries.

※ **The Cradle of Broadcasting**

'Now that the world is one vast whispering gallery' wrote Arthur Mee 'it is difficult to remember that as far as we are concerned it all began in this small Essex village, for **Writtle** was the birthplace of British Broadcasting'.

The man credited with the invention and development of the wireless telegraphy system is **Guglielmo Marconi** (1874–1937), an Italian who became interested in science and electricity at an early age. He conducted experiments at home in Bologna but became obsessed with the idea of being able to send messages across the Atlantic. He came to England and started the Wireless Telegraph and Signal Company – later the **Marconi Wireless Telegraph Company Limited** – in **Chelmsford**. A plaque on the wall in Hall Street commemorates that 'the first Radio Factory in the world' was established there in 1899. In 1902, Marconi built a transmitter that was 100 times more powerful than any previously made and succeeded in receiving signals from across the ocean.

The momentous broadcast that launched radio broadcasting was made on St Valentine's night 1922 from a World War One wooden army hut in a field beside Lawford Lane, Writtle. **Captain Peter Eckersley**, who worked for Marconi, broadcast a One Man Show on **2MT** (Britain's first licensed radio station) set up to test and monitor progress in the knowledge of transmission and antenna technology. The call sign for 2MT, 'Two Emma-Toc-Writtle', was among the first words spoken across the airwaves and laid the foundation for the **British Broadcasting Corporation**.

※ The pioneer radio presenter **Captain Peter 'P.P.' Eckersley** (1892–1963) is credited as being the first-ever radio Disc Jockey. He was a 'natural' broadcaster and was not only one of the first announcers (from 1920–29), but also used to recite poetry and sing songs on air. He subsequently became the first Chief Engineer of the **British Broadcasting Company** (1922–27). However, when Eckersley divorced his wife in 1929 he was sacked by John Reith, Director General of the BBC, who said he had no wish to endure the scandal of employing a divorced man at the BBC.

* Twice a year the **Chelmsford Amateur Radio Society** broadcasts an amateur radio show from the original **2MT** hut, which is now at the **Sandford Mill Museum**.

* Stained-glass windows at All Saints' **Writtle** commemorate 'the birthplace of the BBC' and contain the coat of arms of Marconi and a roundel containing an electric spark. The two windows were designed by Jane Gray and installed in 1992. They also commemorate one of the country's earliest women engineers, Beryl Catherine Myatt, **Baroness Platt of Writtle** (created 1981).

* **Melba Court** in **Writtle** is named for the singer **Dame Nellie Melba**, who sang in a pioneering radio broadcast from the now-famous wooden hut.

* The **Marconi Sailing Club** on the Blackwater was founded for the use of employees working at Marconi's Wireless Telegraph Company. The idea was first mooted in 1950 and two years later the club was established as the sailing section of the **Marconi Athletic and Social Club**.

* **The Essex Frame House**

The county of Essex is famous for its weatherboarded houses, a variation of which is known in America as the **frame house**. A typical array of such cottages is seen at **St Osyth**. The Anchor Inn at **Mistley** is a brick building but was weatherboarded in 1980, thus maintaining the visual tradition. Derek Johnson in *Essex Curiosities* recorded a cottage found in Rowlands Yard, **Dovercourt**, which was built entirely from the decking and timbers of a wrecked ship, 'the stairs and ceilings all bear traces of its former life with hooks and eyelets hanging from the beams'.

❋ Santander backs Essex

In 2009 **Essex County Council** teamed up with the Spanish bank Santander to launch **The Bank of Essex** to assist local businesses during the prevailing economic downturn. Council leader Lord Hanningfield said that the new bank was not a credit union, but a 'proper banking service…Our aim is to be able to lend local businesses and entrepreneurs up to £50,000 at competitive rates'.

Although a Bank of Essex might sound strange, Lord Hanningfield added that giants in the banking industry 'can trace their origins back to a local community bank'.

FOUR
ARTISTIC ESSEX

There could be no definitive list of the historic and modern myriad of writers, poets, artists and musicians who have been connected with the county in one way or another. Here are just a few of those who have passed this way and taken inspiration from Essex.

✵ Ralph of Coggeshall

One of Essex's first chroniclers was **Ralph of Coggeshall** (died after 1227) who became a monk and was afterwards the sixth abbot of the Cistercian Abbey at **Coggeshall** from 1207 to 1218. Ralph amended an existing *Chronicon Anglicanum* (English Chronicle or History), rewriting some of the earlier work and adding his own contribution. He retired as Abbot in 1218 due to ill health. In his writings he refers to a work of visions and miracles that he had compiled but it has not, so far, been discovered. Ralph did not mention contemporary references or documents, but did not shrink from recording his animosity toward King John and singing the praises of Richard I.

✵ The Land of Milk and Honey

In *The Description of Essex* (1594) the topographer **John Norden** (1548–1625) wrote of the county:

'Most fatt, frutefull, and full of profitable things exceeding (as farr as I can finde) anie other shire, for the general comodeties, and the plenty … this shire seemeth to me to deserve this title of the englishe Goshen, the fattest of the Lande; comparable to Palestina, that flowed with milke and hunnye'.

✤ Neither a Borrower Nor a Lender Be!

For centuries the farmer poet **Thomas Tusser** (1524–80) of Lanham Manor, **Rivenhall**, has had an influence on everyday speech, for which he is rarely credited. His long poem *A Hundreth Good Pointes of Husbandrie* (later expanded into *Five Hundred Good Points*) contains an incomparable picture of 16th-century agriculture, but it is for his proverbs that Tusser is best remembered. Among the most famous are 'A fool and his money are soon parted', 'At Christmas play and make good cheer, for Christmas comes but once a year', 'Who goeth a borrowing goeth a sorrowing, few but fools lend their working tools' and 'Seek home for rest, for home is best'.

As a child, Thomas was sent to Berkshire to serve as a chorister and later recalled the harsh treatment meted out to the boys. He was one of the many boys who were taken by licensed officers to serve in the royal choirs, their parents duped into thinking their sons would be cared for by the church and gain career opportunities. Thomas was sent to St Paul's, London and from there to Eton College, where he was unfortunate enough to find himself under the notorious headmaster Nicholas Udall, known for his cruelty to boys in his care. However, by 1543 Thomas had gained sufficient education and musical training for him to be elected to Kings' College Cambridge, where he was, for a short while, happy.

After a serious illness he went into service with Lord Paget of Beaudesert, in whose house he met his future wife. Thomas decided to take a small farm at Cattawade, on the Suffolk side of the River Stour, where he began writing his poem of husbandry points (published in 1557), which was followed by *Ladder of Thrift*, offering yet more good advice to those who would take it. Although he loved farming he was better writing about it than practising it: he lost most of his money and was never able to make it pay. After his wife died he remarried and moved to **Fairstead**, where he again tried farming and again failed. His last years are shrouded in mystery, but he is known to have died in a debtor's prison in London in 1580. Thomas Tusser could show others how to succeed in both farming and business (giving endless advice to women on how they should do everything from running the dairy to managing the servants), but was not able to profit from his own advice.

✵ Among Thomas Tusser's other proverbs is the much-used 'It is an ill wind turns none to good' and he warns about 'Buying and selling of a pig in a poke'.

✵ The playwright, scholar and preacher **Nicholas Udall** (1504–56) had a colourful career as a schoolmaster and was finally forced to leave Eton College after certain charges of sexual and physical abuse of his pupils were brought against him. He has been called 'the famous flogging master' and Thomas Tusser wrote:

> *Where fiftie three stripes given to me*
> *At once I had, for fault but small, or none at all*
> *It came to pass, thus beat I was,*
> *See, Udall, see, the mercie of thee to me, Poor lad.*

In 1538 Udall was licensed to hold the vicarage of **Braintree** with several other benefices. He retained the Braintree living until 1544.

✵ The Father of Electrical Science

The Elizabethan scientist **William Gilbert of Colchester** (1544–1603) was largely responsible for creating the science of magnetism and coined the word 'electricity'. His book *De Magnete* (1600) was the first ever work of experimental physics, and is still regarded as the first great work on the subject.

Gilbert was born in **Colchester**, went up to Cambridge University at the age of 14 and became a physician in 1572. He then began researching magnetism and gained a reputation as one of the great revolutionary thinkers of the age. He was known as the 'father of electrical science' and is credited with discovering the basic laws of magnetism and static electricity.

✵ 'A Steamer from Harwich'

In 1882 the operetta in two acts, *Iolanthe* (or *The Peer and the Peri*) by W.S. Gilbert (1836–1911) and Arthur Sullivan (1842–1900) was first performed in London. The Lord Chancellor's song is a masterpiece of the trials and tribulations of insomnia and contains the lines:

> *For you dream you are crossing the Channel*
> *And tossing about in a steamer from Harwich,*
> *Which is something between a large bathing machine*
> *And a very small second-class carriage.*

By the end of the 19th century the passenger steamers were very popular and highly fashionable. They ran from London to Harwich, stopping off at **Purfleet**, **Grays**, **Tilbury**, **Southend**, **Walton** and **Clacton-on-Sea**. Southend and Tilbury were steamboat stations. By 1900 *Kelly's Directory* was able to record that steamers were also running from **Harwich** to Ipswich (Suffolk).

❋ Billy on the Day Shift
The Trinidadian-born rhythm and blues singer **Billy Ocean** (born Leslie Sebastian Charles) is the most popular popstar to have emerged from Ford's factory at **Dagenham**. Billy, who took his surname from the Ocean Estate where he lived in East London, worked as a session singer while simultaneously employed at the Ford Motor Company. He once said that he took the job because they gave him day shift work that enabled him to do studio work at night. In 1976 he recorded his debut album and he has had four Top Twenty hits and three American number ones.

❋ Brightlingsea Pick Up
One version of the tongue-twisting song *I've Been Everywhere*, written by Australian singer-songwriter Geoff Mack, is by Lucky Starr (born Leslie Morrison in 1940). It came out as a single on the Parlophone label and begins the 'pick-up' at **Brightlingsea** and goes on to mention **Chingford** and other Essex places.

❋ 'Dear, unregarded *Essex*'
In 1954 the distinguished poet, writer and topographer **Sir John Betjeman** (1907–1984) composed the poem *Essex* devoted entirely to the joys of Essex, mentioning **Matching Tye**, **Epping Forest**, the River **Lea** and other places in a county he knew well. *Essex* begins:

> *The vagrant visitor erstwhile,*
> *My colour-plate book says to me,*
> *'Could wend by hedgerow-side and stile,*
> *From Benfleet down to Leigh-on-Sea.*

The final verse, however, regrets that 'now yarrow chokes the railway track' and 'brambles obliterate the stile' and 'No motor coach can take me back to that Edwardian "erstwhile"'.

In 1980 the **Epping Forest Centenary Trust** ran a competition to set Sir John Betjeman's *Essex* to music. It was won by the composer **Adrian Williams**, who later contacted Sir John and was rewarded with a reply that referred to 'dear, unregarded *Essex*' (in which he bemoaned the fact that the poem was unregarded). Sir John wrote that the 'one inch ordnance map of **Southend** [is] my favourite in the series'.

Unfortunately the arrangement of *Essex* (for baritone solo with small chorus and piano) was never performed in its entirety. The organisers of the scheduled debut failed to allow time for the choir to learn the work so the composer had, instead, to improvise at the piano. However, the composer did receive his prize from HRH The Duke of Gloucester but, at the crucial moment, a photographer tripped and fell headlong across the stage in front of them!

✻ **Sir John Betjeman** has particularly strong associations with **Southend**. One of the pier trains bears his name and members of **Southend Poetry Group** frequently gather in his honour beside the bronze bust of him at the Beecroft Art Gallery, **Westcliff on Sea**. In the 1960s, Betjeman visited Southend during filming of a television series *Metroland*, which explored the London suburbs.

✻ **The Martians have Landed!**
H.(Herbert) G.(George) Wells (1866–1946), best known for his novels in the science fiction genre, used **Burnham-on-Crouch** as the setting for *The War of the Worlds* (1898), an apocalyptic vision of the world invaded by Martians.

He also wrote a chapter entitled 'Braintree, Bocking and the Future of the World' in *What is Coming?* (1916) using the two places, geographically divided by only an apparently simple road, to explain the complex difficulties of world peace.

✻ **Flora of Essex**
In 1862 the botanist and philanthropist **George Stacey Gibson** (1818–83) published *Flora of Essex*, the first such work to cover the whole county. Gibson was born in **Saffron Walden**.

❋ Novel Writing at the Griffin Inn

In 1808 the prolific and influential novelist **Sir Walter Scott** (1771–1832) was asked by the publishers John Murray to complete a novel entitled *Queenho Hall*, which had been started (but left unfinished) by **Joseph Strutt** (1749–1802), the Member of Parliament for **Maldon**. Walter Scott stayed at the Griffin Inn at **Danbury**, where he completed the novel, which was his first attempt at fiction writing. He made mention of the Griffin in his later writing and went on to become one of the most widely-read authors of his day and established the form of the historical novel.

❋ *Nearer, my God, to Thee*

Poet and hymn writer **Sarah Fuller Adams** (1805–1848) was born in **Harlow** the daughter of Benjamin Flower (a radical journalist whose views on the politics of the Bishop of Llandaff landed him in prison). Sarah grew up wanting to go on the stage, reasoning that she could spread her strongly-held Unitarian religious views more easily through drama than by the pulpit. Her health, however, was not conducive to the rigours of the theatre and she turned instead to writing, first poetry and then hymns. She and her sister Eliza became friends with the renowned poet **Robert Browning** (1812–1889).

Sarah married William Bridges Adams in 1834 and they set up house at **Loughton**. William was an inventor and engineer and was responsible for devising the 'fishjoint', used to connect rails so that trains could pass safely over the joints. In 1841 Sarah wrote the hymn *Nearer, my God, to Thee*, one of 13 other hymns she contributed to a Unitarian collection for use in the South Place Religious Society in Finsbury, London.

The hymn is based on Jacob's dream at Bethel (recounted in Genesis 28) and when it first appeared was considered by the purists as 'unsuitable for public worship' in Trinitarian churches. Much of Sarah's original hymn was rewritten, but it later reverted to the original and in that form it survives. Sarah died from tuberculosis in 1848.

Benjamin Flower and his two daughters are buried at **Foster Street** (a small hamlet of Harlow).

✳ Much discussion is to be had on whether or not this was the hymn played in the last moments of the sinking *Titanic* (April 1912). It would certainly have been appropriate, but opinions vary almost fifty-fifty!

✳ **The Thomas Hardy of Essex**
The writer and critic **Samuel Levy Bensusan** (1872–1958) was born in London into a family of practising orthodox Jews. His father was an ostrich feather merchant and his mother came from Gibraltar. He did well at school and developed a lifelong love of music and literature and began experimenting in novel writing. He put his knowledge of music to good use by becoming music critic for a number of magazines, including the *Illustrated London News*. As a young man he made his first visit to Essex and it was love at first sight. Although he was to write a large volume of work, he is remembered in Essex for the 24 books and six plays that were inspired by the marshlands of the **Blackwater** estuary and the people he met during his lifelong sojourn in the county. In 1899 he rented a farmhouse at **Asheldham** and then bought Mote Cottage close to **Bradwell-on-Sea**. He later moved to **Great Easton** and then **Langham** before retiring to Sussex, where he died.

Bensusan's work has been described as 'bucolic' and his novels compared to those of Thomas Hardy. He is also known as the Essex Laureate and employed the Dickensian stratagem of using amusing pseudonyms to lightly hide the real people he met in the Queen's Head at Bradwell, such as Solomon Woodpecker, Mrs Wospottle and Martha Ram, among others.

✳ In 1966 the **Albert Sloman Library** at the **University of Essex** acquired the **Samuel Levi Bensusan Collection**, which includes a complete set of his published works, his diaries for the years 1891–1957, and files of published and unpublished works and correspondence.

✳ **Shakespeare in Essex**
One of the most famous Shakespearian references to Essex is that of the **Manningtree Ox**, spoken of by Falstaff in *Henry IV* (1597–98) who says 'that roasted Manningtree ox with a pudding in its belly'. During the annual

mediaeval fairs it was the practice to roast a whole ox in the town. The Ox Sculpture is found on the High Street and was erected by the Rotary Club of Manningtree of the Stour Valley.

❋ In *Richard II* (1595–96) Shakespeare immortalised **Pleshey Castle** when the widowed Duchess of Gloucester bids John of Gaunt commend her to Edward of York and says:

> *With all good speed at Plashey visit me,*
> *Alack! But what shall good old York there see*
> *But empty lodgings, and unfurnished walls,*
> *Unpeopled offices, untrodden stones!*

Pleshey Castle was once one of the most impressive Norman castles in England, but by 1596 it was already in decay.

❋ **The Curate of Wethersfield**

Patrick Brontë (1777–1861) was appointed curate at **Wethersfield** in 1806 and was ordained into the priesthood the following year. Patrick Brunty (he later changed his name) was born in Ireland into a poor family and began life in a two-roomed, mud-floored thatched cabin in County Down. He taught himself to read from the only books in the house – the Bible, *Pilgrim's Progress* and a volume of poems by Robert Burns. A local school teacher gave him the use of his library and taught him Latin and Mathematics so that he was able to take up a post of assistant teacher. Gradually he improved both his learning and opportunities and was enrolled into St John's College, Cambridge, which route led him to Wethersfield.

His vicar at Wethersfield was the Revd Joseph Jowett and he lived in St George's House opposite the church. In due course he fell in love with a local girl, Mary Burder, a member of the Nonconformist church, whose father had died tragically at about the time Patrick arrived. Mary's uncle and guardian, disliking the curate's uncertain future, forbade the relationship. In 1808 Patrick, having written a long diatribe to Miss Burder chastising her for not protesting more to her uncle, accepted the offer of a job in Shropshire. After several more parishes he arrived in Haworth in 1820, where he married and his children Maria, Elizabeth, Patrick Branwell, Emily, Anne and Charlotte were born.

Patrick had allegedly proposed marriage to Mary Burder, but had jilted her when the Shropshire job was offered, but his letter of reproach rather disproves the theory. However, when his wife Maria died in 1821 (leaving him with six children to look after) he remembered his old Essex love and tried to contact her, with a view to taking up where he had left off. Mary Burder, however, declined the offer somewhat tartly. The prospect of a difficult-natured, grieving widower with little money and six small children to support in a remote part of Yorkshire was not appealing.

It would seem that had Mary Burder fought with more vigour for her relationship with Patrick Brontë, the world of literature might well be the poorer.

✴ Goodbye, Mr Chips

The author **James Hilton** (1900–1954) was the son of John Hilton, headmaster of Chapel End School, **Walthamstow**. He wrote *Goodbye Mr Chips* and *Lost Horizon* (which popularised the mythical Shangri-La) and lived in **Woodford Green**. There is a blue plaque at 42 Oak Hill Gardens.

✴ Old Mother Hubbard

Although little is known of **Sarah Catherine Martin** (1768–1826) her intriguing nursery rhyme *Old Mother Hubbard* is as well-known today as when it was first written in 1805. Sarah was born in **Loughton** but the story goes that she actually wrote the rhyme at the house of her brother-in-law, John Pollaxfen Bastard (1756–1816) of Kitley, Member of Parliament for Truro and St Austell (Cornwall). Apparently annoyed by her, he told her to 'run away and write one of your silly little rhymes', which she did.

The Comic Adventures of Old Mother Hubbard and Her Dog (1805) was published by John Harris (London). It became an immediate bestseller and the following year *A Continuation of the Comic Adventures of Old Mother Hubbard and Her Dog* was published. John Harris had a novel way of illustrating his books: the copperplate engravings were over-painted with watercolours by a team of young teenagers sitting around a table. One child would paint in one colour and the next child in another until the image was complete.

The Old Mother Hubbard rhyme has given rise to endless speculation about its inspiration, the chief one being that it refers to the divorce of Henry VIII and Catherine of Aragon. The king is the 'doggie' and the 'bone' is the divorce, with

Cardinal Wolsey as 'Old Mother Hubbard'. Wolsey had been instructed to procure the divorce from the Pope in Rome, but when he returned to the king empty-handed 'the cupboard was bare, so the poor little doggie had none'.

On the other hand, it could refer to a domestic incident that occurred in the house of John Pollaxfen Bastard, and it was he that Sarah turned into 'Old Mother Hubbard'.

Sarah Martin is buried in St Nicholas's churchyard, Loughton.

❋ There was once a public house called Mother Hubbard at **Loughton**.

❋ **The Father of Angling**
Uncountable villages and towns across England claim to have played host to the Father of Angling, **Izaak Walton** (1593–1683), but he is widely celebrated in Essex at **Walthamstow** and **Enfield**. His treatise on fishing, *Compleat Angler* (1653) or *The Contemplative Man's Recreation*, is one of the earliest and most enduring volumes of its kind.

Walthamstow, and the upper reaches of the River **Lea**, attracted Izaak Walton and he is known to have stayed there during his many forays into the county. His working life was spent as an ironmonger, but on retirement in 1644 he took the opportunity to indulge his love of exploring the countryside and writing. He noted practical information, not only on the subject of angling, but also quoted a diversity of other writers, recorded folkloric traditions, songs and ballads and 'glimpses of an idyllic rural life of well-kept inns and tuneful milkmaids'.

❋ The Compleat Angler public house at **Enfield** is a tribute to Izaak Walton, who in 1653 wrote the famous book from which the inn takes its name, as does the **Izaak Walton Hotel**.

❋ The London Angling Association has offices at **Izaak Walton House** in **Waltham Forest**.

❋ **The Peasant Poet**
In 1837 the poet **John Clare** (1793–1864) was admitted to an asylum for the insane at **High Beach** (or High Beech), Epping, where he stayed for almost

five years in the care of Dr Matthew Allen. Clare was born in Northamptonshire, where he had worked as a farm labourer before publishing *Poems Descriptive of Rural Life and Scenery* (1820). Clare had a deep affection for the Essex countryside and Epping Forest and wrote:

> *I love the breakneck hills, that headlong go*
> *And leave me high, and half the world below,*
> *I love to see the Beech Hill mounting high,*
> *The brook without a bridge and nearly dry,*
> *There's Bucket's Hill, a place of furze and clouds,*
> *Which evening in a golden blaze enshrouds.*

As a young man he had been in love with Mary Joyce and, in 1841, he escaped from High Beach to walk the 80 miles back to Northamptonshire. He was deluded into thinking himself married to her and that they would be reunited (which they were not). Part of the old asylum now exists as Lippitts Hill Lodge, in the grounds of which is a group of half-buried catacombs, built in the 1880s with stones from **Chelmsford** prison.

❋ Waltham Abbey Bells

A visitor to Dr Matthew Allen's asylum was **Alfred, Lord Tennyson** (1802–92) who came to High Beach for a fortnight, suffering from depression, and then stayed at nearby Beech Hill Park between 1837 and 1840. He reputedly wrote parts of *In Memoriam* (1850) in High Beach churchyard, where he could hear the sound of the bells of Waltham Abbey. During his time in Essex he was grieving for his close friend, Arthur Hallam, who had died at the age of 22. Perhaps because of his melancholic mood Tennyson wrote that he found the local people 'artificial, frozen, cold and lifeless'. A business venture that he entered into with Dr Allen was unsuccessful, and he lost his capital. While he might not have found Dr Allen's company very conducive, he did, however, enjoy the company of his patients and found them 'most agreeable and most reasonable persons'.

❋ Folk Songs

The composer **Ralph Vaughan Williams** (1872–1958) was renowned for his passionate interest in folk songs. It was at **Ingrave Rectory** in 1903 that the pivotal moment, or epiphany, of his interest took place. He had become friendly with the English folksong collector and researcher Lucy Broadwood, and had embarked on a lecture tour of national songs from the British Isles. He was invited to tea at Ingrave Rectory by the Revd Henry Heatley and his sisters, where he met 74-year-old labourer Charles Potiphar. He later visited Mr Potiphar at his home in Ingrave, where he sang him *Bushes and Briars*. Vaughan Williams was said to be overwhelmed by the experience and felt he had known the song all his life. Thereafter he began to catalogue around 790 folksongs and over 200 texts, many collected in Essex villages, particularly **Little Burstead** and **Chigwell**.

❋ The Ninth Symphony

The first recording of the Ninth Symphony by **Ralph Vaughan Williams** was recorded in **Walthamstow Assembly Hall** the morning after Vaughan Williams's death in 1958. It had been hoped that he would attend and supervise the first recording by the London Philharmonic Orchestra, as was usual, but it was not to be. Sir Adrian Boult issued a spoken tribute and told the musicians that the recording would stand as a tribute to the composer.

❋ The Perfect Fool

The composer **Gustav Holst** (1874–1934) had a lifelong friendship with Ralph Vaughan Williams, which extended to frank and detailed criticism of each other's work, while both shared a deep interest in folk music. Holst lived for a while at **Thaxted**, where he began work on *The Planets* and composed the opera *The Perfect Fool* in a house overlooking the old Guild Hall. Together with the local vicar, the Revd Conrad Noel, Holst organised music festivals in Thaxted Church. Mrs Noel encouraged Morris dancing and the festivals became known as the Thaxted Movement.

❋ Bond Covers

The man nicknamed 'the Bond artist' **Richard 'Dicky' Chopping** (1917–2008) was born in **Colchester** (where his father became Mayor) and from 1944 until his death he lived in an artists' community at **Wivenhoe**. He painted the covers for nine of Ian Fleming's James Bond novels, beginning with *From Russia with Love* in 1957 and *Goldfinger* in 1959. Each of what became iconic watercolours, which made him internationally famous, took a month to complete. He was modestly paid, according to the standards of the time, and never received a royalty. Towards the end of his life he said of his association with Fleming and Bond 'quite honestly, I'm sick of it' and he considered the author 'mean and vain'.

Chopping also had a deep interest in the natural world and one of his first commissions was *Butterflies of Britain* (1943). He also wrote several children's books and published two novels, *The Fly* (1965) and *The Ring* (1967), both described as 'well observed but grim and squalid in content'.

East Anglian Daily Times columnist and poet, Martin Newell, wrote of him: 'with the passing of Dicky Chopping goes not only a part of the 20th century, but also a splash of vibrant colour on the largely monochrome England of his times'.

❋ The Deserted Village
In a small cottage (Dukes Cottages) opposite the village church in **Springfield**, **Oliver Goldsmith** (1730–74) wrote his famous poem *The Deserted Village* (1770). The village of the poem was 'Auburn' and evoked a pastoral idyll which, lamented Goldsmith, only comes from a lack of rural commerce and the resultant depopulation and decline in the English countryside.

❋ Experimental Author
The novelist John Fowles (1926–2005), author of *The French Lieutenant's Woman* (1969), was born at **Leigh on Sea**, though he said of it that 'the rows of respectable little houses inhabited by respectable little people had an early depressive effect on me'. Fowles experimented in writing novels with different endings.

In 1981 the famous film adaptation of *The French Lieutenant's Woman* was made, starring Meryl Streep.

❋ Riddle of the Sands
(Robert) Erskine Childers (1870–1922) was a guest at Bradwell Lodge, **Bradwell-on-Sea** when he wrote *Riddle of the Sands* (1903), a sea story about an amateur yachtsman sailing in the Baltic who discovers plans for a German invasion of England. Childers wanted to draw attention to the fact that the East of England was, in his opinion, badly defended in case of invasion.

❋ **The Creator of Albert Campion**

The crime and mystery writer **Margery Louise Allingham** (1904–66) was born into a literary family in Ealing, London and soon afterwards the family moved to **Layer Breton**. Although Margery moved back to London to study drama and speech-training (she tried to cure a stammer that she had suffered since childhood), she returned to Essex with her husband in the 1930s and stayed for the rest of her life.

They lived first at Viaduct Farm, **Chappel** (where there is a circular Margaret Allingham Walk) and in her novel *The Oaken Heart* (1941) she calls her fictional village 'Pontisbright', which is the old name for Chappel before it became a parish in 1553. She and her husband, Philip Youngman Carter (known as Pip) moved to D'Arcy House, **Tolleshunt D'Arcy** in 1935. Here Margery and Pip enjoyed what her sister later described as 'a life full of writing, art and village cricket'.

Margery Allingham was deeply immersed in Essex life and frequently used local names for her characters or places – **Tollesbury** (and Tollesbury church), **Coggeshall**, **Wivenhoe** and **Stukley-Wivenhoe**. Her first novel, *Blackkerchief Dick* (1923) was written when she was 19 and was set on **Mersea Island**.

It was in 1929 that she published *The Crime at Black Dudley*, which introduced 'Albert Campion'. He was to feature in another 17 novels and over 20 short stories. Although her considerable volume of work is not as enduring, or well known, as that of Agatha Christie (who considered the Allingham novels superior to her own), Margery Allingham nevertheless still has a loyal following. She died of breast cancer in Severalls Hospital, **Colchester**.

❋ The BBC made a series of television adaptations of the 'Campion' novels (1989–90) starring Peter Davison as 'Campion' and Brian Glover as 'Lugg'.

❋ **Dorothy L. Sayers**

In 1925 the author, theologian, playwright and Dante scholar **Dorothy L(eigh) Sayers** (1893–1957) bought numbers 20–24 Newlands Street, **Witham**, for her mother to live in. When she died in 1929 Dorothy put the two together (now called Sunnyside Cottage) and lived there with her husband until her own death in 1957.

The daughter of a Fenland clergyman, Dorothy had a series of love affairs before marrying journalist O.A. Fleming in 1926. She was one of the first women to receive a degree from Oxford University, but although she had finished with first-class honours in 1916 she had to wait some years before receiving the award, as women were not then awarded degrees. Although she was a noted theologian and devoted the final years of her life to a translation of Dante's *Divina Commedia*, she is most popularly known for her fictional detective, Lord Peter Wimsey, man-about-town and amateur sleuth. The best known of the Wimsey titles is *The Nine Tailors* (1934), which involves long (and complicated) passages relating to bell-ringing, the title itself referring to the ringing of church bells to indicate a death in the parish. Although Dorothy was not a ringer herself, she was fascinated by the subject and claimed not to be able to understand complaints about the noise. She wrote 'it seems strange that a generation which tolerates the uproar of the internal combustion engine and the wailing of the jazz band should be so sensitive to the one loud noise that is made to the glory of God'.

Her female character, Harriett Vane, features in four novels and is considered to have been autobiographical. Harriett Vane and Lord Peter Wimsey meet in *Strong Poison* (1930) and eventually marry.

❋ **Witham Library** holds a large volume of reference works in the **Dorothy L. Sayers Centre**. A statue of Dorothy and her cat, Blitz, is located opposite the building.

❋ *The Hundred and One Dalmatians*
The third in the trinity of women writers closely associated with Essex is **Dodie Smith** (1896–1990), born Dorothy Gladys Smith, who lived at Barretts, **Finchingfield**, on and off from 1934 until her death. She first described Finchingfield, one of the most picturesque and photographed villages in Essex, as having 'an almost indescribable rightness about the composition of the place, just as one finds in great works of art'. Five roads lead to a green and a pond, surrounded by cottages, but in 1934, Dodie did not like her very run-down cottage when she first saw it in what was then a

terrible state of repair, with 'the aroma of hens and tramps' about it. Although she enjoyed visiting churches she never once set foot in Finchingfield church (she was a Christian Scientist).

Dodie's two most enduring works are her first novel, *I Capture the Castle* (1948) and *The Hundred and One Dalmatians* (1956). She had always liked black and white; her clothes were monochrome and her flat was the same. In 1934 she received a Dalmatian puppy for her birthday, which she named Pongo, and thereafter she always had a Dalmatian dog, the last being Charley.

✤ The first film version of *The Hundred and One Dalmatians* was a Walt Disney animation in 1961. In 1996 another film was made starring Glenn Close as the evil Cruella de Vil and Joan Plowright as the Nanny.

✤ Doctor Salter's Diary

The Georgian-fronted D'Arcy House lived in by Margery Allingham at **Tolleshunt D'Arcy** was previously owned by **John Henry Salter, JP, MRCS** (1841–1932), who kept a diary from 1848 until his death, covering around 30,000 days. It was written in 80 volumes and ran to about ten million words. Dr Salter took up his practice in 1864 and recorded in his diary that he was 'received with great cheering at the entrance to the village'.

Dr Salter's diary was a classic of its kind and reflected his many and varied interests in life – medicine, prize fighting, horticulture, fishing, dog breeding and Freemasonry. He is reputed to have bred over 2,500 dogs from 44 different breeds, most of them sporting or gun dogs, for export all over the world. His interest in prize fighting extended to taking part in the ring and he once fought in Hogini's Circus (Ireland) as Jack O'Reilly. He took particular care to include the minutiae of everyday life, even recording details of fights between the local fishermen and the 'landlubbers' outside the Queen's Head.

✤ The Puritan Farmer and Diarist

Although many clergymen were evicted from their livings during the 17th-century Civil War there were some who retained their positions by slanting their beliefs towards Puritanism. One such was the **Revd Ralph Josselin** (1616–83) of **Earls Colne**, who kept a diary for most of his life entitled *A*

Thankfull Observacon of Divine Providence & Goodness towards Mee & a Summary View of My Life by Mee Ralph Josselin (observacon being an old word for observation). After being educated at Bishops Stortford and Jesus College, Cambridge, Josselin came to Earls Colne in March 1641 at the instigation of Richard Harlakenden, a relative of the Parliamentarian Oliver Cromwell. He went only to preach a single sermon, but the parishioners 'desired mee I would come and live with them as their Minister', which he did, for the sum of £80 per annum. They seemed undeterred (according to him) that his sermons could last up to three hours and in appreciation often sent him gifts of fruit and other food. He wrote of his 'serious exhortation to lay aside ye jollity…and keep the Sabbath better which is the Lord's day we are commanded to observe.'

Josselin did not hesitate to comply with orders from London that the churches should be stripped of 'all images and pictures and such like glass' and recorded it in his diary, almost as an observer rather than as a participant. He had, by this time, acquired a wife and a daughter (there were to be nine more children) and Earls Colne became a 'Puritan stronghold'. Josselin had been perturbed by the news of Charles I's execution, writing 'I was much troubled with the blacke providence of putting the King to death'. He faithfully recorded the various troop movements from the outbreak of the Civil War in 1642 onwards and wrote commendably of the New Model Army soldiers, but he viewed the restoration of Charles II with little emotion. 19 May 1661, a few days after the king rode into London to reclaim the throne, was declared a day of national thanksgiving for the restored monarch, but although Josselin preached that day there were 'very few hearers'.

Josselin had very firm views on the behaviour of children and was not enamoured of those who played rowdy games on the village green and severely chastised them, lamenting the fact that their parents sat at home while their children made merry in the streets.

He wrote once or twice a week, in very small handwriting, and included everyday events and incidents, making it an important document of the 17th century. Having bought a small farm in 1645, he always took care to record the seasons and the final entry in his diary stops in mid-sentence – 'We begun harvest July 27 reaping and mowing. God send us…' and shortly afterwards he died.

❋ **Sylvia Pankhurst and The Stone Bomb**
The writer, suffragette and Third World activist **Estelle Sylvia Pankhurst** (1882–1960) was the daughter of the legendary Mrs Emmeline Pankhurst. After a colourful career as an activist in the Votes for Women campaign of the first two decades of the 20th century, Sylvia came to live in **Woodford Wells** at Vine Cottage (which she renamed Red Cottage). In 1924, shortly after serving a six-month prison sentence for incitement to sedition, Sylvia and her lover, Silvio Corio, an Italian radical, scandalised the local community by moving in together and living openly without being married. They incurred further displeasure by producing a son, Richard, in 1927. Even her mother Emmeline was shocked at such unconventional behaviour and refused to speak to her for the rest of her life.

Sylvia's first love was painting (she won a scholarship to London's Royal Academy in 1902), but she chose instead to join the Women's Social and Political Union (WSPU) in support of women's rights. She was imprisoned and, like many other suffragettes, went on hunger strike and endured force-feeding. However, she disliked the militancy of the WSPU and in 1914 founded the East London Federation of Suffragettes, which promoted socialism and pacifism. She started *Woman's Dreadnought* (the mouthpiece of the Workers' Socialist Federation) and in 1936 *The New Times and Ethiopian News* (which was printed in **Walthamstow**). She also wrote many works in support of Ethiopia, histories of the Suffragette Movement (1912 and 1931) and several other books including *Save the Mothers* (1930), *The Ethiopian People* (1946) and *Cultural History of Ethiopia* (1955). She adopted Ethiopia as her particular cause and raised money for a hospital in Addis Ababa. She and Silvio also opened a cafe in the Red Cottage with a printing press at the back and later ran a nursery school for disadvantaged children.

In 1933 Sylvia, Silvio and Richard moved to a house near Woodford station. Two years after Silvio died (1954) she moved to Ethiopia. She never returned to England and died in 1960.

❋ Sylvia Pankhurst is unique in commissioning a memorial against aerial warfare in a future war. The Stone Bomb (or torpedo) statue, executed by Eric Benfield, was unveiled in **Woodford Green** on 5 May 1935 as a protest against Mussolini's bombing attack on Ethiopia and the World Disarmament Conference of 1932 that 'upheld the right to use bombing planes'. She wrote 'There are thousands of memorials in every town and village to the dead but not one as a reminder of the danger of future wars'. The Stone Bomb was vandalised (not for the first time) in 1996 but retrieved and reinstated.

❋ Sylvia's house is long gone, but the green opposite the flats where it stood is named **Pankhurst Green**.

❋ **Actress and Suffragette**
One of the most militant suffragettes of the early 1900s was the actress and music hall entertainer **Kitty Marion** (1871–1944) from **Great Dunmow**. Kitty was born Katherina Schafer in Germany, but when her mother died in 1873 she fled from an authoritarian father and came to live with an aunt in Essex. Having shown talent as a singer and dancer, Kitty learned English and decided to work as a travelling actress. But before she could set out on a music hall career she needed stage experience and a new name. Having abandoned her birth name she took the stage name Kitty Marion, which she kept for the rest of her life. Her first stage appearance was at the **Southend Hippodrome**, followed shortly afterwards by performances at the Grand Theatre, **Colchester**. When she began to travel she was disgusted at the way the actresses were exploited and helped to found the Actresses' Franchise League. In 1908 she latched on to the Votes for Women movement, then beginning to gain momentum, and joined the militant WSPU. In 1911 she appeared as a 'Music Hall Artiste and Militant Suffragette' at the annual meeting of the Colchester Liberal Unionist Association and was praised for the quality of her voice.

In due course Kitty became involved in the WSPU's arson campaign and gave up her stage career. She also formed close connections with the Pankhursts. She used her abilities as a performer in her campaigning and was imprisoned several times under the Cat and Mouse Act (1913). It was calculated that Kitty endured 200 force-feedings in prison while on hunger strike. However, when World War One broke out she became worried that she would be regarded as a German spy and in 1914 briefly resumed her theatrical career. She appeared on stage in London and organised a choir to sing carols in the streets to raise money for Sylvia Pankhurst's East End children. When it came to a compulsory registration with the British authorities she knew her suffragette record would go against her so she left for America, where she again became involved in politics and was imprisoned in 1916. She visited London in 1930 but returned to New York and died there in 1944. Shortly before her death she wrote her autobiography and, although it was never published, the Kitty Marion Papers are held by the New York Public Library.

❊ William Morris – Home Maker

The designer, socialist, poet and one of the founders of the Arts and Crafts Movement **William Morris** (1834–96) was born at **Walthamstow** (now part of the London Borough of Waltham Forest). As a boy he wandered freely in **Epping Forest** and developed a love of nature, and trees in particular, that would in later life influence the development of his artistic designs. In 1834 Walthamstow was a rural idyll, the forest to the east and on the west the River Lea and its haunting marshlands. In his mid-twenties Morris married and when it came to setting up home he could find no contemporary designs for the interior that would match his new house, so he designed his own. Almost immediately his designs were taken up and became highly fashionable. This encouraged him to start a business producing wallpaper, tapestries, metal and glass work, furniture and artistic tiles to 'properly enhance a fashionable 19th century home'. His dream was of good craftsmanship for the masses and he defined art as 'man's expression of his joy in labour'.

❊ The **William Morris Gallery** at Walthamstow is in Lloyd Park, once the gardens of Water House, where the Morris family lived when William was a child. A Blue Plaque is found on the present fire station that records the site of his birthplace, Elm House.

❊ Paddington Bear

The famous character of **Paddington Bear** (from the books by Michael Bond) was originally illustrated by the Essex artist **Peggy Fortnum** (born 1919), who lives in **West Mersea**. She visited London Zoo to study bears and submitted sketches to the publishers, who liked them instantly. Peggy always wanted Paddington to look like a real bear, not a toy one. Paddington Bear turned 50 in 2008.

❋ Sunrise-Land

In 1893 **Arthur Rackham** (1867–1939) embarked on an artistic tour of the eastern counties that was to result in the publication of *Sunrise-Land* (1894), the start of a distinguished career as a book illustrator. Publishers Jarrold and Sons commissioned Annie Berlyn to write a comprehensive, fully-illustrated guide to East Anglia, for which she and two young artists (M.M. Blake and Rackham) collected material throughout 1893–94. They travelled through **Dedham**, **Harwich**, **Manningtree**, **Colchester**, **Brightlingsea**, **Chelmsford** and **Hadleigh**, Annie Berlyn writing the text and Rackham and Blake sketching and drawing everything they saw. The three always put up in the best hotels and enjoyed top-quality cuisine wherever they stayed. *Sunrise-Land* was published to great acclaim. In 1900 Rackham illustrated Grimms' *Fairy Tales* and in 1906 gained considerable fame with his watercolours for J.M. Barrie's *Peter Pan in Kensington Gardens*.

❋ Ten Years on the Mud

One of the most exceptional Victorian clerics among many such men was the novelist, hagiographer, biographer, antiquarian, folklorist and hymn writer **Sabine Baring Gould** (1834–1924) who was Rector of St Edmund King and Martyr **East Mersea** between 1871 and 1881. His industry can only be viewed with dazed admiration: a bibliography extending to over 1,240 diverse publications (including 16 volumes of *The Lives of the Saints*), a collection of songs and ballads that were the first to be published for the mass market, numerous ghost stories, 30 novels and a number of hymns including *Onward Christian Soldiers* and *Now the Day is Over*. He always wrote standing up.

Never a man to do things by halves, he fathered 15 children (all but one surviving to adulthood), although he understandably had trouble remembering them all. Sabine once attended a children's party and indulgently asked a child 'And whose little girl are you?' whereupon the child dissolved into tears and sobbed 'I'm yours, Papa!'

Sabine had a lifelong love affair with his beautiful wife, Grace Taylor, whom he met as a curate in West Yorkshire. The 16-year-old Grace was the illegitimate daughter of a mill hand and he fell passionately in love. Sabine sent her to York for two years to learn 'proper manners' and they married in 1868 (she was 18, he was 34). The marriage lasted for 48 years and when Grace died in 1916 he carved on her tombstone *Dimidium Animae Meae* (half my soul).

As eccentric as any of his ilk, Sabine is said have had a pet bat which, when not on his shoulder, lived in an old sock in his room. It was eventually killed by a housemaid who inadvertently trod on the sock and squashed the bat.

Having been born in Devon, and spent most of his young life travelling the spas and cities of Europe with his parents, Sabine found the Essex marshlands oppressive and cold and was not taken with his new parishioners, whom he thought 'dull, shy, reserved and suspicious'. The islanders were not too keen on him, either, and Sabine complained that his parish clerk, 'Ellis by name', was a frequenter of the Dog and Pheasant. Ellis's idea of a rector was one who gave a single service on Sundays; he recalled that the previous rector 'grew very good taters [potatoes], and he left us gloriously alone'.

Sabine suffered considerably from the dank atmosphere and low-lying mists of the Mersea Flats though, nothing wasted, he used the landscape and characters in many of his novels, principally *Mehalah: A Story of the Salt Marshes*. 'A more desolate region can scarce be conceived' he wrote, 'and it is not without beauty. In summer the thrift mantles the marshes…a purple glow steals over the waste as the sea-lavender bursts into flower, and simultaneously every creek and pool is royally fringed with sea-aster'. The heroine of the story was said to live on **Ray Island**, which stands proud of the marshes near to the Mersea Strood crossing.

His flock were largely Dissenters, and not kindly disposed to the Anglican Church, though this did not bother him as it gave him time to research *The Lives of the Saints*, most of which was written at East Mersea, as were his autobiographical works, *Ten Years On The Mud* and *Early Reminiscences*. He considered wildfowling, a popular indulgence of the day, a contributing factor to his parishioners' continual ill health. He never let accuracy get in the way of a good story and, although he could be scathing about the 'ignorant' fishermen and farmers, compared himself to Thomas Hardy as having 'the same love of the English peasant in common'.

In 1881 Sabine inherited the family property at Lewtrenchard (Devon) and returned there, where he continued to write, run the estate and carry on his pastoral duties. In 1906 his death was mistakenly reported and he was able, somewhat curiously, to read his own obituary. He died in 1924 aged 90.

❋ The Dedham Vale

The landscape artist **John Constable** (1776–1837) wrote of the **Dedham Vale** 'I associate my careless boyhood with all that lies on the banks of the Stour. Those scenes made me a painter'. Constable is ranked as one of the greatest British landscape artists. Many places and people of the Stour Valley are found in Constable's art, but perhaps his most famous painting is *The Hay Wain* (1821), which typified the scenes that he would have been familiar with at his father's mills at Flatford (Suffolk) and Dedham. He said of Essex 'I love every stile and stump…as long as I am able to hold a brush I shall never cease to paint them'.

The Ascension by John Constable is on permanent display in the parish church. It is the best of only three religious paintings and was commissioned in 1821 as an altarpiece for St Michael's **Manningtree**. The other two paintings were for Brantham (Suffolk) and **Nayland**.

❋ The House of my Dreams

Constable was not the only artist to be inspired by the Dedham Vale. **Sir Alfred Munnings, KCVO, PRA** (1878–1959) moved into Castle House, **Dedham**, in 1919, calling it 'the house of my dreams'. He lived and worked there for 40 years. Following his death, Sir Alfred's widow, Lady Violet, turned the house into a museum to celebrate her husband's life and work.

Alfred Munnings was born into a farming and milling family on the Suffolk-Norfolk border and showed outstanding artistic ability from an early age. When only 14 he took his first job, as a poster artist for Page Brothers, spending his spare time at Norwich School of Art. It was clear that his future lay in the artistic presentation of agriculture as opposed to practical participation. By the age of 20 he had successfully submitted a picture for the

Royal Academy's annual exhibition, the first of 230 Munnings pictures that were accepted by the Academy. In the same year he lost the sight in his right eye after an accident that happened when lifting a dog over a stile.

His most celebrated paintings are those that portray East Anglian rural life, but he drew horses throughout his life and is famous for his racehorse and equestrian paintings. Critics, however, have observed that his pictures became 'slick and repetitive' and his enduring popularity is more with lovers of horses than of paintings. His wife, Violet McBridge, was a champion horsewoman, and although she helped him tirelessly with both his art and business she did remark that he was not such a 'good painter after he married me. He had establishments to keep up and more expenses to meet. It meant painting for money'.

When he accepted the Chair of the Royal Academy (1944–49) it was not a happy experience for either Sir Alfred or the Academy, as he was an outspoken critic of modern art. His final speech at the Royal Academy Banquet was highly controversial as he openly decried artistic modernity in the bluntest of terms and said he thought painting should be a 'representative art'. He later said 'What are pictures for? To fill a man's soul with admiration and sheer joy, not to bewilder and daze him.'

❋ 'Chigwell…is the Greatest Place in the World'

It is well known that **Charles Dickens** (1812–70) spent much time in Essex and used innumerable places and people in his novels. However, he had a special affection for **Chigwell** and in 1844 wrote to his friend (and later biographer) John Forster, 'Chigwell, my dear fellow, is the greatest place in the world…such a delicious old inn facing the church – such a lovely ride – such forest scenery – such an out-of-the way rural place.'

The King's Head is called the 'Maypole' in *Barnaby Rudge: A Tale of the Riots of 'Eighty* (1840–41) and it is likely that, while the name was taken from the Maypole Inn on Chigwell Row, the description is more of the King's Head. In the book the Maypole is said 'not always to have been an inn' and indeed it was once a ladies' school. It was a very ancient building and Forest Courts were held there until the reign of George III.

Much of *Barnaby Rudge* was written at the King's Head, where the chimneys and gables have been identified, while the cellars and porch belong to the Maypole Inn. A new public house was built on what was once the village green (where the London coaches used to stand in the 1840s) and it, too, was called the Maypole (and is still there).

❋ **The Great Bardfield Artists**
The artistic community at **Great Bardfield** has been home to many artists since it was set up in the 1930s. Chief among the artists was **Edward Bawden, RA** (1903–89) who was born in **Braintree**. Bawden worked as a war artist from 1940 to 1944 and made two tours of duty in the Middle East. He travelled through Saudi Arabia, Iran and Iraq and was awarded a CBE for his services.

The Great Bardfield Artists' heyday was between 1945 and 1970, when artists were drawn there from all over Britain. They had large open-house exhibitions, which attracted national and international interest as critics enjoyed the novelty of viewing the work in the artists' own homes.

❋ The **Fry Public Art Gallery** in **Saffron Walden** has a unique collection of paintings, prints, books and ceramics by artists who lived in and around Great Bardfield (and **Tilty**) from the 1930s to 1980s and others currently working in the area. It also houses the **North West Essex Collection**, which comprises over 1,700 items.

FIVE
WHY IS IT CALLED THAT?

Across the county there are clues to its history in place or street names that commemorate an event, occupation, person or family important in some way to those who lived there. Essex is packed full of such 'signposts to the past' – here are just a few.

❋ **Hatfield Broad Oak**
The *Victoria History of the County of Essex* records that **Hatfield Broad Oak** was formerly known as 'Hatfield Regis, King's Hatfield, Hatfield Regis atte Broad Oak, or Hatfield Chipping' and took its eventual name **Hatfield Broad Oak** from the veteran oak tree that once stood in **Hatfield Forest**. Hatfield Broad Oak was one of the largest settlements in Saxon Essex: in 1086 it had a population of 115, making it the ninth largest in the county.

❋ **Hatfield Forest** is a rare surviving example of a mediaeval Royal Hunting Forest where there are still over 1,000 acres of ancient woodland and pasture.

❋ Another famous tree was the **Doodle Oak** and, although it too no longer exists, the site is marked in the north-west corner of **Hatfield Forest** on the edge of **Elmans Green**. The Doodle Oak was one of the stoutest-ever trees in England and measured 60ft in circumference in its prime. It was already a landmark in 1630 and was 'Giraffe Pollard-cut high' in typical Tudor fashion. When the remains of the stump were excavated in 1949, 850 annual rings were found. Three hundred people turned out to see it felled in 1859. The Doodle Oak gate does not mark the site of the ancient tree, but rather the inn of the same name, now a private house. The name is likely to be a derivative of 'Doole', a boundary stone or wooden stake (usually marking the limits of Church lands). The oak might also have provided coppicing for stakes.

❋ St Peter's Boats

The Peter Boat inn at **Leigh-on-Sea** takes its name from the type of fishing vessel used off the Essex coast from as early as 1580. The boats were only 20-30ft long and could manoeuvre around the shallow mudbanks of Leigh and **Grays**, the stem and stern being alike. The boats took their name from Petermen, a term once used for fishermen after St Peter (died AD 64), a Galilean fisherman and the Patron Saint of fishermen.

❋ Where Salt was Made

The village of **Salcott** (now **Salcott-cum-Virley**) recalls the heyday of the long-lived and commercially valuable salt industry that goes back to at least Roman times (see also Chapter Three, The Red Hills of Essex). Salcott stands at the head of a creek, and navigable channel, to which it gives (or from which it takes) its name. Ekwall's *English Place-Names* confirms that in the 13th century Salcott was exactly what it says – 'a cottage where salt was made or stored'.

❋ Bilge Water

Thurrock takes its name from the Old English or Saxon word meaning 'bottom of a ship, where dirt collects'. It appears as Thurrucca in the Domesday Book and by the 13th century had evolved to Turroch. As the Thurrocks (Grays, Little and West) are at a bend of the Thames, it is probable that the water there was stagnant and thought to resemble bilge water. Ekwall's *English Place-Names* suggests an alternative meaning of 'drain', which could indicate it was a point where the water ran off the land into the river. In 1968, Norman Scarfe thought that although 'Thurrock is grimy [the] Saxon description is now too strong.'

❋ Doctor's Pond

No one is quite sure why the **Doctor's Pond** at **Great Dunmow** is so named, although there are three possible explanations. The first comes from a local doctor who used the pond for breeding and keeping leeches when they were used in medicine, and the second from two doctors who lived in Brick House opposite the pond. There was also a Dr Rayner in Great Dunmow in the 18th century, who used to care for the pond and keep it stocked with fish.

※ **The Cutlers**
The importance of cutlery manufacture at **Thaxted** in the 14th century is remembered in the **Cutlers Guildhall** and the nearby hamlet of **Cutlers Green**. In the Poll Tax Return of 1381 over one-third of the adult male population was described as 'cutlers'. Cutlers made, repaired or dealt in knives (and later other cutlery) and this, combined with employment in the woollen industry, made Thaxted a very prosperous town and attracted many immigrant workers. The industry continued until the 16th century, when it suffered a rapid decline. Superior grinding facilities in Sheffield, and a deliberate concentration by the new manufacturers on the lower end of the market, enabled the Sheffield cutlers to undercut the smaller centres such as Thaxted.

※ The extent of mediaeval prosperity at **Thaxted** is seen in the size of the Parish Church, dedicated to St John the Baptist, Our Lady and St Laurence, the latter being the **Patron Saint of Cutlers**.

※ **The Two Wendens**
There were once two villages called Wenden, Great and Little, but they were joined in 1662 to form **Wendens Ambo**, meaning 'both Wendens'. There is a neighbouring parish named **Wenden Lofts**. The Wendens have been inhabited since prehistoric days and have yielded ancient finds including bronze hoards and flint tools from 300–200 BC.

※ **Jumbo**
The 'Jumbo' water tower on **Balkerne Hill** in **Colchester** is named after **Jumbo** (1861–1885), an elephant born in French Sudan and brought to France, where he was raised in the Paris Zoo. When young he was sold to the Royal Zoological Society in London, but as Jumbo grew he developed an

uncertain temper and the Society was fearful he could cause considerable mayhem should he ever wish to do so. He was then bought by Phineas Taylor Barnum (1810–1891), ostensibly for his Hippodrome at Madison Square Gardens, New York, but in reality to help generate interest in Barnum and Bailey's English Circus. He launched a campaign to persuade people that if Jumbo was exported to America they would be losing a 'national treasure'. The plan worked and 'Jumbo Mania' ensued. Even Queen Victoria and the Prince of Wales expressed interest in the fate of the elephant. Children's toys showing Jumbo on wheels soon appeared in the shops, as well as Jumbo-shaped soaps, advertising posters and promotional souvenirs.

The excitement attracted the attention of the Revd Canon Irvine, Rector of St Mary-at-the-Walls, who had an altogether different take on 'Jumbo Mania'. When plans were drawn up for the building of the water tower he wrote to the *Essex Standard* complaining about the 'Jumbo' construction that was to be built within 60ft of his rectory, thereby creating the tower's nickname.

Unfortunately for Jumbo fans, Phineas Barnum was a businessman and decided to export Jumbo to America to drum up business at the Hippodrome as 'the largest beast in captivity'. He dismissed Jumbo's faithful keeper, Matthew 'Scotty' Scott, who had looked after him for 20 years. Jumbo, though, was more loyal and immediately went on a week-long sit-down strike until Scotty was restored to him.

In America, Jumbo proved as much of a crowd-puller as he had been in England, but in 1885 he was involved in an accident on a Canadian railway line and died. It took 160 men to drag him off the line. He was removed to a taxidermist, who stuffed and mounted the hide. Thus Jumbo remained in the public eye until 1975, when his remains were destroyed in a fire.

The Balkerne Water Tower was started in 1881 and completed two years later at a cost exceeding £10,000, over-budget and well over time. Originally it was designed to hold 220,000 gallons of water, but it never reached that capacity as later engineers decided that the structure was too weak to carry the weight. In 1884 the **Colchester Earthquake** weakened it still further. Around 1.2 million bricks, 450 tonnes of cement and 369 tonnes of stone were used in the construction. The *Little Guide* (1909) regretted that 'it is not beautiful…but it is eminently utilitarian and has the distinction of being the second largest water tower in England'.

It ceased being a water tower in 1987, since when it has changed hands several times and, although several alternative uses have been proposed, none has so far been accepted or implemented. It is now considered to be the largest surviving Victorian water tower and is a Grade II listed monument.

❋ The Witchfinder's Way

A cycle ride that starts at Iconfield Park, **Harwich**, goes through the small port of **Mistley** and returns to Harwich via **Wix**, **Great Oakley** and **Little Oakley**: it is called **The Witchfinder's Way**.

The Witchfinder belongs to a dark period of Essex history when, between 1645 and 1646, the zealot **Matthew Hopkins** (1620–1647) claimed he was employed to hunt out witches (though he was never officially engaged by any governmental office). The son of a Puritan clergyman, Hopkins was born at Great Wenham (Suffolk), but by 1644 was living in **Manningtree**. Religious and political upheaval was rife and the **Tendring Hundred** was dominated by Puritan ideals. The reign of James I saw the Elizabethan laws against witchcraft strengthened, encouraging hysteria and suspicion, especially in country areas where superstition thrived. The king himself wrote a book on demonology and confirmed the suitability of the death penalty in cases where guilt could be established, while ordinary people were encouraged to pursue malefactors.

In 1645 Tendring was manorially weak: the staunchly Puritan lord of the manor, Sir Harbottle Grimston (1569–1648), was permanently away from his seat at **Bradfield Hall**, allowing authority to lapse. Tradition holds that Hopkins was a failed lawyer, though there is little to confirm that he ever qualified, but in his mid-twenties he took advantage of the near anarchy brought about by the political confusion of the outbreak of Civil War (1642). He began his witch hunts aided by the equally sadistic John Stearne.

Hopkins started with **Elizabeth Clarke** (*c.*1565–1645), known as Mother Clarke of **Colchester**, who 'confessed' to being a witch after being deprived of sleep for three nights. She was said to have incriminated others and Hopkins rounded up 25 old women who were dragged to **Chelmsford** to stand trial. 'Evidence' was provided by Rebecca West, a daughter of one of the accused, in return for a reprieve for her mother, Anne West. At the time she was hanged, Mother Clarke was over 80 years of age, infirm and with only one leg.

As the hysteria increased women from **Mistley**, **St Osyth** and **Thorpe-le-Soken** were implicated. By 1645 there were 34 women incarcerated in a filthy dungeon at **Colchester Castle** awaiting trial. The war was creating chaos in the courts and the judges were not professional men but Puritan soldiers. Brutal interrogations took place across Essex and Suffolk and the hunt for witches spiralled out of control. The Chelmsford court upheld many indictments of 'communion with the devil', 'nourishing imps', and other charges of women 'working mischief on both animals and people in the neighbourhood'. Clergy appeared in the witness box for the prosecution and spewed out the most extraordinary instances of imagined witchery. One said he was assailed by 'four black rabbits' and accused women of employing black magic. Accusations were often used to explain personal adversity, many linked to the malice of a disgruntled neighbour. In the 1640s witchery was a logical reason for otherwise inexplicable misfortune.

Some women died on their way to the gallows, but four were burnt at the stake. Three women from **Maldon** were hanged in front of Chelmsford Town Hall. Others were strung up on the green at Manningtree.

By 1646, however, Hopkins's hysterical fervour began to scare some of the clergy and the courts turned against such trials. He returned to Manningtree discredited and died there the following year. His grave is unknown, but some say he was buried in the old church at Mistley and others that he was buried on Mistley Heath.

* The Thorn Hotel **Mistley** was once used as an office by Matthew Hopkins.

* The horror film *Witchfinder General* (1968) was based on Ronald Bassett's 1966 book of the same title and starred Vincent Price as Matthew Hopkins, Ian Ogilvy as Richard Marshall and Rupert Davies as John Lowes. Shortly after release it was voted the year's most violent film. In America it was renamed *The Conqueror Worm* to link it with Edgar

Allen Poe's poem, but the title had little to do with the poem and even less to do with Matthew Hopkins.

❊ The Magnificent Hireling

Hawkwood Road and the **Hawkwood Memorial Chapel** in **Sible Hedingham** commemorate **Sir John Hawkwood** (1320–94), who was one of the most famous, yet feared, of the English mercenaries of the period. Arthur Mee calls him 'the magnificent hireling…a towering lawless man who became the wonder and terror of mediaeval Italy'. In Italy he was notorious as a *condottiero* (mercenary leader) of a band of wandering mercenaries, whose shining breastplates caused them to be known as the White Company. It had some 5,000 horsemen and 1,500 foot soldiers, who would fight on the side of the highest bidder. In France Sir John was called *Haccoude* and in Italy *Giovanni Acuto* (John the Keen One). These were the days when countries did not have standing armies and relied instead on raising forces only when they were needed.

Sir John was born in Sible Hedingham, the son of a prosperous tanner who held large swathes of land and lordship of two manors. His father sent him to London where it was intended he should be apprenticed to a tailor, but instead he joined the army of Edward III (1312–77) whose claim to the French throne sowed the seed of what became the Anglo-French Hundred Years War (1337–1453). John Hawkwood took to soldiering with a vengeance and showed a natural talent as a commander of men. He became a captain in a company of archers and before long was serving with the Black Prince (1330–76) at Poitiers. After leaving the king's army he went to Italy, where he fought at Padua, Milan and Florence, changing sides when necessary, fighting under different banners, always with an eye to the main chance. So began his career as a *condottiero*, which was enhanced by his marrying into the ruling Visconti family of Milan.

Myths and legends of his adventures are legion, but there is no proof that he was ever knighted by an English king. Some historians say that he was so honoured by the Black Prince, or one of the Florentine kings, and others that he might have given himself the title to gain authority over his troops. He openly declared that he lived 'avowedly to foment war, regular or guerrilla'. He reputedly told a monk that he lived on war and 'that peace would undo me'. If anyone failed to pay him he would take forceful revenge on the debtor and, being illiterate, he learned never to rely on the written word. Any contract he may have been offered was read to him by his advisers, but he preferred cash to contracts.

Sir John Hawkwood finally settled down in Italy as General of the Florentine forces. He died there in 1394 and was given a state funeral. His final resting place is in Florence's Duomo. Rumours persisted that Sir John's body was brought back to Sible Hedingham at the request of Richard II and reinterred in the parish church. However, it is generally accepted that the memorial in the church is a cenotaph and not a grave. There are several hawk references in the church and, over a canopied recess in the south aisle, an allusion to his name: the 'Hawkes' that fly in a 'Wood'.

* A book that tells the story of Sir John Hawkwood *Mediaeval Mercenary: Sir John Hawkwood of Essex* by Dr Christopher Starr was published in 2008 by the Essex Record Office.

* **Sir John Hawkwood** was the inspiration for a character in *The White Company*, a novel by Arthur Conan Doyle published in 1891.

* In the novel *This Side of Paradise* (1920) by F. Scott Fitzgerald, the character 'Amor Blaine' is said to be reading *The White Company*.

* **The Knight of Aveley**

The **Knight of Aveley** public house in **South Ockenden** is a reminder of the crusading fervour that swept England in the 14th century. A knight of the Crusades, **Ralph de Knevynton** (died 1370), has a brass in St Michael's **Aveley** that bears the inscription *Deus id Vult* (God wills it), the war cry of the crusaders. The Knights Hospitaller held rents at Aveley and in 1303 owned 'one Knight's fee' of the parish.

The 62cm-long 14th-century Flemish brass shows *Radulphus de Knevynton* in armour under a canopy with a dog wearing a collar at his feet. The Latin inscription reads *Here lies Ralph de Knevynton, who died on the Thursday before the feast of St Nicholas the Bishop, in the year 1370 when the Dominical letter was F.*

It is exceedingly rare for a brass to carry a Dominical letter. In the church calendar, the year was allocated one of seven Dominical letters, A to G, employing the letter corresponding to the day on which the first Sunday fell.

❋ **Home of the Saffron Industry**
There is no secret about how **Saffron Walden** got its name, or why its coat of arms carries saffron flowers 'walled in' (a pun derived from Walden). The walls with four towers, gateway and portcullis enclosing three saffron flowers first appeared on a charter granted by Edward VI in 1549. The saffron or autumn crocus (*crocus sativus*) became an increasing source of wealth and importance for the town from the late 1300s onwards until, by the early 1500s, it was the centre of the English saffron industry. The town was called **Walden**, then **Chipping Walden** and by the 16th century had become **Saffron Walden**.

The small Saxon settlement here in Roman times was called *weala-denu* (Valley of the Britons) but in around 1130 the Norman Lord of the Manor, **Geoffrey de Mandeville, 3rd Earl of Essex**, founded a Benedictine Priory and built a castle nearby. No one is sure how the saffron crocus first came to Essex, but there is evidence that it was brought in by the Romans. However, it was not until the reign of Edward III (1327–77) that it was farmed commercially. Saffron's many uses – as a condiment, a dye and in medicine – meant that it had several markets. Culpeper's *Complete Herbal* noted that 'not above ten grains must be given at one time; a cordial if taken in an immoderate quantity, hurts the heart instead of helping it'.

By 1726 **Littlebury** was the only place still growing saffron, and by the end of that century it had virtually disappeared. Medicine moved away from that based on folklore, cooks no longer sought its yellow properties, and cheap imports of yellow dye sounded the final death knell.

❋ In 1909 the *Little Guide* recorded that 'no fewer than twenty Essex parishes still bear field names such as **Saffron Grounds**, **Saffron Piece** or **Saffron Fields**, which speak clearly of a former commerce'.

❋ Those that tended the **crocus gardens** were called **crokers**.

❋ The saffron crocus was adopted by St Mary the Virgin **Saffron Walden** as its emblem. Windows in the North Chapel contain crocuses set in scallops and the crocus theme is also found in the design of the Communion Rail, as a decorative motif on the Altar Table, and in the spandrels of the arcade opposite the South Porch.

❋ The **saffron crocus**, with three stigmas, is a common pargetting motif (both old and new) in the Saffron Walden area.

❋ Presents of saffron were made by the **Corporation of Saffron Walden** to distinguished visitors including James I and Charles I. Saffron was presented to Charles II at **Audley End** and to William III when he, too, came to Audley End in 1689. One of the last was to George I in 1717 when over £4 was paid 'for a silver salver to present some saffron to King George'.

❋ In Tudor times, Henry VIII decreed that saffron should only be used for dyeing luxurious garments for the nobility. However, it was legal for the common man to use it in cooking, as in Shakespeare's *The Winter's Tale*. The Clown plans a sheep-shearing feast and declares 'I must have saffron, to colour the warden pies'.

❋ **Judge Tindal**

Both Tindal Street and the Judge Tindal public house in **Chelmsford** take their name from **Sir Nicholas Conyngham Tindal** (1776–1846) the celebrated lawyer who in 1820 successfully defended Caroline, queen of George IV, at her trial for adultery. Judge Tindal was born at **Moulsham** (where Moulsham Street is today) and was a member of the long-standing Tindal family of **Maplestead**. He was educated at the King Edward VI Grammar School in Chelmsford and later at Trinity College, Cambridge.

During the course of his legal career he was always popular among the public, who saw him as a fearless upholder of the universal application of the law.

One of his most enduring legal achievements was the reform of the application of criminal law in respect of the verdict 'not guilty on the grounds of insanity' and a defence plea of provocation for murder.

✱ The statue of **Judge Tindal** was erected by subscription in 1850 and has been moved from its original site (in the Conduit) into the centre of Chelmsford. The epitaph reads:
To preserve for all time the image of a judge whose administration of English law, directed by serene wisdom, animated by purest love of justice, endeared by unwearied kindness, and graced by the most lucid style will be held in his country in undying remembrance.

✱ **The Peasants' Revolt**
Wat Tyler Country Park on **Pitsea Hall Island** comes from one of the 14th-century leaders of the Peasants' Revolt (1381), which began with unrest in the **Fobbing** area. **Wat Tyler** (1341–81) and the Revd **John Ball** (1338–81) a Lollard priest and one-time rector of St James' **Colchester**, were the leaders of unrest sparked by the imposition of a Poll Tax in Essex. The Park was previously known as **Pitsea Hall Park**, but was renamed 'as a memorial dedicated to those people of Essex and Kent who in the cause of liberty took part in the Peasants' Revolt of 1381'.

The depletion of the workforce following the Black Death (1348–49) contributed to the confidence of the workers and artisans to buck the hitherto unassailable system of serfdom. A third of the population had succumbed to the plague and in 1355 a new underground movement simmered until, in 1380, a third Poll Tax was imposed. Money was wanted by Richard II for the French wars and, although taxation was already burdensome, the king demanded one shilling per head of the population over 16 years of age. Only the destitute were exempt. Land, and those who owned and worked it, was always seen as a convenient source of revenue, but, although the aftermath of the Black Death had seen a certain improvement in the rural economy, the serfs were unable and unwilling to pay.

John Ball preached that all men were born equal, but in 1366 was prohibited by the church from sermonizing. In 1381 he was excommunicated for advocating 'ecclesiastical poverty and social equality', although he continued to hold impromptu meetings in town squares and became a potent voice of the people.

In 1381 one of the greatest mass rebellions in English history commenced when John Bampton, Justice of the Peace and former Sheriff of

Essex, came to Fobbing to investigate Poll Tax avoidance. Rioters set about systematically destroying all the Poll Tax records and went on a rampage of violence and destruction across the county. They pillaged manor houses, opened gaols and burned property indiscriminately. Wat Tyler, John Ball and Jack Straw (from Kent) led protestors towards London, where they rioted, murdering many Flemish immigrants in the process. They stormed Lambeth Palace and beheaded **Archbishop Simon of Sudbury**, who was instrumental in imposing the tax.

The ferocity of the rebels took the government by surprise and the king conceded to their demands, although he ordered that Wat Tyler be arrested. In the confusion Tyler was killed. John Ball was later sentenced to be hung, drawn, and quartered.

❋ The **Peasants' Revolt Monument** (1990) is in the Recreation Ground at **Fobbing** and depicts the events of 1381.

❋ **Old Siege House**

The 15th-century **Old Siege House** at **Colchester** has timbers peppered with bullet holes that are the legacy of fighting that took place there in 1648 during skirmishes between Royalists and Parliamentarians in the Civil War (1642–49). The **Siege of Colchester** began in early July and involved the Royalist Sir Charles Lucas, whose family had acquired **St John's Abbey** at the Dissolution of the Monasteries. In 1642, however, that property and family graves in the nearby St Giles's Church were sacked by townspeople who supported the Parliamentary cause. Thus the town was split between the two causes of Charles I and the Parliamentarians led by Oliver Cromwell. On 11 June 1648 the Roundheads (as the Parliamentarians were called) failed to stop Sir Charles and some 5,000 of his troops from entering Colchester and using St John's as a temporary sanctuary.

Meanwhile, Lord Thomas Fairfax (1612–71), commander-in-chief of the New Model Army, was alerted to the Royalist 'nest' and hastened to Colchester. Setting up his headquarters at **Lexden**, he sent troops to secure **Mersea Island** so as to cover the Colne estuary.

Early in July Parliamentary firepower was boosted by the arrival of 40 guns from the Tower of London and Fairfax began a steady bombardment of the town. Skirmishes took place continually in the suburbs, around Head Gate and Shere Gate, and men on both sides were killed and prisoners taken. Almost 200 houses were set alight and others plundered. One of these skirmishes was the **East Street Sortie**, where the Parliamentarians had seized and garrisoned the Old Siege House, knowing it to be of strategic importance. Its position at the foot of East Hill was close to the bridge that spanned the River Colne and the river crossing was crucial to forces entering or leaving Colchester. On 5 July Sir Charles Lucas led the sortie with 200 cavalry and Sir George Lisle with 500 foot soldiers. They charged down the hill and rushed the footbridge, dispersing the Parliamentarians, who then rallied and drove the Royalists back, only for the Parliamentarians to regroup, forcing the Royalists to retreat into the town.

With East Street secure, Fairfax gradually encircled the Royalist troops, closing off exit routes where he could. Comprehending Fairfax's siege tactics, Sir Charles Lucas sent men to ransack the Hythe. Stores of corn, fish, wine and ammunition were commandeered and stored in the town. The Balkerne Gate was fortified and various small forts constructed. The Royalists made occasional forays out into the countryside, on one occasion via the North Gate, boosting their rations with cattle, sheep, corn and other provisions.

However, by the middle of July the Royalists knew it was only a matter of time before they would have to surrender. Food was running low and conditions in the town were deteriorating badly. Horses were killed for food (it is said over 800) and troops were forced to eat cats, dogs, rats and whatever else they could find, including soap and candles. By August the remaining townspeople began to harass the Royalist commanders, demanding that they surrender and accept Fairfax's terms. Messages were sent between Sir Charles Lucas and Fairfax but, with no agreement, rumours were rife among the ranks and there was talk of desertion among the Royalist lines. On 23 August it was found that there was only one day's supply of food left and on 28 August, 3,531 Royalist men surrendered.

Fairfax entered Colchester on the afternoon of 18 August and immediately had Sir Charles Lucas, Sir George Lisle and Sir Bernard Gascoigne imprisoned and condemned to be shot forthwith. They were taken to the castle and that evening Sir Charles was shot first and then Sir

George. Sir Bernard was reprieved as he was an Italian and Fairfax feared that his death would have repercussions in Europe. The two Royalist commanders were buried privately in St Giles' churchyard. A public funeral was held in June 1661 at the Restoration, when a grave slab was carved commemorating their 'eminent loyalty to their soverain', recording that they were 'in cold blood barbarously murdered' by Fairfax.

The common soldiers fared little better as they were stripped of everything they owned, including their clothes, and sent out in heavy rain. Many died, being already half starved. Some were sold for transportation to the West Indies. Huge fines were imposed on the town.

An obelisk stands in the grounds of **Colchester Castle** on the spot where the two knights were executed and it is said that the grass does not grow on that spot.

✱ The damage wrought on **Colchester** during the siege left its mark for years to come. St John's House was all but destroyed and the Romanesque priory-front of St Botolph's was in ruins, as was St Mary's church. In 1656 John Evelyn found Colchester still 'wretchedly demolished by the late Siege', and in 1698, 50 years after the 1648 siege, the traveller Celia Fiennes visited the town. She wrote that 'formerly there were 16 churches tho' now much of it is ruinated'.

✱ In 1724, Daniel Defoe published a detailed account of the **Siege of Colchester** from a diary 'of the most remarkable passages' by an unknown Royalist eyewitness. He wrote that the town 'still mourns, in the ruins of a civil war'.

✱ **Humpty Dumpty**

One of the Royalist cannons is said to have been nicknamed **Humpty Dumpty** and was placed on a wall near St Mary's Church, where a defensive fort had been hurriedly erected. An attack by the Parliamentarians on 14 July 1648 dislodged the wall, bringing the cannon down, so that the Royalists, 'all the king's horses and all the king's men', could not put him back on the wall or repair the cannon. The Humpty Dumpty cannon was reputedly manned by a Royalist gunner named 'One-eyed' Thompson. The ditty was Parliamentarian propaganda to show how easily the Royalist defences had been breached.

It was in 1871 that Humpty Dumpty assumed the personage of an egg, when Sir John Tenniel illustrated *Through the Looking Glass and What Alice Found There* by Lewis Carroll (1832–98).

※ **The Sarah Moore**

A public house on Elm Street **Leigh on Sea** is called the **Sarah Moore** after an evil-smelling sea witch who sold 'fair wind' to sailors. Anyone foolish enough not to cross her palm with coins was cursed. One such curse, it is claimed, remains on one old Leigh family to this day. Sarah Moore was described as having a hooked nose, a harelip and always giving off a horrible smell!

※ **Rigby Avenue, Mistley**

The Rigby family were merchant drapers in the City of London and landowners in **Mistley** and Manningtree. **Richard Rigby** (1690–1730) made his fortune in the South Sea Company and fortuitously sold his share before the 'bubble' burst in 1720. His son, also **Richard Rigby** (1722–88), was known as the playboy squire of Mistley Hall, who embarked on an ambitious plan to continue his father's transformation of Mistley by converting it into a spa town. The family name gives rise to **Rigby Avenue** and **Rigby Road**.

When the young French tourist, François de La Rochefoucauld, visited Mistley in 1784 he found that it was 'a very small place, fifty houses at most, which are so well built and so spruce that you see at a glance that they all belong to the same owners. Mr Rigby owns the whole town and a superb house and fine park'. However, not everyone in Mistley was enamoured of Mr Rigby. There was one house that did not belong to the squire and its owner 'would never sell it to him'. So that strangers would not think that he had, the man painted the house red when the others were all white.

Richard Rigby invested heavily in **Mistley Hall**, which was constructed of white brick, surrounded by pleasure gardens and built to take in a view of the estuary. Its interior was sumptuous in the extreme. In addition to the formal gardens and the farm there was a nine-acre kitchen garden with hot houses, fruit trees and vines. Rigby spent much of his fortune rebuilding Mistley Church (designed by Robert Adam in 1777) and through his government contacts brought corn and coal trade to Mistley quay.

The hall was the scene of wild, extravagant parties which attracted many celebrities of the day, including the actor David Garrick, François de La Rochefoucauld and his entourage, and the celebrated architect Robert Adam. According to one account 'brandy was drunk at Mistley Hall as other men drink small beer'. Rigby had a successful political career, becoming a Member of Parliament in 1745. In 1755 he became a junior minister in the Board of Trade and was appointed Master of the Rolls for Ireland in 1759, which brought political guests aplenty. Such was the local interest in the notables arriving at Mistley Hall that people lined the road to watch them. On winter evenings Richard Rigby would sometimes send his steward out with hot punch to sustain the onlookers.

Unfortunately Richard Rigby was not as careful with the family fortune as previous generations and his close friend the Duke of Bedford had to lend him £5,000 to clear his debts. However, as Rigby was Paymaster to the Forces (1768–84) it was reckoned that he had misappropriated large chunks of government money so that when he died it was said that 'he left near half a million of public money'.

Richard Rigby's dream of a spa at Mistley was not realised, but there is still much to show for the family tenure: Robert Adam's church towers, the Thorn Inn, the Swan fountain, and several Georgian houses and quay buildings commissioned by one or other of the Rigbys. Rigby himself suffered for his indulgent lifestyle and, having retired to Bath on doctor's orders in 1785, died in 1788 unmarried and with no heirs or successors. Mistley Hall was demolished in 1844.

✳ Dickens of a Place

Chelmsford has very strong connections with Charles Dickens's famous *Pickwick Papers* (1836–37), as shown by **Havisham Way**, **Estella Mead**, **Copperfield Road**, **Oliver Way** and **Dickens Place**. The Black Boy coaching inn that stood next to Grays Brewery features in the book when

Mr Weller Senior describes how he transported Job Trotter and Charles Fitz-Marshall from 'The Black Boy at Chelmsford, the wery place they'd come to, I took 'em up, right through to Ipswich'. Dickens often stayed at the inn on his way from to London from Norwich, but it was pulled down in 1857 having suffered a drastic lack of custom after the railways opened in 1843. The inn site was redeveloped in 1982 and it was discovered that a hostelry had stood there since the 14th century.

SIX
ESSEX PEOPLE

✳ **Ealdorman Byrhtnoth**

The 10th-century Ealdorman of Essex, **Byrhtnoth** (born *c.*961) was one of the county's first heroes, defending his people against the invading Danes. Arthur Mee calls him 'one of our forgotten heroes, a wise and gallant warrior'. He is said to have stood over 6ft in height and his Old English name reveals the esteem in which he was held – *beorht* (bright) and *noth* (courage).

The prosperity of the late Saxon port of **Maldon** on the River **Blackwater** attracted the attention of the Scandinavian raiders, who had already begun renewed attacks on settlements along the Essex and Suffolk coasts. In the 890s the Danes had made considerable inroads but Edward the Elder (900–924), son of Alfred the Great, reclaimed many of the Anglo-Danish lands and built a small castle at Maldon in 916. However, in 991 the Danes came to resettle their lands. News arrived of a planned skirmish at Maldon. A party of Danes had landed and encamped at **Northey Island** and Byrhtnoth knew he had to prevent them from crossing the causeway to Maldon and reaching mainland Essex. He hurriedly gathered a small army, recruiting men from wherever he could, but was hampered in his choice by Saxon law, which required fighting men to be 'mootworthy, foldworthy and fyrdworth', that is, upstanding citizens who not only attended the courts, but were also skilled farmers. The common man was not eligible.

With forces thought to be almost 4,000-strong, the Danish raiders were more than a match for Byrhtnoth's untrained followers and within a few hours of the start of the **Battle of Maldon**, he was dead. His army was hard-pressed to contain the foe and, although the Saxons put up a determined and courageous fight, after three days of skirmishing the Danes won the day. However, they had sustained heavy casualties and instead of capitalising on their victory and forcing their way into the mainland, they were obliged to retreat and regroup. It had always been the intention of the Saxons to prevent the incursion so in that respect, at least, they had achieved their purpose and Byrhtnoth was hailed a hero.

* The site of the three-day **Battle of Maldon** (991) is recognised by English Heritage. It is not only the only known battle site in Essex, but is also the earliest confirmed battlefield in England.

* The Danish leader, Olaf Tryggvason, is said to have used Byrhtnoth's head as a tankard.

* There is a statue of **Ealdorman Byrhtnoth** in a recess at All Saints' **Maldon**. A somewhat larger statue stands in Promenade Park. The 10ft tall figure defiantly brandishes a sword, raised in his right hand, and is now a familiar landmark for those approaching by way of the River Blackwater. The statue was erected in October 2006 and, although controversial at the time, has since grown in the public's affection.

* The village of **Danbury** is said to mean 'hill of the Danes', who camped there during their campaign of 991, but Ekwall in *Dictionary of English Place-Names* (1936) prefers 'the burgh of Dene's people'.

* Physician and Naturalist

Allan Maclean (1796–1869) was a physician at the Essex and Colchester Hospital (1821) and a naturalist of some repute. He raised the first white pelargonium and first variegated gladiolus. He is also credited with inventing a special butterfly net (known as Maclean's elastic net) and carried out extensive propagation and conservation of the Purple Admiral butterfly.

* Founder of a London Hospital

Benjamin Golding (1793–1863) of **St Osyth** founded **Charing Cross Hospital**. He spent his student days at St Thomas's and later became physician for the West London Infirmary. He later transformed the infirmary into the famous Charing Cross Hospital in the heart of London. There is a monument to Benjamin Golding on the wall of the north aisle of the church of St Peter and St Paul **St Osyth**.

❋ The Greatest of all Field Naturalists

The son of a village blacksmith, **John Ray** (1627–1705) was a pioneering botanist described as 'the greatest of all field naturalists' and was inspired by his mother, who was skilled in the use of herbal medicine. He was born at **Black Notley** and attended **Braintree** Grammar School before going on to Trinity College, Cambridge. There began his lifelong interest in the natural world and, finding that botanical literature was both scant and inaccurate, he set about a methodical and scientific study of his own.

John Ray's *Historia Plantarum* (History of Plants) was published in three volumes between 1686 and 1704. In it he devised a system of classification of plants that remained in use for over 200 years. He also compiled notes on around 11,000 different insect species with special emphasis on beetles (of which he identified 300 kinds), bees and spiders.

He died at Black Notley and an obelisk to him stands near the church of St Peter and St Paul (paid for by the Bishop of London). Although the tomb sustained damage in 1943, when the church was bombed, it was restored by members of the Ray Society.

❋ One of **John Ray's** hobbies was collecting and recording Essex proverbs or jingles, one of which was:

> ***Braintree*** *for the pure, and **Bocking** for the poor;*
> ***Cog'shall*** *for the jeering town, and **Kelvedon** for the whore.*

However, he commented that 'jeering' Coggeshall 'is no proverb but an ignominious epithet fastened on the place by their neighbours'!

❋ Robert Miller Christy

One of the many Victorian writers and antiquarians to explore and record the archaeology of Essex was **Robert Miller Christy, FLS** (1861–1928), born in **Chignal St James** in 1861. *The Times* obituary column described him as 'an authority on Essex Archaeology and on many out-of-the-way subjects of interest to collectors and connoisseurs'. Among his best-known works are *Handbook of Essex* (1887), *Trade Signs of Essex* (1887) and *Birds of Essex* (1890). He was a member of the Council of the **Essex Archaeological Society** and in 1927 superintended the excavation of the Roman temple foundations at **Harlow**. He also compiled entries for the *Dictionary of National Biography*.

❋ The Great Bright of Maldon

When **Edward Bright** (1721–1750) died in 1750 he weighed so much and was so large that a special coffin was made for him. A note in the parish burial register recorded: '*A way was cut through the wall and staircase to let [the coffin] down into the shop; it was drawn upon a carriage to the church and slid upon rollers to the vault made of brickwork, and interred by the help of a triangle and pulley. He was a very honest tradesman, a facetious companion, comely in his person, affable in his temper, a tender father and valuable friend*'.

Though only 29 he died leaving a wife and five children at Church House on the High Street, **Maldon**. Bright, a descendant of Oliver Cromwell's sister, was a post boy in his youth and later a candle manufacturer and grocer at Church House. By the time he was 11 he weighed 10 stone and at 22 he was 30 stone. A year before he died his weight was said to be '584lbs or nearly 42 stones…he measured 5ft 9in in height and round the chest measured 5ft 6in and the stomach 6ft 11in'.

He was, though, a kind husband and father and a good friend to those in need. The press dubbed him the Great Bright.

Shortly after Edward Bright died a wager was made between Mr Codd and Mr Hants, patrons of the **Black Bull** public house. They bet that five hundred men could be buttoned into Bright's green baize waistcoat 'without breaking a single stitch'. Thinking it impossible many took the bet but were duped when not five but seven 'hundred' men managed to squeeze in, but since they were all from the Dengie Hundred, seven 'hundred' men had indeed fitted in.

A replica of Bright's waistcoat and a sculpture of the '700 men' can be seen at Maldon Museum, where he is celebrated as a local hero.

❋ In 2003 the **Maldon Brewing Company** launched **Edward Brights Stout** at the **Maldon Beer Festival** (started in 2002) in celebration of the Great Bright.

- **Captain Cook at Barking**
Seaman and explorer **Captain James Cook** (1728–79) married Elizabeth Batts at **Barking** on 21 December 1762. Elizabeth was born in Barking, the daughter of Samuel Batts, proprietor of the Bell Inn, Execution Dock, Wapping. Captain Cook, having joined the navy in 1755, took lodging at the inn and he and Elizabeth were married shortly afterwards. Unfortunately they spent little of their married life together as Cook spent most of his time at sea, but they nevertheless managed to have six children (two sons drowned at sea when young). After Captain Cook was killed, his wife moved to London and lived to the grand old age of 93.

- The **Captain Cook** pub in Axe Street is a reminder of his association with **Barking**.

- At St Mary and St Mary Magdalene **Wethersfield** there is a tablet monument to **Captain Charles Clerke** (1741–1779), who sailed round the world four times, his last three voyages with **Captain Cook**. Captain Clerke was born in Wethersfield, the son of a gentleman farmer, but studied at the Royal Naval Academy in Portsmouth from the age of 13. After joining an expedition to explore the Pacific in 1764, he became master's mate on Cook's *Endeavour* in 1768. When Cook was killed in Hawaii, Captain Clerke took command of HMS *Resolution* and got the ship to safety. Due to a stint in the Fleet debtor's prison, for the debt of one of his brothers, his health had suffered and he became ill shortly after assuming command. He died of tuberculosis before the voyage was ended, aged only 38, and was buried at Petropavlovsk (Russia).

- **The Father of Modern Surgery**
The surgeon and founder of antiseptic surgery, **Dr Joseph Lister**, 1st Baron Lister of Lyme Regis (1827–1912) was born at **Upton** (Forest Gate) and raised as a Quaker. Lister was greatly influenced by his father's interest in botany and by Louis Pasteur's work on bacteria. In the course of his work as a surgeon at the Glasgow Royal Infirmary he introduced the use of carbolic acid dressings to reduce the risk of infection. He realised the need for surgical cleanliness and that germs were responsible for the chronically high

death rates following surgery, which could be anything up to 80 per cent. As his methods took effect the death rate began to fall. In spite of his success he was treated with a measure of professional scepticism and jealousy, but he persisted with what a poet later described as 'faultless patience'. In 1868 he became Professor of Clinical Surgery at Edinburgh and in 1897 was created Baron Lister of Lyme Regis.

❋ The Courtaulds

The name Courtauld is readily associated with Essex, several generations of the family having lived and prospered in the county since the late 1700s (most of them confusingly called Samuel or George). Descended from Huguenot émigrés, the first to set up business in Essex was **George Courtauld**. He had been adventuring in the New World but returned to England in the late 1790s and started a silk mill at **Pebmarsh**. He went back to America in 1818, by which time his son **Samuel** (1793–1881) was operating his own silk mill at **Braintree**. The family business was expanded by bringing in more family members and converting the former corn mill at **Halstead** (Townford Mill on the River **Colne**) in 1825 and at **Bocking** they leased a water-powered mill (which became one of the first to be steam-operated).

In 1861 the Prince Consort died and Queen Victoria went into mourning for the rest of her long life, thereby setting the fashion for women's mourning dresses. Happily for Courtaulds, one of their mills specialised in manufacturing black mourning crepe, which provided them with an on-going and highly lucrative market.

Samuel Courtauld had a country estate at **Gosfield** with a large park edged by a long lake. He had intended to retire there, but when the time came he could not let go the reins and maintained a controlling interest in the company right up until his death in 1881. Samuel built many timber-framed cottages in the village and is said to have had a lifelong wish that when he died 'I should like to have written on my tomb, *He built good cottages*'.

❋ Samuel's great nephew **Samuel Courtauld** (1876–1947) was Chairman between 1921 and 1946 but is remembered today as the founder of the

Courtauld Institute of Art in London. In 1931, when his wife died, he made over his house in Portman Square to the Institute, complete with his considerable art collection. Many other family members were benefactors of the arts and, during the 1930s, **William Julien Courtauld** gave artworks to **Essex County Council** at **Chelmsford** and the Town Hall at **Braintree**.

* In 1838, over 92 per cent of the Courtauld workforce was female and by 1850 there were around 2,000 women working in the three silk mills.

* Many episodes of the long-running television antiques series *Lovejoy* were filmed at **Halstead's Townford Mill**, starring Ian McShane (Lovejoy) and Phyllis Logan (Lady Jane Felsham). The series was based on the books by Jonathan Gash.

* **The Man on the Icecap**
Augustine 'August' Courtauld (1904–1959) was born at **Bocking**, the eldest son of **Samuel Augustine Courtauld** and a descendant of George Courtauld, who had gone to America in the late 1700s. August was an idealist and led a life full of adventure and daring. As well as taking part in four expeditions to Greenland (in the 1920s and 30s), August was a navigator, sailor, climber and explorer. His outstanding achievement was as a member of the Gino Watkins' British Arctic Air Route Expedition (1930–31) that went to observe and record the weather at an altitude of over 8,000ft on the Greenland icecap. The advances made in air travel had opened up the possibilities of an air route to America via Iceland, but since no one knew what the weather would be like in winter the expedition was sent to find out.

The expedition reached its destination and set up the station, but due to a shortage of rations it was impossible for the entire team to stay for the winter. Bad weather delayed the trip and most of the food had been eaten. August, claiming afterwards that it was because he had frostbite and did not relish the trip back, volunteered to stay alone at the station to make the necessary meteorological observations. He would have five months alone on the icecap with frostbitten toes and meagre rations. The story of his survival was later told in *Man on the Icecap, Life of August Courtauld* by Nicholas Wollaston (1980).

In 1932 August married Mollie Montgomerie (1907–2009) of **Castle Hedingham** and set up home at Spencers, **Great Yeldham**. She was a friend of August's sister, Betty Courtauld, and they had met socially for several years before marrying. Mollie accompanied August on the British East Greenland Expedition (1935–36), spending many months at sea in polar conditions. The marriage was an outstanding success and they had six children.

August distinguished himself in 1939 when he joined the Special Operations Executive (SOE) and, at the request of Naval Intelligence, took his yacht *Duet* along the Norwegian coast, observing and recording the harbours and factories along the way. He later worked for the Admiralty and eventually served in ships in Atlantic convoys.

His final years were tragically afflicted by multiple sclerosis. He was only 54 when he died and was buried at sea from the lifeboat he had donated to the **Walton and Frinton Station** in memory of his mother. Like all the Courtaulds he had a well-developed streak of altruism and a strong sense of community. He was chairman of the Essex Association of Boys' Clubs, Justice of the Peace, and High Sheriff of Essex in 1953. He had also been one of his generation's most daring explorers and gave quiet but effective war service.

※ **The Best Prime Minister we never had!**
Six months after the death of **August Courtauld** his widow married **Richard Austen 'Rab' Butler** (1902–82), then Home Secretary, Leader of the House of Commons and chairman of the Conservative Party. There were raised eyebrows at the speed of their marriage so soon after her husband's death, but she later wrote in *August and Rab, A Memoir* (1987) that 'they did not know how long ago August had left me'. Mollie and Rab had known each other for many years, having Courtauld relations in common (their children were second cousins) and her home at **Great Yeldham** was not far from **Stanstead Hall, Halstead**, home of the Butlers.

Rab Butler was born in India and after a distinguished academic career entered government as Under Secretary of State in the India Office in 1932. In 1926 he married the heiress **Sydney Courtauld**, only child of Samuel Courtauld (another descendant of the George who went to America). They set up home at Stanstead Hall and shortly afterwards he became the Member of Parliament for **Saffron Walden** (1929) and held the seat until his retirement in 1965.

During the 1930s Rab Butler became involved in the long-running dispute between the Church of England and the tithepayers, known as the **Tithe War**. His constituency was primarily rural and large numbers of his constituent farmers were liable to pay sums of money to tithe holders *in lieu* of tithe, a tenth part of a man's income due to the church at that time. In 1836 this tenth share of farm produce – the tenth pig, wheat sheaf, fodder, eggs, milk and every other fruit of the land – was converted into a fixed cash liability that did not depend on income or the ability to pay. The amount took no account of the season's vagaries or religious persuasion of the tithepayers, but by the 1930s affected only those farmers and landowners on land where tithe had not already been redeemed. A meeting was held at **Radwinter** and a Tithepayers' Association was formed. It attracted the attention of Rab Butler, who offered to chair the initial meeting and gave his full support to the 'war'.

Protests continued throughout the 1930s, the many Essex associations joining the larger National Tithepayers' Association, but it was not until 1976 that the government finally allowed full redemption of the remaining tithes. Rab Butler supported the farmers throughout and spent many hours receiving deputations and writing letters to his parliamentary colleagues. He also enjoyed chatting with the farmers and was a familiar figure at the local cattle markets.

In 1954 Rab's wife Sydney died of a distressing form of cancer, leaving him bereft and lonely. He married the recently-bereaved Mollie Courtauld in 1959. She wrote 'he and I turned towards each other for mutual comfort, and in doing so found a depth of devotion which was to last for the rest of our lives'.

Throughout his distinguished political career he held numerous governmental posts, including the offices of Home Secretary and Foreign Secretary. As President of the Board of Education he proved himself a radical reforming minister and the 1944 Education Act became known as the Butler Education Act. In 1963, as deputy Prime Minister, he was involved in a leadership struggle that ended in his being passed over in favour of Sir

Alec Douglas-Home, a repeat of the disappointment in 1957 when he had lost out to Harold Macmillan. He was described by many as 'the best Prime Minister we never had'.

At the time of his retirement Rab Butler was the longest continuously serving member of the Commons and had held Saffron Walden for 36 years.

The Banner of the Most Noble Order of the Garter, which hangs at the west end of the nave of St Mary the Virgin **Saffron Walden**, belongs to Rab Butler, 'Lord Butler of Saffron Walden KG, CH, DL, PC'.

Lord Butler is the only person to have been buried in the Saffron Walden churchyard for over 100 years.

❋ At St John the Baptist **Finchingfield** can be found an unusual reference to tithe before it was converted into a cash payment. At the top of one of the chancel pillars is a stone carving of a priest holding his breviary in one hand and a tithe pig in the other. Quite possibly the mason who carved this figure was a tithepayer and it is to be wondered whether his parish priest knew of the carving.

❋ **The Fighting Parson**

On a promontory between the Blackwater estuary and the sea stands **Bradwell Lodge**, once the home of **Revd Sir Henry Bate Dudley** (1745–1824), rector, magistrate, public servant, journalist, playwright and squire of **Bradwell-on-Sea**.

Born Henry Bate, the son of a clergyman, he was educated at Queen's College, Oxford. As a student, and then a curate, he was always a colourful character and while living in London took part in at least two duels. The first was over derogatory remarks about the Countess of Strathmore, which was settled with pistols; the second was over remarks made to his sister-in-law Mrs Hartley, an actress. This he resolved with his bare fists and the fight, combined with other 'fisticuff' incidents, earned him the nickname 'The Fighting Parson'.

After a stint as editor of the *Morning Post* (which he founded in 1772) Henry worked on several newspapers and became known for his 'daring approach' to both politics and society. In 1780 he was sentenced to 12 months in the King's Bench Prison after publishing an inflammatory and libellous article about the Duke of Richmond. Thinking he might lie low for a while, he came to Bradwell as curate in 1871.

However, he was not a man to take life quietly at any level. Few country parsons of the 18th century had such a colourful lifestyle as Sir Henry, who moved in elevated society circles and numbered Thomas Gainsborough, William Hogarth, George Selwyn and the actress Mrs Sarah Siddons among his friends. The Lodge, previously the rectory, was greatly enhanced at his expense and was the scene of lavish dinner parties. In 1784 he inherited a substantial fortune, but only on the condition that he added Dudley to his name, which he did, and he used the money to reinforce his position not only in Essex (where he made improvements to the run-down parish church), but also in London society. He married Mary White, whose sister was the well-known actress over whose honour he had fought, and thereby became friends with the actor and theatre manager David Garrick. The saying 'Wonders will never cease' is attributed to Sir Henry and was later used by Garrick in one of his plays. Sir Henry also wrote a number of plays and comic operas, some of which were performed at London's Theatre Royal.

In common with many country parsons of his day, Sir Henry was master of a pack of foxhounds. On one famous occasion the fox made a bid for safety at **Creeksea** church by climbing up the ivy onto the buttress of the roof, pursued by Sir Henry and several hounds.

Sir Henry (the baronetcy was conferred on him in 1813 by the Prince Regent) cultivated a particular friendship with the painter and portraitist Thomas Gainsborough. Four portraits of Sir Henry and his wife painted at Bradwell Lodge are now in the National Gallery. The Georgian wing was added in the 1780s (designed by John Johnson, the county surveyor of Essex, supposedly so that Sir Henry could keep a watch out for smugglers) and here Gainsborough had a studio, said to be one of his favourites.

During the Napoleonic Wars Sir Henry took an active role in organising the defence of the Essex coastline. He also resolved to improve the roads thereabouts and compelled the parish councils to see that the work was carried out. In later life he began reclaiming some of the marshy glebe land at Bradwell, turning it to agriculture, though this was not enough to convince the Bishop of London to admit him as incumbent of Bradwell, as he believed Henry guilty of simony.

In 1823 he retired and moved to Cheltenham, where he died soon afterwards.

❋ **Bate Dudley Drive** in **Bradwell-on-Sea** is named for Sir Henry.

❋ The Tudor version of **Bradwell Lodge** was part of the divorce settlement between Henry VIII and his fourth wife, Anne of Cleves (died 1557). After the divorce Anne of Cleves 'retired' to **Hadleigh Castle**, which had been rebuilt in 1365 during the reign of Edward III.

❋ **A Spy at Bradwell Lodge**
In the 1930s, **Bradwell Lodge** was home to another characterful occupant, the journalist and left-wing Member of Parliament **Thomas Driberg, Baron Bradwell** (1905–1976).

Tom Driberg came to prominence as a journalist on the *Daily Express,* where he started the successful William Hickey gossip column. Always a controversial and flamboyant figure, he was flagrantly homosexual (at a time when it was illegal) and had extensive links with Communist Russia.

He became Member of Parliament for **Maldon** (1942–55) in a by-election as an independent candidate but took the Labour whip in 1945. He retained the seat until 1955 and in 1959 was elected the Member for **Barking** (1959–74), though he was said to be a not very successful representative 'since his Socialism was of the champagne variety'. He became Chairman of the Labour Party (1957–58) and, in spite of his constant notoriety and outrageous behaviour, alienating many he worked with, Harold Wilson gave him a peerage in 1975. Rumours that he was a member of the Russian KGB were constant and his visits to Moscow did nothing to dispel the general opinion that he was a Russian spy. A few years after his death it was revealed that he was, in fact, a KGB spy, codenamed 'Lepage'. It was not state secrets as such that he passed on, since he had limited ministerial information, but he was an inveterate gossip and provided personal information about prominent people which could have been used for blackmail purposes.

Tom Driberg bought Bradwell Lodge just after World War Two and subsequently entertained celebrities of the day including Edith Sitwell, John

Betjeman, Lord Beaverbrook, Mick Jagger and Joan Littlewood (with her Theatre Workshop). In the late 1950s, John Betjeman joined Driberg in organising a petition against the building of the **Bradwell Nuclear Power Station**, saying that it would spoil that part of the Blackwater. He raised the subject several times in the House of Commons and, once it was clear that it would be built, attempted to get assurances about its safety with particular reference to possible leakages. He was adamantly anti-nuclear and spoke out regularly against the defensive use of 'the bomb'.

He always referred to Bradwell as 'Bradwell-juxta-Mare' and complained regularly that the nearest post-box was too small for his letters.

✳ The Beautiful Bigamist

In 1743 a beautiful young woman named **Catherine 'Kitty' Canham** of **Thorpe-le-Soken** married the Revd Alexander Gough, a much older man with a very bad temper. Kitty was the daughter of a tenant farmer who lived at **Beaumont Hall** and in her teens became the toast of the neighbourhood. By marrying she had thought to widen her circle of friends, but her husband was scholarly and wanted the gregarious, fun-loving Kitty to sit quietly at home rather than be off to one of the numerous parties that she had previously enjoyed. The marriage was not a success and after a few years Kitty could stand it no longer and moved to London, where she resumed her social life. Then she met **John Primrose, Lord Dalmeny** (1725–1755) and they fell in love. John was the eldest son and heir of the 2nd Earl of Roseberry and a man of considerable culture and social standing, not only in London but also in his native Scotland. Kitty and John decided to elope to Verona in Italy, though whether or not John knew then that she was already married can only be a matter for speculation. Knowingly, or otherwise, John married 'Catherine Canham' in Verona in 1748 and after travelling around Europe they settled back in Italy, where for some years they lived happily together as man and wife.

In August 1753, however, Kitty became ill and told John that if she died she wanted to be buried at Thorpe-le-Soken. It is to be wondered if she then told him about her first husband and, if so, why he agreed to return her to Essex, where he would surely be faced with a charge of bigamy. However, when Kitty died he had her body embalmed and encased in a lead coffin and set out for Thorpe-le-Soken. Unfortunately, as he approached the Essex coast, a storm blew his boat off course and he was intercepted by Customs and Excise officers, who discovered his wife's body and accused him of murder. He managed to convince them of his innocence, but the Revd Alexander Gough was summoned. It is still not clear whether John knew of Kitty's deception, as he might just have been asking for the church rector with a view to arranging the funeral.

The two husbands quickly discovered the truth and Alexander had to be persuaded not to challenge Lord Dalmeny to a duel. Instead they called a truce and agreed to give Kitty the funeral and burial she had requested. John and Alexander walked behind the coffin, allegedly hand-in-hand.

It is entirely possible that Lord Dalmeny had no idea that he was married bigamously until Alexander identified his wife. In view of his position as heir to the Earldom of Roseberry, he must surely have come in for some censure from his family. Whatever the truth, he only lived two more years, dying when only 30 years old.

❉ The ghost of Kitty Canham reputedly haunts the Bell Inn at **Thorpe-le-Soken**, which stands beside the churchyard and was originally the Guild Hall. In the mid-1800s renovations were carried out at the church and some of the graves were disturbed, including Kitty's. Ever since, her restless soul walks the corridors of the inn and plays pranks on guests and scares any dogs or cats in the neighbourhood. In 1972 Kitty was blamed for the mysterious movement of a very heavy wardrobe from one side of a bedroom to the other during the night, unheard and unobserved. Guests have reported seeing a shadowy female figure, which moves silently round the room then melts through closed doors. Although fire ravaged the inn in 2001, the picture of Kitty remained undamaged.

❉ **A Cunning Man**

In *Essex, Its Forest, Folk and Folklore* (1923) Caroline Craven Mason tells of **James 'Cunning' Murrell** (1780–1860), an 18th-century white witch who was born at **Rayleigh** (or **Rochford**, no one is sure) but settled in **Hadleigh**. Cunning Murrell, as he was called, was the seventh son of a seventh son and was reputed to be able to call out the **Canewdon** witches (of which there were many) at will. One of these witches was supposed to have been the parson's wife, another the butcher's wife and yet another a Canewdon girl who went to keep house for her uncle at **Woodham Ferrers** (but the poor man 'knew no peace for after she came into the house nothing in it would keep still').

Cunning men, also known as wizards, were practitioners of folk magic and villagers thought that they would protect them from evil through the use of charms and herbs. Because he was the seventh son James's father knew he would be a witch and he was the only one in his family to be given an education. He moved to London to gain knowledge and experience in the occult and astrology and amassed a comprehensive reference library. Once back in Hadleigh he rented a cottage and, rather peculiarly, began work as a cobbler. However, he simultaneously began to build a reputation as a herbalist and breaker of evil spells and so earned the name 'Cunning'. He kept one of the rooms for consulting and there laid out the tools of his trade, bunches of herbs, a human skull and a magical mirror and telescope.

Murrell seemed to be able to recover stolen property. On one occasion a man lost his horse and he told him that it was at a certain place in Suffolk and so it proved to be. If children or animals were bewitched, he would be consulted and would often put some of their hair and nail clippings into a witch bottle and bury it, saying that the spell would lose its power.

Inevitably Cunning Murrell made enemies as well as friends and, as he became more famous, clients came from wide and far to consult him. In 1860 he became ill and foretold his own death. Tales abound as to how this came about. One version states that a local man had a donkey that he believed to have been bewitched and held Cunning Murrell responsible. Playing him at his own game the man took hair from the donkey and put it in a witch bottle, which he then consigned to the fire. Very soon afterwards James Murrell was found dead.

* Another equally famous Cunning Man was **George Pickingill** (1816–1909) of **Canewdon**. He managed to practice his folk magic for an astounding 90-odd years and is believed to have been the last of the Master Witches of Canewdon.

❋ Stand and Deliver!

The highwayman **Richard 'Dick' Turpin** (1706–39) of **Hempstead** was a housebreaker, cattle and horse thief, smuggler and murderer and no more should have been heard of him after he was hanged at York for the murder of an **Epping** innkeeper in 1739. However, in 1834 the novelist William Harrison Ainsworth (1805–82) wrote *Rookwood*, an historical novel with an elaborate and highly impractical plot (called a 'gothic horror' by the critics). In it was a chapter describing a thrilling night ride that 'Jack Palmer' (alias Dick Turpin) took from London to York on his mare, Black Bess, in order to establish an alibi. *The Ride to York* was so gripping that it was published separately and became immensely popular, spawning a succession of highwayman stories, which romanticised the 'adventures' of the open road. *The Ride to York* was, of course, a work of fiction and never took place, but the fictional legend of Dick Turpin was glorified to the extent that *The Ride to York* was assumed to be a true and accepted chapter in the history of highway robbery. It was to Dick Turpin that film makers attributed the famous lines 'Stand and deliver…Your money or your life!'

Dick Turpin's father was the landlord of the Bell Inn, Hempstead (which later became the Crown, then the Rose and Crown, then the Bell and Crown and currently the Bluebell Inn). Dick was apprenticed to a local butcher, but before long he was involved in a shooting incident in which a man was killed. Soon afterwards he joined a gang of deer-stealers led by a blacksmith, Samuel Gregory, and ultimately became a career villain. No one was immune from his thievery and no one was safe if they stood in his way. Coaches leaving London and passing through the Essex forests proved rich pickings for Turpin and his like.

Turpin evaded capture for some time, once by using the alias 'Palmer' (his wife's maiden name), but was eventually condemned to be hanged for horse stealing and murder.

❋ Patrons of the Rose and Crown public house at **Hempstead** used to be shown the knot-hole in the floorboard of the bedroom above the tap room, through which the young Dick Turpin reputedly listened to the gossip about the highway robberies which persuaded him to become a so-called 'gentleman of the road'.

- There were other Essex highwaymen who did not gain such notoriety as Dick Turpin, many of them working in gangs. The **Waltham Blacks** who operated in **Epping** in the 1690s took the name from their habit of blacking their faces to disguise their appearance. These were not the loveable rogues of fiction, but disillusioned ex-soldiers who could not find work and instead took to crime.

- Interestingly, highwaymen did not only steal from travellers, but also from smugglers, who landed their booty on the Essex coast and sent it inland.

- **16-String Jack**

One who haunted the byways of **Epping** in the 1770s was **John Rann**, otherwise known as '16-String Jack' on account of the eight coloured ribbons that fluttered from each knee of his breeches. He wore ostentatious clothing with a scarlet waistcoat, while his favoured headgear was a top hat festooned with buttons and silver strings. As highwaymen went, he was outwardly amiable but described by victims as 'impudent and arrogant'. That he was a thief and common criminal is not in doubt, but he is credited with a degree of wit and nerve when faced with the Bow Street magistrates. On one occasion he was accused of stealing a gold watch, but when asked for his defence Jack Rann answered that he knew 'no more of the matter than you'. For the court appearance he sported a large bunch of flowers pinned to his coat, 'almost as big as a broom', and a number of bright blue bows tied to his leg irons. He admitted nothing and since no evidence, only conjecture, could be presented by the prosecution, he was released without charge. Once freed he reverted to his trade but one day stole another watch, this time from a Dr Bell, a man of some influence and standing. This time no amount of bright blue bows could save him. He was hanged at Tyburn in November 1774 for highway robbery in, it was said, as jovial a mood as he had lived, commenting that he had 'long expected to see' the gallows.

- Many a tale is told of another highwayman, **Stephen Bunce** of Romford. He fell in with the notorious Jack Hall and Dick Low, who robbed and pillaged for many years before finally being caught and convicted. The three died together on the gallows at Tyburn in December 1707.

✻ Winstanley's Wonders

One of the best known Essex eccentrics is **Henry Winstanley** (1644–1703) of **Littlebury**, a village a mile or two north of **Audley End**. Henry Winstanley was a designer of considerable talent, but he was also imbued with a highly developed sense of fun and fantasy, probably influenced by his grandfather, who entertained his grandchildren by telling them fairy stories, ancient legends and fantastic tales of imagination by the evening fireside in his farmhouse at **Quendon**.

Henry Winstanley's father had connections at **Audley End** (purchased from the Earl of Suffolk by Charles II in 1666) and, when he was only 25, Henry was made Clerk of Works for the king at Audley End and Newmarket (Suffolk). His ingenuity and resourcefulness soon became apparent and he began to take an interest in engineering. He travelled to Europe, where he was fascinated by mechanical devices, and in 1679 he constructed a set of clockwork hammers for the church clock at **Saffron Walden**. He learned copper line engraving and produced intricate woodcuts of his own design. His Audley End connections gave him access to the movers and shakers of his day, making him ambitious for social advancement and a place in posterity.

Soon after his marriage he moved to Littlebury with the clear intention of building his own spectacular house and gardens, into which the public would be invited for a fee of one shilling each. A turnstile was erected at the gate and visitors were invited to partake of what Henry called 'Winstanley's Wonders', at what became known as the 'Essex House of Wonders'. An enormous light was fixed onto the roof to attract visitors 'like fireflies'.

Among the visitors to the Wonder House was the writer Daniel Defoe (1660–1731), who reported that Henry had 'made many odd contrivances of chairs running on springs, etc., which usually much surprised strangers who came to see the House.' The visitor was invited to sit in a chair which, the spring being touched, clasped the occupant and whisked him or her backwards through the house and into the garden, finally suspending the sitter above an artificial stream.

Unfortunately for Celia Fiennes, when she visited Littlebury in 1697 she found 'a house with abundance of fine curiosities all performed by Clockwork and such like which appears very strange to the beholders' but Mr Winstanley was not at home so they did not meet.

People came from near and far to view Henry's various clockwork amusements. A device named the Water Theatre was packed with ingenious contrivances to delight and entertain his customers. The novelty of distorting mirrors, which transformed visitors' shapes much as they do on fairgrounds today, was then new and particularly popular, as was the slipper that gave whosoever picked it up a shock. In 1696 Henry invented 'The Wonderful Barrel', which served visitors with hot and cold drinks from the same 'barrel'.

Henry Winstanley's climb up the social ladder went very well and he began to describe himself as 'Gentleman'. He expanded his operation to London's Piccadilly, where he opened a Mathematical Water Theatre to great acclaim, adding the convenience of refreshments where tea was accompanied by flaming torches and flying dragons, out of whose mouths were disgorged balls of fire.

Closer to home, he designed a lantern for the spire of **Saffron Walden** church, plus an elaborate church clock with a dial that indicated the rising and setting of the sun and moon. The lantern was the forerunner of Henry Winstanley's Great Idea – to build a lighthouse on Eddystone Rock, 14 miles off Plymouth, which was the graveyard of many ships. He began construction in 1696 and in 1698, after a series of adventures (including Winstanley being kidnapped by a French naval ship, Britain and France being then at war), and a phenomenal amount of work, the 120ft-high wooden lighthouse was complete. Bad weather caused damage during the winter of 1698–99, but Henry rebuilt it with extra stonework and even more elaborate decoration. But worse was to come: in 1703 a huge storm blew up. Henry wanted to fulfil his ambition of being in the lighthouse during 'the greatest storm that ever was'. On the night of 27 November, the ferocious seas dashed not only the lighthouse into the raging waters, but also its creator and five others. No debris was found, nor was Henry's body ever retrieved. Two days later the brig *Winchelsea* was dashed against the rock and was lost with all hands, the first ship to perish on the Eddystone rocks since Henry had built his lighthouse.

Although he died with his great invention, Henry had proved the worth of such a light. Three more lighthouses followed, the last being James Douglass's (1882), which is still in use. Before Henry Winstanley's Eddystone Lighthouse no one had thought it possible to construct such a thing on a rock in the middle of intemperate and perilous seas.

❊ The Barking Record Breaker

The **Barking Abbey School** was the first co-educational grammar school in England (established in 1922) and its first headmaster was **Colonel Ernest Achey Loftus, OBE** (1884–1987) the holder of two world records. The first concerns his diary (the world's longest personal diary), which he began in 1896, at the age of 12, and maintained until his death in 1987, aged 103. Guinness World Records does not register diary length in words, but the chronicle is listed as the longest diary measured by duration. It is held by Thurrock Library. The second is as holder of the title 'the oldest known schoolteacher'. Colonel Loftus did not retire officially until his 96th year and was known to still be teaching at the age of 100 in Harare (Zimbabwe), where he spent much of his later life (he died there in 1987). Colonel Loftus wrote *A History of Barking Abbey* (1954) and his ashes are buried in St Margaret's churchyard, Barking Abbey.

❊ Clean Up TV Campaign!

In 1976 **Mary Whitehouse** (1910–2001) and her husband Ernest moved to **Ardleigh**. As founder of the Clean Up TV Campaign in 1964 (later the National Viewers' and Listeners' Association and now Media Watch) she was already a household name, her reputation as the antithesis of the Swinging Sixties and a self-proclaimed guardian of public morals firmly established.

Among the more famous moments from a colourful career as a crusading campaigner against the use of bad language and sexual content in television programmes was her objection to the word 'knickers' in the Beatles' lyrics to *I am the Walrus* (1967). She considered the BBC, and its Director General in particular, 'responsible for the moral collapse in this country' and, as result of her campaign, the BBC banned the video *School's Out* by Alice Cooper in 1972. Cooper later sent her flowers in thanks 'for the publicity'. One of her last campaigns was in 1995 when she attempted to get the film *Four Weddings and a Funeral* (1994) banned on account of its use of 'bad language'. She said: 'I haven't seen it, of course, but I've heard that the opening three minutes contain a stream of four-letter obscenities'.

Mary wrote many articles, and gave many interviews, and was the author of three books including *Who Does She Think She Is?* (1971) and *Whatever Happened to Sex?* (1977).

❋ In 2008 the BBC screened *Filth: The Mary Whitehouse Experience* (by Amanda Coe) which dramatised the Clean Up Television campaign instigated by Mary Whitehouse and her relationship with the then Director General of the BBC, Hugh Carleton Greene. Mary Whitehouse was played by Julie Walters and husband Ernest by Alun Armstrong.

❋ **International Plantswoman**

The author, garden designer and plantswoman **Beth Chatto OBE** (born 1923) created the internationally famous **Beth Chatto Gardens** at **Elmstead Market** in 1960 at the back of her husband's fruit farm. She uses the principles of 'the right plants for the right place' in five acres of informal gardens designed to harmonise with the surrounding countryside. A specially constructed Gravel Garden emulates a winding dried-up river bed, while five ponds have been shaped into a Water Garden.

Beth Chatto Gardens is a regular winner at horticultural and flower shows, an exhibit of 'Unusual Plants' being awarded 10 consecutive Gold Medals at the Chelsea Flower Show from 1977 to 1987.

In 2002, Beth Chatto was awarded the OBE in the Queen's Birthday Honours.

❋ **Marathon Man**

Lloyd Scott MBE (born 1961) from **Rainham** is known as **Marathon Man**. He came to the public's attention when he took part in the 2002 London Marathon in a diving suit and again in 2008 dressed as the title character from the film *The Iron Giant* when he wore a nine-foot-tall iron costume. He wore the same diving suit at the Edinburgh Marathon and set a world record for the slowest marathon time of six days, four hours, 30 minutes and 56 seconds. In 2007 Lloyd visited Australia and travelled 2,700 miles from Perth to Sydney on a penny farthing while dressed as Sherlock Holmes.

Lloyd has been running marathons since 1989 when he was diagnosed with leukaemia and has raised more than £4 million for charity. He was awarded the MBE in 2005 and joked that the letters should stand for 'Mad, Bonkers and Eccentric'.

SEVEN
CHAPELS AND CHURCHES

The chapels and churches of Essex are not by some standards grandiose, but they are diverse and beautiful almost without exception. Some are gloriously eccentric configurations and others almost quirky, with a fine array of timbered towers and shingled spires. Many still stand in remote isolation and there is not one the same as all the others. The county has also, within its embrace, two of the oldest and most important ecclesiastical structures in English Christendom: the Chapel of St Peter on the Wall **Bradwell** is the most ancient church in Essex, and St Andrew **Greensted juxta Ongar** is probably the oldest surviving timber-built church in the world.

Due to a lack of local stone (apart from a vein of septaria), the early church builders had to improvise: there was no abundance of any one material – except wood and later brick – that would give the county's churches a distinctive character. Bricks became an important ingredient in church buildings from the 13th century onward and the Gate Chapel of St Nicholas at **Little Coggeshall** contains some of the earliest mediaeval brickwork in England.

Each building has evolved over the length of its existence, many in an admirably idiosyncratic fashion. There is no better example of the latter than St Leonard **Southminster**, which has defied polite description from all the famous commentators, yet is loved by those who tend it and astounds those who see it for the first time. Hundreds of mediaeval churches still stand resolutely amid modern developments with styles of architecture ranging from the mediaeval timber-framed Black Chapel in the hamlet of **North End** (for which there is no known dedication and it now lies outside the jurisdiction of the Church of England) to the Tudor brickwork at **Gestingthorpe** and **East Horndon** (said by Norman Scarfe to be 'an essay in red brick'). For a real mix of style there is the almost unbelievable church of St Nicholas **Fyfield**, not least because of its outer coating of cement, described by Pevsner as 'interesting but not an attractive exterior'. On the approach to St Margaret's **Bowers Gifford** is seen a huge diagonal buttress and an equally large electricity pylon in the background, yet its charm is not diminished.

At last count, there were some 400 listed Anglican churches in the county (plus almost 100 in the parishes lost to Greater London), and around 50 listed Nonconformist chapels and Catholic churches. All creeds and shades of religion are represented, particularly those of Nonconformity, which gave rise to a sprinkling of chapels throughout towns and villages that continue to enrich the county's architecture. As long ago as 1698, the writer and traveller Celia Fiennes noted that **Colchester** was 'a town full of dissenters, besides Anabaptists and Quakers'.

The Anglican **Diocese of Chelmsford** (created in 1914) has care of over 600 churches, of which 410 represent mediaeval parishes, some of which once belonged to one or other of the Roman Catholic pre-Reformation monastic houses. Several of the mediaeval churches, which bear testimony to over a thousand years of Christianity, are now in the care of conservation bodies, while others are deconsecrated and adapted as private homes. They remain visible in the modern landscape and inspire a feeling of continuity and permanence, as well as providing clues to the past while acting as potted parish histories. The size of the churches of **Thaxted** and **Saffron Walden** illustrates their historic prosperity, while every brass, plaque or monument shows former fashions and customs. The imprint of Norman influence is evident in churches across Essex and, as remarked by the founder of historical genealogy, J. Horace Round (1854–1928) 'there is no county perhaps that bears more clearly than Essex the imprint of the Norman Conquest'.

There is no substitute for hours, or even a lifetime, of church crawling, but here are just a few stories about the chapels and churches of Essex.

❋ The churches of **Willingale Doe** (St Christopher's) and **Willingale Spain** (St Andrew's) are unique in standing together in the same churchyard. The layout is not repeated anywhere else in Essex. Until 1929 the two churches operated independently, but the two are now united in the same parish of **Willingdale**. St Andrew's, the older of the two, is currently under the care of the Churches Conservation Trust.

✽ **A Good View**
From the tower of St Mary **Buttsbury** can be seen the spires of seven other churches. Norman Scarfe (incredibly, he says) gives Buttsbury's mediaeval name as Ging-Joyberd-Laundry.

✽ **Yak hair for Church Walls**
Hair cut from yaks in Tibet was used to hold together a new coat of rendering at All Saints' **Wrabness**, parts of which date back to 1120. In 1995 the architects decided that the church walls were too thick, old and full of rubble for a damp-proof course to be inserted and decided instead to render the inside with yak hair in lime putty, which allows the walls to breathe and the salts to disperse.

✽ In the churchyard at All Saints' **Wrabness** stands a 17th-century wooden bell cage, which houses a solitary bell, that was built after the church tower collapsed. Pevsner described it as looking like 'a village lock-up'. In January 2000 over 50 parishioners – with ages spanning nine decades – took turns at ringing in the New Year…new century…and new millennium on the bell in the churchyard bell cage. There is a similar bell cage at nearby **Wix**.

✽ **Fake Norman Wheel**
The Norman wheel window in the east end of St Nicholas **Castle Hedingham** is one of only five such windows in the whole country. During 19th-century restoration it was discovered that one of the eight radiating shafts was wooden, not stone.

✽ **A Church Reborn**
One of the few parish churches to be destroyed during World War One, St Peter and St Paul **Little Horkesley** was originally built in the 14th century but was obliterated by a German bomb in September 1940. Not to be

defeated, the parish embarked on rebuilding and in 1958 a new church was consecrated. A few mediaeval monuments were restored, including three wooden effigies to the de Horkesley family, who were Lords of the Manor until 1322. It was built to resemble the old building and is frequently mistaken for an original church.

❋ Grade II Listing for Our Lady of Fatima

The Catholic Church of Our Lady of Fatima **Harlow** was given Grade II listed status in 2000. Built in 1958–60 to the designs of the architect Gerard Goalen, it is designed to reflect the growth of the Liturgical Movement in England, allowing the Mass to be celebrated facing the congregation. Dom Charles Norris, of the Order of St Benedict at Buckfast Abbey, made the stained glass in a slab and fused glass system. The fixtures were also designed by Goalen and are seen as a coherent set of works in modern art inspired by the French Art Sacré movement.

❋ St Helen's Chapel

The ancient chapel dedicated to St Helen (or Helena, Patron Saint of Colchester) in **Colchester** started life in Saxon times (possibly on Roman foundations). It ceased to be a place of worship at the Reformation and has since had a variety of uses, including as a workshop and a private house. In the 18th century it became a **Quaker Meeting House** and later a parish hall, but in 2000 was restored as a place of worship by the **Greek Orthodox Church**.

❋ Holy Innocents

There are only five churches in England with the Holy Innocents dedication, one of which is at **Lamarsh**.

❋ Feathered Vandals

In 2000 the village of **Great Henny** was forced to confront the problem caused by male green woodpeckers using the spire of St Mary's Church as a sounding board to attract females. They were found to be completely wrecking many of the cedar shingles fitted only 25 years previously. It was decided to fit new oak roofing tiles that would blunt the beaks of amorous woodpeckers, at a cost of over £30,000. It is hoped that the new tiles will last for the next 60 years and that the woodpeckers will be able to hammer away to their hearts content!

✻ St Mary's **Great Henny** features in one of Thomas Gainsborough's finest paintings *Cornard Wood*, which hangs in London's National Gallery.

✻ Christopher Columbus is Innocent

The pitted bones of a young woman who was buried in St Mary and All Saints' **Rivenhall** during the 13th or 14th century have disproved the long-held theory that Christopher Columbus (1451–1506) was responsible for bringing syphilis to Europe after his forays into the New World. In 2001 scientists revealed that tests carried out on the girl's bones showed that syphilis (or the 'pox' as it was commonly known) was rife in England long before Columbus discovered America in 1492.

Dr Simon Mays, a human skeletal biologist, thought that the disease could have been brought to Europe 'not by Columbus but by the Crusaders in the 11th and 12th centuries'.

The girl's bones were among 400 plastic bags full of bones from the church environs, first discovered in 1970. They vary in date between 1295 and 1445 and were stored in the church crypt for some time before finally being examined and then re-interred.

St Mary and All Saints' is built on the site of a large Roman villa and incorporates some of its remains. The churchyard has been used for burials for almost 1,500 years.

✻ Essex Stonehenge

In 2001 a team of geologists pronounced that a group of seven hard sandstone 'sarsens' found in the grounds of St Barnabas **Alphamstone** might form a miniature Stonehenge dating back to the Ice Age. Over the years numerous theories have been put forward as to their purpose, but it has recently been suggested they were used as part of a pagan spiritual ritual. Two of the stones are built into the church wall. The church itself is built over a Bronze Age barrow on top of a hill overlooking the **Stour Valley**. The largest stone is approximately 150cm long. Although the stones are not in a ring, it is thought that others which lie beneath the surface could complete a circle. The Alphamstone stones form one of the largest collections of sarsens outside Wiltshire. Sarsens are sometimes called Druid Stones, or even Saracen Stones, but the etymology is uncertain.

❋ The Leper Stone at **Newport** is the largest standing stone in Essex.

❋ **The Skin Door**
One of the south doors of St Nicholas **Castle Hedingham** is known as the Skin Door. Legend has it that human skin was nailed to the door during early mediaeval times when those who desecrated or robbed a church had their skin 'nailed to the church door'. The legend does not say whether the thief was still in his skin at the time.

Hundreds of rusting nail stubs can still be seen hammered into the wood and the legend is similar to others in Essex churches including **Copford** and **East Thurrock**.

❋ At **Hadstock** the story goes that it was a Dane who committed sacrilege. He was flayed alive and his skin nailed to the 11th-century door (thought to be one of the oldest in England). During repair to the door hinges a piece of human skin was found and is now in the museum at **Saffron Walden**.

❋ *The Darts have it!*
In 1943, members of the Congregational church at **Ridgewell** were split 50–50 on the subject of whether or not darts should be allowed in the canteen provided for the men of the United States Air Force. At a hastily convened church meeting it was put to the vote: the result was tied with 14 votes each way. The Minister had the casting vote and came down firmly on the side of having a dart board!

❋ *Four Weddings and a Funeral*
St Clement **West Thurrock** was used to film the funeral of Gareth (Simon Callow) in the film *Four Weddings and a Funeral* (1994), starring Hugh Grant. The church has a peculiarly surreal setting in that it is adjacent to the **Procter and Gamble** factory. The church, though, owes its continued existence to Procter and Gamble. It was declared redundant in 1977 and in 1987 the firm offered to take responsibility for

it and immediately set about repairing the years of damage caused by vandalism and neglect. The proximity of church and factory are incongruous in appearance, yet one would not survive without the other in modern industrial Essex.

❉ Elizabethan Rarity

The church of St Michael the Archangel **Woodham Walter** is the only church to have been built in Essex during the reign of Elizabeth I and one of only six such examples in England. Built of red brick, it was consecrated by the Archdeacon of Essex in 1564, only six years into the Queen's reign.

❉ Donkey Power

The Victorian composer and organologist Dr **Leighton George Hayne** (1836–83) was not a man to do things by halves. When he was appointed Rector of **Mistley** with **Bradfield** in 1871 he brought with him a large five-manual organ that he had built while organist and precentor of Queen's College, Oxford (with considerable additions during his time as succentor of Eton in 1867). Instead of leaving the organ behind, and as he considered it his own property, it was brought to Essex in 10 large railway trucks. In 1961, Denis Bayley, Curate of Mistley and President of the Essex Archaeological Society, discovered that the organ was originally erected in a specially built room behind the stables of Hayne's house, where 'three donkeys were used to work the apparatus for blowing the organ'.

At around the same time, an organ built in the Albert Hall (London) was completed and claimed as the largest in the world. Hayne promptly added four more stops to his 'chamber' organ so that his should be larger and he could thus claim the title.

Later great disruption was caused to the Bradfield chancel when Dr Hayne built and rebuilt parts of the church so that his organ could be accommodated. Monumental brasses and ledger stones were removed under cover of darkness, Dr Hayne doing the work himself with the help of a village builder, Mr Puxley. Denis Bayley recounts 'some of the wooden pipes were of immense size; known as Hayne's tubs, some of them served at a later date for tables and benches for the Sunday School treat, while the swell-box is said to have become eventually a receptacle at a maltings'.

* The Bradfield organ survives, albeit in an altered form. Dr Hayne was an organ enthusiast *extraordinaire* and when he died his library was dispersed, but his notebook passed to St Michael's College, Tenbury and is now at the Bodleian Library.

* **The Hospitallers Church**

There are only five mediaeval circular churches in England and one of them is St John the Baptist **Little Maplestead**. It is the smallest of them all, but contains the oldest font in Essex (Pevsner says 'it may well be 11th century'). Known as the Round Church, it was modelled on the Holy Sepulchre in Jerusalem and was given to the Order of St John of Jerusalem (known as the Hospitallers) in 1186 by Lady Juliana Audelin, who owned both the manor and the church. The Order was founded by an Essex man, Jordan Briset, at Clerkenwell after the capture of Jerusalem by the Saracens in 1076 and its members became renowned warrior-monks who exercised political influence throughout Europe. They, with the Teutonic Knights and the Knights Templar, were the most powerful orders of chivalry to emanate from the Crusades. The Order set up a commandery here (a manorial estate and hospice) and, although never a large community, it was part of a much wider property holding in Essex. In 1310 the Knights Templar were disbanded and their lands and holdings given to the Hospitallers.

The Order of St John was dissolved in 1540, along with others at the Dissolution. The Round Church now falls within the Benefice of the Knights and Hospitallers Churches and members of the Order of St John process once a year in full robes.

* Part of the manor of **Layer-de-la-Haye** is named **Blind Knights** and a house by the same name was a hospital for knights who were blinded or lost limbs in the Crusades. The name appears in a document dated 1364.

* **Firewood!**

At All Saints **Messing** it was recorded by **Robert Miller Christy** (1861–1928) that in the recess of the north wall had once stood a wooden cross-legged effigy of a knight in mail. 'It was burned' wrote Mr Christy 'as firewood by order of a late vicar!'

CHAPELS AND CHURCHES

❋ The Smallest Cathedral
In 1914 the Anglican **Diocese of Chelmsford** was formed and the first bishop, John Watts-Ditchfield, took his seat here. There are 660 churches in the diocese, which serves a population of 2,500,000. The perpendicular Gothic parish church of St Mary the Virgin was raised to cathedral status when the new Diocese was created.

In 1954 the cathedral was rededicated to **St Mary, St Peter and St Cedd**. It is the second smallest Church of England cathedral in England (after that in Derby) and is also the second-largest diocese in the country.

❋ St Peter's **Coggeshall** is one of the largest churches in Essex and was considered as a possible cathedral for Essex (Chelmsford being finally chosen).

❋ Mayflower Hall
The United Reform Church's **Mayflower Hall** at **Billericay** was built in 1927 at a cost of £4,000 as a memorial to the Pilgrim Fathers. 1920 was the tercentenary of the expedition and, as five of the pilgrims were from Billericay (the fifth one was added later, after the original plaque was erected), it was decided to name the hall in their honour.

In the 17th century the founders of what is now **Billericay United Reformed Church** worshipped in a barn (in Chapel Street) but by 1716 there were around 400 church members and it was decided that a brick Meeting House was needed. In 1725 a site was obtained and the church built. The present Meeting House is only a few metres south of the one erected in the 18th century. In the middle of the 19th century church members joined the Congregational Union.

❋ First Marriage
The first Church of England marriage ceremony to be celebrated by a woman priest was held at St Stephen's **Cold Norton**.

❋ Unique Board Game
A unique example of an Elizabethan board game, **Nine Men's Morris**, is scratched in a window ledge (possibly two ledges, it is difficult to discern

now) in the south aisle at St John the Baptist **Finchingfield**. The game of Nine Men's Morris is very old: it was a favourite with the Romans and particularly popular during Elizabethan times. Two players, each with nine 'men' (or pieces), manoeuvre around a board with 24 intersections, making chequer-like moves until one player sees off the other's men.

Such a gaming board is not found in any other East Anglian church and it is to be wondered who made it, and why it was not discovered and rubbed out by a disapproving Victorian vicar. Arthur Mee asks 'did the village boys of Shakespeare's time shelter here, we wonder, playing this old game when the rain was falling in the churchyard?'

Nine Men's Morris has nothing to do with Morris Dancing, but comes from the Latin *merellus* meaning a gaming piece or counter. It appears most famously in Shakespeare's *A Midsummer Night's Dream* (1596) when Titania bemoans the fact that 'the nine men's morris is fill'd up with mud'.

✸ The Earliest Essex Brass

One of the few military brasses in England to date from the early part of the 14th century is found at St John the Baptist **Pebmarsh** and is the earliest in any Essex church. It is also one of the first to illustrate the transition from chain mail to plate armour. The figure is **William Fitzralph**, who fought in Edward I's army against the Scots, dying in 1323. He is portrayed wearing full armour and chain mail and has a long coat tied at the waist. Behind his crossed and pointed feet lies a patient-looking, long-eared dog. Some of Sir William's heraldic glass is in the north chancel window.

✸ The brass of Sir John Gifford (1348) at St Margaret of Antioch's **Bowers Gifford** is the third-oldest military brass in Essex. The brass is mutilated, the figure of Sir John having lost a leg and his head.

✸ Triangular Tower

All Saints' **Maldon** church has a triangular-shaped west tower, carrying a shingled spire and three smaller spires. It dates from the 13th century and is unique in Western Europe. The fabric contains Norman stones and later adjustments were made to the nave in order to accommodate the old fish market (that was once held in **Silver Street**).

✻ The Brightlingsea Tiles

All Saints' **Brightlingsea** has a unique collection of memorial tablets to parishioners who lost their lives at sea – 213 tiles set into the nave walls. The tradition of the tiles was started by a late 19th-century vicar, the Revd Arthur Pertwee, who in stormy weather could be seen standing on the 94ft-high church tower with a lighted lantern in his hand to guide local fishermen to safety. In 1883 a storm claimed the lives of over 200 mariners, 19 of them from Brightlingsea. Arthur Pertwee decided to record parishioners 'lost at sea' from the time of his incumbency by tiles bearing the name, age, date and circumstances of the loss. The first tile is dedicated to William Day and his son David, who were drowned off Hartlepool in 1872, the year that Arthur Pertwee became vicar of the parish.

The names reflect a long history of tragedy among Brightlingsea's seafaring men and women, including Charles Barber, aged 46, who perished in his smack *Greyhound* in the 'Swim' in September 1884; Frank Mills, aged 22, who was lost on HMS *Queen Mary* at the Battle of Jutland in 1916; Walter Dines, aged 29, accidentally killed while on patrol aboard the yacht *Clementina*; and Sidney Conrad Siebert, aged 30, who perished in the wreck of SS *Titanic* in the Atlantic on 15 April 1912. One of the most recent tiles is to David E. Clifford, aged 21, who was murdered by a Portuguese cook while on duty in MV *Union Jupiter* in December 1988.

✻ Arts and Crafts for Chapel

When the **United Reform Church** in **Dedham** closed its doors in 1979 a new use was sought for the building. Plans were submitted for conversion to an **Arts and Craft Centre**, but it was April 1984 before they came to fruition. The existing chapel was built in 1871 and replaced an older one that was started in 1738 on land purchased by the owner of the Sun Inn, Timothy Peacock. The first sermon was delivered in 1739 by the Revd Benjamin Vowell of **Colchester**. A crowd of around 400 gathered for the opening service and 'the church was inconveniently crowded'. The centre is home to several local artists and craftsmen, who exhibit on two floors.

✻ The Glass Tortoise

In a window of the south isle of St Mary the Virgin **Kelvedon** a pet tortoise is depicted in stained glass in one of two windows gifted in 1938 by **Ada Cecilia Lance** (1866–1954) of Kelvedon. The windows were made by J. Powell & Sons of Whitefriars and their trademark, a white and cowelled friar, is found in the right-hand window. Powells were heavily influenced by the Arts and Crafts movement, which is seen in the homely composition and natural colouring of the windows.

Miss Lance was the granddaughter of the artist George Lance (1802–1864), who was born at **Little Easton**. 'Felix', as the tortoise is reputedly called, was the model for the glass design and is the only pet tortoise to be so depicted in any East Anglian church. When the church guide was written (it is undated), Felix was still alive and over 90 years old!

✻ The Easter Sepulchre

At St Katharine **Little Bardfield** is found an **Easter Sepulchre** on the north side of the altar. In mediaeval times the Blessed Sacrament was buried in the walls of many churches on Good Friday and brought out during the mass on Easter Morning with considerable ceremony. Watchmen were employed to guard the Easter Sepulchre and were rewarded with ale and a brazier to keep them warm during their watch. Another such sepulchre can be found at **Layer-de-la-Haye**.

✻ The Hostages Windows

The west and south windows at St Mary the Virgin **Broxted** are entitled The Captivity and The Freedom windows and were dedicated on 31 January 1993 to commemorate the Beirut Hostages – Brian Keenan, John McCarthy and Terry Waite. The windows were designed by John Clarke. That part of the church is now called the **Journalists' Corner** in order to remember all journalists who risk their lives and freedom in the course of their work. Between 1985 and 1991 the three men were held captive in the Lebanon and as John McCarthy's parents, Patrick and Sheila, lived in part of what is now the Whitehall Hotel (next to the church), the village became involved in the five-year struggle for their release. Sheila McCarthy, who died before she heard that her son was safe, is buried in the churchyard. The McCarthy

Hatchment on the west wall was made by the Royal College of Arms and presented to the church in her memory.

❋ Roodscreen Rarities

St Mary the Virgin **Stebbing** has a very rare mediaeval stone roodscreen, one of only three in northern Europe, the second being at St Mary the Virgin **Great Bardfield** and the third in Norway. The Great Bardfield screen has a corbel face on either side which represents Edward III and his Queen Philippa.

❋ The Chapel Without the Walls

The mediaeval monastery gatehouse chapel of St Nicholas **Little Coggeshall** is part of the ruined 12th-century Cistercian Abbey founded by King Stephen (1135–54). Called **The Chapel Without the Walls** (*capella extra muros*), it now stands on the edge of a field, surrounded on three sides by pastureland. It was used as a barn during the 16th century, which may be the reason that, unlike the abbey itself, it escaped destruction at the Dissolution of the Monasteries. In 1897 the chapel was in a bad state of repair but was rescued and restored by a group of parishioners. A curate was appointed and it was again used for services. When, in 1940, the parish church of St Peter was hit by a bomb, parishioners moved to St Nicholas. Monthly services are still held in the chapel.

The rectangular-shaped chapel contains some of the earliest mediaeval brickwork in Essex, and possibly England. They can be seen as dressings round the lancet windows, the threshold of the doorway, and elsewhere in the mixed fabric of the construction. The pink bricks are approximately 2in thick and have been dated to 1220 during the time of Abbott Benedict.

A 19th-century print shows the chapel to have been thatched with a rustic porch on the south wall and still being used as a barn.

❋ Another gatehouse chapel that once served the Cistercian Abbey at **Tilty** is now the parish church of St Mary the Virgin.

❋ Britain's Oldest Saxon Church

The Chapel of St Peter-on-the-Wall (*Ad Muram*) **Bradwell-on-Sea** (Bradwell *juxta Mare*) is the oldest church in Essex and one of the oldest in England. It was built on the wall of the Roman fort **Othona**, which had been erected towards the end of the third century as one of the defensive forts of the **Saxon Shore** (a half-circle of forts from the Wash to the Isle of Wight) and intended to deter a Saxon invasion. An overseer of the fort was appointed, to be known as the Count of the Saxon Shore (*Comes Littoris Saxonici*). The first of these officers was Carausius, described as 'a Belgic coastal pilot, a barbarian from the Low Countries', whose job it was to defend the coast and maintain dominion over his province. Unfortunately Carausius later fell foul of the Emperor Maximian, who accused him of allowing pirates into the Channel. He was finally murdered in 293 by one of his own officers.

When the Romans left Essex in 450 the village was known as **Ythancestrir** and identified as such by the Venerable Bede in *The Ecclesiastical History of the English People*. It was to Ythancestrir that **St Cedd** came from Lindisfarne in Northumbria at the invitation of King Sigeberht to reintroduce Christianity into Essex, which had lapsed back into paganism in the late seventh century. Cedd landed at Ythancestrir and travelled round the kingdom of the East Saxons before returning to the old fort and causing the chapel to be built. He dedicated it to St Peter in AD 654 using tiles and stone from the ruins of the old Roman buildings. When Cedd was consecrated Bishop of the East Saxons (654–64) St Peter's became his cathedral, making it the earliest cathedral in England.

St Peter's fell into disuse at the time of the Viking raids, but by the middle of the 15th century had been restored to use by the Bishop of London (in whose diocese it then was). The chapel survived into the 20th century when in 1920 it was again restored and rededicated by the Bishop of **Chelmsford**.

* An Annual Pilgrimage to the chapel takes place on the first Saturday in July. On the **Bradwell Pilgrimage** of July 1985 the chapel altar was consecrated by the Bishop of Chelmsford and the Bishop of Brentwood. One of the altar stones is a gift from Holy Island Lindisfarne, where Cedd was trained by St Aidan, Apostle of the North.

* **The World's Oldest Wooden Church**

The village of **Greensted juxta Ongar**, writes Arthur Mee, 'is unique in its sylvan setting and unique in one of its possessions, a wooden church with

Saxon timbers built into its walls'. St Andrew's Church has the oldest oak log walls in Europe and is believed to be the oldest wooden church in the world. The first church here might not have been a church at all, but a pagan shrine. Work is thought to have begun on a church here in about 654 and an archaeological dig in 1960 revealed a simple wooden building under the present chancel floor. Some time after St Cedd arrived in 654 it was converted into a Christian building and dedicated to St Andrew, a Celtic saint and popular choice for Anglo-Saxon church dedications. The diagonal cross of St Andrew is found in the south-facing chancel window.

✳ Tradition has it that Alwyn, the Benedictine monk who was guardian of the body of **St Edmund, King of the East Angles** (841–69), rested here in 1013 on his way back to Bury St Edmunds. Alwyn had taken the relics of the Saxon martyr to London in 1010 when the Danish again began to ravage East Anglia. St Edmund was seen as a symbol of the Saxon resistance and it would have been a coup for the Danish King Sweyn to have seized his remains.

✳ A Pirate's Grave?

Much is made of the crossed bones which are to be seen on a weatherworn tombstone in the ruined St Peter's **Alresford Old Church**. The inscription is to 'Robert Bray, 1724' but there are no pirate legends to go with the crossed bones and no tales of derring-do at sea. It would be interesting to know where in the churchyard Robert Bray is buried – if on the north side it would be fitting for a pirate, since this is the Devil's side and was used for burials of excommunicants and the unbaptized, though it is doubtful if such a man would have had a headstone at all. More likely he died of an infectious disease and the bones (perhaps once accompanied by a skull) were to warn others away from his grave.

The mystery of the 'pirate's grave' continues even though the church is in a ruinous state. It was originally erected in about 1300 by Audrey de Staunton on the site of an even older building, but was destroyed by arson in 1971. It was considered to be too badly damaged and was not rebuilt. The fire, however, exposed parts of the walls not previously seen, thus confirming its antiquity. In 1975 it was replaced by the Essex-barn style church of St Andrew closer to the village.

Ghost hunters allegedly visit the churchyard of St Peter's, perhaps to discover the secret of the pirate's tomb.

❊ Hanging Hats
Under the tower at St George the Martyr **Great Bromley** can be found a small collection of hats that belonged to successive Tower Masters and Captains of the bell ringers, dating from the 19th and 20th century. When a captain dies his hat is dated and hung with the others. The oldest hat is around 300 years old.

❊ Largest Church in Essex
St Mary the Virgin **Saffron Walden** is the largest parish church in Essex. Its earliest features date from 1250, but most of its present fabric was built in the Perpendicular style between 1470 and 1525. Its size reflects the wealth of the town, derived from both the mediaeval local wool trade and the saffron trade (see also Chapter Three, Why is it Called That?).

❊ Mounting Steps
On the outside of the church wall at St Thomas's **Bradwell-on-Sea** can be seen five very well-worn 18th-century stone steps with an iron post on top, to assist churchgoers who arrived at the church by coach or on horseback.

❊ Patron Saint of Agricultural Workers
There are only three representations in Essex of **St Walstan** (died 1016), the Anglo-Saxon **Patron Saint of Agriculture and Farm Workers**, whose iconography is found exclusively in the eastern counties. The early 16th-century screen painting at St Peter and St Paul **Foxearth** is the only extant pre-Reformation icon of St Walstan outside Suffolk and Norfolk. The church was dramatically restored in the 19th century by the Revd John Foster, who was Rector from 1845 until his death in 1892. Foster was a high churchman in the Tractarian tradition, a philanthropist who inherited a fortune from his mother and spent much of it in the parish of Foxearth. As well as effecting the internal decoration of the church and the rectory, he also built the village school.

At St Margaret's **Stanford Rivers** the east window (1952) is in memory of a local farmer, **Henry Millbank** (1880–1950), who was Churchwarden from 1906 until 1950. Henry Millbank was also a founder member of the **Ongar Young Farmers Club**, a prominent and long-standing member of the National Farmers' Union and Justice of the Peace.

The depiction of St Walstan in stained glass at St Michael's **Kirby-le-Soken** (1953) is unusual in that it has no direct agricultural connection. The Cheeld family, to whom the window is dedicated, came to Essex in the mid-1800s and lived at **Clacton-on-Sea**, where they were involved in the catering industry.

❋ Mosaic Fish

In St Catherine's **East Tilbury** a mosaic fish can be found set into the floor beside the lectern. It was both designed and executed by pupils of **East Tilbury School** in 1966. The fish is a symbol from the earliest times of Christianity and was used as a secret sign of communication between church members at times of persecution.

❋ Little Sodom

During the early 19th century the village of **Abridge** was known as 'Little Sodom', declared so in 1833 by the *Wesleyan Methodist Magazine*. The inhabitants of Sodom were, according to the Bible, destroyed by brimstone and fire 'from the Lord out of heaven' and the name is synonymous with impenitent sin. Obviously it was a place badly in need of a Wesleyan chapel and so it was that, following the building of a chapel and the arrival of a Methodist minister later that year, Abridge was 'saved' from the obvious dangers of brimstone and fire.

❋ The Arquebus Window

In St Laurence **Upminster** is a 17th-century window in the antechamber of the north aisle that contains in its design a partridge, butterflies, a family walking in the garden and the figures of two soldiers each carrying an arquebus (an early muzzle-loaded firearm). The armorial bearings in the window are those of the Stanley, Engaine, Deincourt and Latham families. The window is dated 1630, the year in which Hamlet Clarke, father-in-law (or stepfather) of Serjeant Ralph Latham of the Manor of Gaynes, renovated the Gaynes chapel. Some of the painted armorial glass was installed then and no doubt one of the soldiers is Serjeant Latham, who held the post of Common Serjeant of London. The Gaynes Estate once covered most of the south half of the parish.

❋ A Scratched Ship
On the wall of the rood loft staircase at St Helen and St Giles **Rainham** is a rare mediaeval scratch-drawing of a fully rigged ship. **The Ship Centre**, named after the ship scratching, is operated by the church community and was opened in 1995.

❋ The Heart of a Queen
The legend that the severed head of **Anne Boleyn** (1507–36), second wife of Henry VIII and mother of Elizabeth I, is buried under the altar in All Saints' **East Horndon** is long-held. Anne, the daughter of Sir Thomas Boleyn, was crowned in June 1533, the last Queen Consort to have been crowned separately from her husband. It was thought that her head was smuggled out of the Tower of London soon after her execution and brought to East Horndon, where it was buried in secret. The answer to the question of why here, and not at **Rochford** (the family home of the Boleyns, Sir Thomas being created Viscount Rochford in 1525) appears to be that Sir Thomas had friends at nearby **Corringham** and thought Rochford too obvious a burial place should there be further political fall-out from Anne's execution. Immediately after her death rumours and myths proliferated. She was reputed to have six fingers on one hand, at a time when any physical deformity was interpreted as a sign of evil.

It is to be wondered whether or not her daughter Elizabeth I knew of the legend when she passed that way to **Tilbury** in 1588 to rally the English troops. Officially, Henry VIII refused to provide a coffin for Anne and she was therefore buried in an unmarked grave in London. Elizabeth is said to have stayed at Arden Hall **Horndon-on-the-Hill** the night before her Eve of Armada speech and, although the actual house is a matter of dispute, the fact that she passed this way is not.

All Saints' is currently under the care of the Churches Conservation Trust.

❋ Best for Brass
Essex is second in the country for the number of surviving monumental church brasses – around 500, of which nearly 300 have one or more

engraved figures. There are only 10 extant English brasses dating from before the Black Death (1348–49) and three of them are found in Essex at **Pebmarsh**, **Wimbish** and **Bowers Gifford**. Another rarity is at **Chrishall**, where Sir John de la Pole (1380) is seen clasping his wife Joan's hand. His feet are on a lion (for valour) and hers on a dog (fidelity). A favourite among students of heraldic dress is the brass at **Ingrave** that shows Sir Richard FitzLewes (died 1528) with his four wives.

❋ **Rare Vaulting**

The 12th-century church at **Copford** is an extraordinary rarity among English parish churches. Its Norman vaulting is highly unusual and especially rare as it forms a tunnel vault. Apart from London's Tower Chapel, no other English tunnel-vaulted church nave exists. Copford church is also noted for the remains of wall paintings which were discovered first in 1690 and rediscovered in 1871. They were subsequently restored (with varying degrees of success) to appear as they might have done in around 1150 when they were first painted. Pevsner calls them 'by far the most important mediaeval wall paintings in Essex'.

In 1880 the church was dedicated to St Michael and all Angels (but usually called St Michael's) as the original dedication is lost, possibly because it was built as a private chapel to the Bishop of London. It might at one time have been known as 'Our Lady at Copford'.

❋ **Have Another Glass!**

Beside the pulpit at St Mary Magdalen **Thorrington** is a 17th-century wrought-iron hourglass stand, a reminder of the days when an hourglass was used to measure the length of the sermons. Really keen preachers would turn the glass upside down and invite the congregation to 'stay and have another glass'. Before the advent of watches the congregation had no other way of knowing the length of a sermon, which on average would last an hour. In the 17th century it was not only compulsory to attend church, but also for preachers to lecture for at least that length of time.

❋ Hourglass stands are also found at **Abbess Roding**, **Ingatestone** and **Norton Mandeville**.

❋ Strict Morals for Dedham

In *A Foot in Essex* (1968) Frank Daws tells of the **Dedham Classis**, an association founded in 1582 by ministers with puritanical leanings. A Minute Book was compiled for the parish of Dedham in 1585 which contained Rules for the Church and Town of Dedham. It listed 15 items concerning the strict observance of the Lord's Day and Item 10 demanded 'that all the householders frequent the two lectures read every week with some of their servants, at the least as many as may be spared in regard to their trades and callings'.

Item 15, however, was very specific in regard to the parish morals – 'that if any be known to have known one another carnally before the celebrating of their marriage, that none accompany them to the church nor from the church, nor dine with them that day: and that the pastor at the baptizing of the children of any such as be known to have committed such filthiness…do publicly note and declare out the fault to all the congregation, to the humbling of the parties and terrifying of others from the like filthy profaning of marriage'.

❋ The Dedham Lectureship

Monuments in St Mary's **Dedham** attest to the advanced Puritanisation of the area and celebrate the preachers and holders of the **Dedham Lectureship**, founded in 1577. Before the destruction of the religious orders by Henry VIII at the Reformation, the itinerant friars would preach for their living. With the professional preachers gone it became clear that the untrained clergy could not preach. Parishes, therefore, started to look to Town Preachers, or Lecturers, to fill the gap.

People flocked to Dedham church at eight o'clock in the morning on Sundays and Tuesdays (market day) to hear the lectures. Many walked miles to attend and others would arrive by carriage, enhancing market day as a highly commercial event.

The first lecturer was an Elizabethan Puritan, **Edmund Chapman** (died 1602), who was appointed in 1577. His epitaph ends 'the shepherd asleep among his lambs', indicating his desire to be buried in the churchyard, among the congregation, rather than in the church with the clergy.

His successor **John Rogers** (1572–1636) – known as 'Roaring Rogers' – was lecturer until his death in 1636 and known as 'one of the most awakening divine of the age'. He preached from a turret adjoining the church porch roof. Roaring Rogers has a bust in the chancel where he is seen wearing his skull cap and ruff. An elegy written for him reads:

> *A person grave, a patron rare,*
> *Most humble, godly, wise*
> *Whose presence made the wicked fear*
> *When they beheld his eyes.*

When the lectures were banned in 1662 (the vicar and lecturer ejected by the Commonwealth Government), Dedham's economy suffered, the wool trade having also been in decline, as fewer came to the weekly market.

In 1692, however, **William Birkitt** (lecturer and vicar from 1692–1703) decided to revive the Lectureship and raised an endowment by public subscription to secure its future. He died in 1703 but left his house and some land in his will to ensure that the lectureship continued, albeit in an altered form, as by the 1690s the parish was impoverished and found it hard to maintain the voluntary sponsorship and payments. Birkitt's legacy, however, continued into the 20th century. In 1906 it was agreed that the vicar should *ex officio* also hold the office of lecturer.

A list of lecturers and vicar-lecturers is found inside the church.

❋ A Persian Inscription

On the west side of the vestry at St Mary the Virgin **Dedham** is found what is believed to be the only Persian inscription in a British church. It is worked into a stone slab and was placed there as a covenant to pray for the conversion of a particular person, but serves as a testimony to any who may read it: 'Ask, and it shall be given you; seek, and you shall find.' (St Luke 11:9).

❋ The Danbury Knight

In 1779 a curious discovery was made in the north aisle of St John the Baptist **Danbury**. Some workmen were digging a grave for the recently deceased lady of the manor, Mrs Frances Ffytche, when they found a leaden coffin without any inscription. It was beneath an effigy of a man in armour, leading the rector to think that this could be the body of one of the three knights of the Sinclair family (known locally as St Clere), although there was no name on the coffin lid. Three wooden effigies are among the treasures of Danbury: they date from the 13th and 14th century and one of them is William St Clere.

The rector, assisted by the churchwarden Mr White and watched by the workmen, decided to open the coffin. Inside they found an elm coffin, still entire, and within that a shell about three-quarters of an inch thick. The rector removed the lid. Inside was the body of a man preserved, or perhaps pickled, in murky liquor said by an eyewitness to resemble 'mushroom ketchup'. The body wore a linen shirt with a collar of lace sewn with bold stitches, and except for the face and throat, the flesh appeared 'exceedingly white and firm', his teeth almost perfect and his limbs in 'excellent symmetry'. The body had, it seemed, been preserved in the liquid that still half-filled the coffin and on which flowers and herbs still floated. The churchwarden, being without a sense of smell, tasted the liquor. He found it aromatic, 'though not very pungent', with a suggestion of Spanish olives.

The parishioners of Maldon were alerted to the goings-on in the church and several made their way to the north aisle to view the spectacle, one man even prodding the body with his walking stick. It was agreed that the body 'conveyed the idea of hearty youth, not in the least emaciated by sickness.' Curiosity satisfied, the rector decreed that the coffin lids should be replaced and the lid soldered on. Things were left exactly as they were found.

* Was the **Danbury Knight** one of the St Clere family, or was he in fact a Knight Templar? If he had not been sick, how did he die? The Member of Parliament for Maldon, **Joseph Strutt** (1758–1845) disputed the Knight Templar angle and decided to write a novel about what might have happened to the man, calling it *Queenhoo Hall* (see also Chapter Four, Artistic Essex).

* **Greek Orthodox**

The parish church at **Tolleshunt Knights** dates from the 12th century and was sold by the Church of England to the **Greek Orthodox Church** in 1958. It has been restored as a chapel to the Orthodox Monastery of St John the Baptist in the grounds of the old rectory.

* **Timber Tower**

St Lawrence **Blackmore** has a wooden tower that was built using timbers dating from 1400. There are 10 internal posts and Pevsner wrote that 'it is a most elaborate piece of carpentry and looks very powerful'.

EIGHT
EPITAPHS AND MEMORIALS

An epitaph is usually an inscription that commemorates a person or event and is not only genealogically interesting, but also gives insight into the life and times of both the rich and powerful and the common men and women. Some are affectionate, like that to Sarah Rickett at **Barking**, and others amusing, like that at **High Laver**, where the benefactor's name has been forgotten. Many recall great deeds or commemorate friendship, such as that in the south porch of **Chelmsford Cathedral**, where the link between wartime Essex and the United States of America is remembered. It is to be expected that important historical figures find a place in posterity, but the joy of the many thousands of ordinary memorials in the county's parish churches is that they give immortality to the likes of young Rice Parry of **Great Clacton**, and Midshipman Nicholson of **Wendens Ambo**, who would otherwise be eclipsed from memory. Needless to say, there are hundreds of such epitaphs and memorials to be discovered and those listed here are only a taste.

❋ An Early Ford
Given the 20th-century connection with the **Ford Motor Company** a monument in St Peter and St Paul **Dagenham** is of special interest. It is to **William Ford**, who died almost a hundred years before Ford set up shop in Dagenham.

In the year 1825, William Ford, Farmer,
By his will gave the munificent sum of

> *Ten thousand pounds*
> *To found a free school in this parish, to be conducted upon the principles of the*
> *Established Church of England.*
> *And the interest of the sum of one thousand pounds*
> *To supply warm clothing to the aged poor.*

A stipulation in the will, however, was that no person bearing the name Fanshawe was to be involved with the running of the school. It would be intriguing, no doubt, to discover what the Fanshawes had done to William Ford to provoke such a stricture!

※ **An Officer and a Gentleman**

In St Lawrence **Bradfield** is a memorial to **Squadron Commander Edwin Harris Dunning, DSC, RN** (1892–1917), second son of Sir Edwin Harris Dunning of **Jacques Hall**. While bombing enemy territory on 20 June 1916, Squadron Commander Dunning was wounded in a fight with enemy seaplanes and awarded the DSC for gallantry. A year later he became the first pilot to land an aircraft on a moving ship.

A brass plaque carries a long epitaph and tells the story of Edwin Dunning's feat of landing his Sopwith Pup on HMS *Furious* in Scapa Flow, Orkney, on 2 August 1917, while the ship was underway. This had never been done before and the data obtained was 'of the utmost value…it will make aeroplanes indispensable to a fleet and possibly revolutionise naval warfare'.

Although he had already made two successful landings, Dunning expressed a wish to land again and in this last run he was killed. A tyre burst, throwing his plane overboard. He was knocked unconscious and drowned in the cockpit. The Admiralty was fulsome in its praise for such bravery and 'my Lords desire to place on record their sense of the loss to the Naval Service of this gallant officer'. His Captain wrote that he admired his keenness and enthusiasm 'and such an excellent and capable fellow in every way'. Both the officers and men serving under him lamented the death 'of so fine an Officer and Gentleman'.

※ There is also an obelisk in the churchyard with doves of peace on each side and inscribed:

> *This memorial with the ground and enclosing wall*
> *Is presented to Bradfield by Sir Edwin Dunning Kt*
> *In the hope that the parishioners will show due reverence for God's acre and all within it, 1918.*

It also serves as a war memorial and carries the names of 156 parishioners who served in the armed forces during World War One. The column is on the site of the former Plough Inn, which had been purchased by Edwin Dunning's father.

❃ Gone but not Forgotten

In All Saints' **High Laver** there is a board which reads:

> *A Benefactor*
> *Whose name by some misfortune or neglect is now unknown gave a field called Bell acre containing nearly two acres, situated in this Parish, by the roadside about a mile West of Matching Green, leading to Moreton for the perpetual repairing this Church.*

A case of gone but not forgotten.

❃ Always the Same!

Sarah Rickett of **Barking** died aged 58 in 1767 and her epitaph reads:

> *Here honest Sarah Rickett lies*
> *By many much esteemed*
> *Who really was no otherwise*
> *Than what she ever seemed.*

Her family obviously remembered her fondly with simple and fitting sentiment.

❃ Anchor Fence

Close to the south porch of St Michael's **Ramsey** is a large and very prominent memorial to 24-year-old Edward Francis Burbidge, who died in November 1854. The inscription reads:

> *His years few*
> *His deeds of Boundless Generosity many.*
> *This monument is erected by his widow as the last token of Gratitude and Love.*

The draped urn is surrounded by 24 iron anchors.

❋ Perished at Sea

In St John's **Great Clacton** is found a memorial to 17-year-old Rice Parry, who died on 10 March 1891:

Perished at sea tied to the rigging of ship 'J W Babel' of Beaumaris which was wrecked on Fund Fleet Sands.

In those days sailors stranded on wrecked vessels would tie themselves high in the rigging to avoid the rising tide and prevent themselves from falling into the sea if they should become unconscious. Young Rice Parry tied himself to his ship and waited for help to arrive, but he died of exposure before he could be rescued.

❋ A Renowned Esquire

In the transept of **Chelmsford Cathedral** is a monument to **Thomas Mildmay Esquire** and 41 members of the Mildmay family who died between 1544 and 1798. The (Latin) inscription to Thomas and his wife reads:

He was a renowned esquire
She a daughter and lovely branch of William Gunson, Esq,
And they had fifteen pledges of their prosperous love,
Seven whereof were females, eight were males.

Thomas was granted the Manor of **Moulsham** by Henry VIII and in return he founded a grammar school in the town.

❋ The Gravestone with Double Dates

A rare inscription on a gravestone at St Peter and St Paul **St Osyth** records the double dates that prevailed in the nation's calendar from the late 16th century until, in 1752, the Gregorian Calendar replaced the ancient Julian Calendar that had been in use since the time of Julius Caesar. However, while the Gregorian Calendar supplanted the Julian calendar throughout Catholic Europe in 1582 (it was instigated by Pope Gregory XIII, hence Gregorian) it did not happen in Britain (Henry VIII having broken with the Papacy) until 1752. By 1752, however, the two calendars were adrift by 11 days. In order to bring the two into line Britain 'lost' 11 days between 3 and 14 September and at the same time changed the start of the official year from 25 March to 1 January.

The inscription at St Osyth shows that Ann, Wife of William P (the rest illegible), departed this life on the 17th day of February in the year 1734/5. Fortuitously, Derek Johnson was able to include a photograph of the gravestone in *Essex Curiosities* (1973) before it became too badly eroded. The date signifies the overlapping of the two years which, a few years later, was put right.

※ **Robert Bucke, Benefactor**

On a board in St Peter's **Ugley** is a precise record of the village benefactor, Mr **Robert Bucke, Draper**. Robert Bucke of **Bollinger Hall** was born at Ugley and in his will (proved on 27 November 1620) he gave to the Draper's Company a messuage and land in the parish of Langley (Kent) in trust to pay for the purchase of clothing which should be sent to the parish of Ugley (for so long as those with the surname Bucke shall inhabit Bollinger Hall) to defray the cost of:

3 suits of clothes to 3 poor Men and 3 suits to 3 poor Women with Hats, and 3 pounds in Money…to be given at the Discretion of the ChurchWardens at Ugley every 3rd Year for Ever.

Ugley was to receive the bequest in the first year, the (now lost) parish of Manendine in the second, and **Stansted Mountfichett** in the third year. The trust was to be administered by the Draper's Company, London.

※ A previous bequest was made by John Bucke (in 1558) for an area of land just over seven acres in size, the rent for which should go towards clothing the poor parishioners of Ugley. According to *White's Directory*, in 1848 the amount of rent amounted to £15 10s a year.

※ **The Old Lady of Mark's Hall**

Mary Honeywood (1527–1620) lived at **Markshall** (Mark's Hall) on the Honeywood Estate. She was born Mary Atwater (or Waters, it is not clear) in Kent and before she married into the influential Honeywood family (sometimes Honywood) in 1543 was styled Mary, Lady Mildmay Atwater. She was the daughter and co-heir of Robert Atwater (or Waters). She and her husband **Robert Honeywood** set up house at Mark's Hall (built in 1605–09), where they had 19 children. Robert died in 1576 and was buried at Lenham (Kent), where he was born and the seat of the Honeywood family, leaving Mary to wear a widow's cap for over 40 years.

Mary Honeywood was one of the most formidable and courageous women of her age and visited prisons, at great danger to herself, during the religious turmoil and persecution of Mary Tudor's reign (1553–58). At one point in her life she suffered from religious melancholy and was visited by John Foxe (1516–87), the martyrologist, but he unsurprisingly failed to cheer her up. He wrote lurid accounts of the sufferings of the Protestant martyrs and she herself had witnessed the burning of the martyr Mr Bradford at Smithfield, whose story is recounted in *Foxe's Book of Martyrs* (1563). In spite of Foxe's entreaties, Mrs Honeywood continued to believe that some humans were predestined to endless misery and that she was one of them. Having a drinking glass in her hand she once dashed it to the floor, saying 'I shall be dammed as surely as this is smashed'. The glass rebounded and did not break. Quite soon afterwards she announced that 'God had suddenly shot comfort like lightning' into her soul so that she lived the remainder of her life 'in spiritual gladness'.

When she died in 1620 – at 93 years of age – she had lived under five different monarchs and survived extraordinarily turbulent years during which the Catholic religion was dismantled by Henry VIII and reinstated by Mary I, only for Protestantism to be finally established by Elizabeth I. Although she died in Essex her body was returned to Lenham to lie beside that of her husband.

- ✻ For many years there were memorials to the Honeywood family in St Margaret's **Markshall** (erected by Mary's son and heir, Robert), but when it was demolished in 1933 some were removed to the **Hollytrees Museum** (Colchester) and the Honeywood Tablet was taken to the church of St Peter ad Vincula, **Great Coggeshall**. It records that Mary left four generations, '16 of her owne body', 144 grandchildren, 228 great-grandchildren and nine great-great-grandchildren, '367 in all'. Shortly before her death a banquet was given in her honour by 200 of her descendants.

- ✻ Remnants of the old Markshall church foundations and part of the churchyard can still be seen at **Mark's Hall Gardens and Arboretum**. The gardens contain a double border that stretches nearly 450ft and is one of the longest in East Anglia.

❋ The famous **Honeywood Oak** on the **Mark's Hall Estate** is thought to be around 700 years old and would have been over 200 years old when Robert and Mary Honeywood lived there.

❋ **Boy Cornwell, VC**

Boy Seaman 1st Class **John 'Jack' Travers Cornwell** (1900–1916) was a young man with a clear sense of duty. The epitaph on his grave in **Manor Park Cemetery** (London) reads:

It is not wealth or ancestry but honourable conduct and a noble disposition that maketh men great.

Jack was born at **Leyton** (now in Greater London), though the family later moved to **East Ham**. He left school aged 14 to be a delivery boy and became a Boy Scout in the **Little Ilford** troop. At the outbreak of World War One his father (who fought in France under Lord Kitchener) and his brother (who served in an infantry regiment in Flanders) volunteered and in October 1915 Jack gave up his job to enlist in the Royal Navy. He had references from his school and employer, but his father was unaware that his son had joined up. In April 1916 Jack was assigned to HMS *Chester* and was in the Battle of Jutland. The ship sustained horrific gunfire from four German cruisers and, although severely wounded, Jack stayed at his gun post until the *Chester* retired from the battle. She had sustained 18 direct hits, but the ship was saved by her hull armour. The gun crew were not so lucky and Jack was found to be the sole survivor among the dead, still at his post though badly injured by shards of steel that had punctured his chest, and awaiting further orders. Captain Robert Lawson instructed that Jack be taken to Grimsby General Hospital, but he died before his mother Lily arrived.

A month or so later the story broke that Jack had been buried at **Manor Park Cemetery** in a common grave without a headstone. The *Daily Sketch* campaigned against such scant respect for the young war hero and his body was reinterred, with full military honours, in July 1916. The First Lord of the Admiralty delivered the funeral oration. The monument stone was erected by scholars and ex-scholars of schools in East Ham and Jack Cornwell's portrait hung in many school halls.

In November 1916 Jack Cornwell's mother received the posthumous Victoria Cross from King George V. The citation described how Jack, though mortally wounded, 'nevertheless remained standing alone at a most exposed post, quietly awaiting orders till the end of the action, with the gun's crew and wounded around him'. He was the youngest person to receive a VC in World War One. He was just 16 years old. His father died a few months later and a younger brother in 1918, both in action.

Court painter Frank O. Salisbury made a portrait of Jack (using his brother as a model) and the *Boy Cornwell Memorial Fund* was founded by the Lord Mayor of London.

* Jack Cornwell Street in **Newham** is named in his honour and a nearby public house is named the Victoria Cross.

* A group of cottages in **Hornchurch** also bears the Cornwell name.

* The Scouting movement created the **Cornwell Decoration**, often known as the 'Scout VC', which is awarded by scout troops all over the world.

* **The Scouting Brothers**

More scouting heroism is found at **Chelmsford**, where two brothers are honoured for gallantry. One is 16-year-old **Scout George Dawson** of the **6th Chelmsford (Cathedral) Troop**, who lost his life 'in a gallant, but vain, attempt to save a brother scout from drowning in Belgium in 1929'. He was doubly a hero, having rescued a boy from drowning in Chelmsford in 1928. The second is George's brother **Pilot-Officer Norman F. Dawson RAFVR**, aged 21, who lost his life on 28 April 1941 when his aircraft, on escort duty for Convoy FN 59 in the North Sea, crashed killing all three on board. Norman had been called up at the outbreak of World War Two and was granted his commission in August 1940. The *Chelmsford Chronicle* described him as 'a former Scout and all-round athlete' who engaged in cricket, football, hockey and swimming.

The brothers were buried in the same grave in the Borough Cemetery, where the poignant memorial includes their parents George Dawson (died 1974, aged 85) and Susan (died 1977, aged 91) who had many years in which to mourn their sons.

An account of George Dawson's heroism is found in Chelmsford Cathedral and a plaque, dedicated by the Cathedral Troop of Boy Scouts, is on the tower arch.

❋ Essex has had a long association with the Scouting Movement and at St Nicholas **Castle Hedingham** a modern carving illustrates the long connection between scouting and Hedingham Castle over the last 50 years. It is in a panel in the side chapel and replaces a 16th-century Flemish carving that was stolen from the church in 1978.

❋ **Mrs Smith has All the Money!**

The orator, mathematician, philosopher and linguist Sir Thomas Smith (died 1577) of **Theydon Mount** was a member of the Smith family, who lived in the Theydons for almost 300 years. The family built the church of St Michael the Archangel at Theydon Mount (1611–14) and Sir Thomas himself built Hill's Farm, **Theydon Garnon**. Sir Thomas's wife was obviously a woman of some character as he wrote of her in his diary: 'My wife does not go so gorgeously as some would have her. If that be a fault, let her bear it. She hath all my money!'

❋ **A Judicious Man**

In St Mary the Virgin **Broxted** is a memorial plaque to **Thomas Bush**, who died on 22 February 1791, aged 71.

> Who by Diligent Attention to Business,
> Acquired an Ample Fortune,
> Which he judiciously bequeathed
> Amongst his Relatives in such Manner
> As to place them Above the Cares
> But below the dangerous Indulgencies of Life.

Thomas, late of the parish of St James's Westminster, obviously knew of the dangers of inherited wealth!

❋ The Seven-Year Penance

The story goes that William Kempe (1555–1628) of Spains Hall **Finchingfield** was a happily married man. Spains Hall was named after Hervey de Ispania, but early in the 15th century it passed into the Kempe family when Margaret de Ispania married Nicholas Kempe. His descendant William had a daughter and all seemed to be going well until he had an argument with his wife and falsely accused her of adultery. So horrified was he at having wronged her that he vowed not to speak for seven years. His family and staff were informed and legend has it that he had a new pond dug for each of the seven years. Even when his wife died (in 1623) he maintained his self-imposed penance in her memory.

When the seven years were up he attempted to speak but the effort killed him. It is possible that his wife might well have settled for a simple 'sorry'!

The story of William Kempe's seven-year penance is found in the Kempe Chapel in the parish church (written in Latin).

❋ The Swearing Font

St Mary the Virgin **Tollesbury** has an 18th-century font that is known as the Swearing Font. It was paid for in penitence by John Norman, who came to Tollesbury in 1718, who had entered the church 'and cursed and talked loud in the time of Divine service'. An inscription on the font (put there by churchwarden Robert Joyce) reads:

Good people all I pray take care
That in ye church you do not swear
As this man did.

John Norman's £5 fine was used to pay for the font by way of penance, but chiefly to avoid prosecution in the ecclesiastical courts. The parish registers show that the first child to be baptised in the font in August 1718 was Elizabeth, daughter of Robert and Eliza Wood.

❋ Persecuted by Gog and Magog

In order that his story survived his death, the **Revd Simon Lynch** (1600–1660) composed his own epitaph, which was to be inscribed on his tombstone, now in the Priory Church of St Lawrence **Blackmore.** In his will (dated 1659) he specified the following:

Here lyeth the body of Simon Lynch, Rector of Runwell
Who for fearing God and the King was sequestered prosecuted and persecuted
To the day of his death
By Gog and Magog.

Simon Lynch was appointed Rector of **Runwell** at a time when Charles I's relationship with Parliament was coming under severe strain. The clergy were starting to divide into those siding with Parliament and others who stayed loyal to the Crown. During the Civil War more loyalist preachers were ejected from their livings in Essex, and replaced by Puritans, than in any English county. Simon Lynch was a royalist and his appointment as curate of **Blackmore** was not welcomed in the pro-Puritan parish. Essex was a stronghold of the Parliamentarian cause and, like many other such rectors, Simon Lynch was 'admonished and dismissed' from Runwell after the execution of the king.

The reference to Gog and Magog, who were the powers represented in the Apocalypse as the Satanic forces at Armageddon, indicates that he saw himself hounded by such forces and determined that posterity should know of his plight and loyalty to the anointed king. When he wrote his will he was not to know that on 29 May 1660, only a few weeks before his own death on 19 June, the restored King Charles II would ride through London to the accompaniment of church bells and bonfires on street corners. By his burial at Blackmore, where he was only curate, rather than Runwell where he had held the rectorship, it is probable that the Revd Lynch never recovered from his ordeal at the hands of the Puritan supporters when they ejected him in favour of Mr Oakley, described as 'a godly, able preaching minister'.

✴ Unworthy Bishop of Chichester

The brass to **Samuel Harsnett** (1561–1631) in St Mary's **Chigwell** bears the inscription (in Latin):

Here lies Samuel Harsnett, formerly vicar of this church. First the unworthy Bishop of Chichester, then the more unworthy Bishop of Norwich, at the last a very unworthy Archbishop of York.

The effigy is almost life-size and is often cited as evidence of a post-Reformation use of the 'proper and ancient Episcopal vestments'. The Archbishop, who was born in **Colchester**, is depicted wearing cope, alb, mitre, dalmatic and stole, all of which could be thought to belong to the Roman Catholic faith, abolished at the Dissolution of the Monasteries, rather than to the new Elizabethan Protestantism of his ministry. Indeed, at the start of his career the Archbishop was denounced for Popery and he, in turn, denounced aspects of Calvinism and wrote a book discrediting the 'puritan agenda'. When vice-chancellor of Cambridge University he was accused, among other things, of Romanising tendencies. However, in spite of his colourful religious pronouncements, scepticisms and contradictions, and being disciplined by the Church for preaching against predestination, he found favour with James I and successfully ascended the Episcopal ladder. In 1603, perhaps to ingratiate himself with the newly enthroned king, Harsnett wrote *Declaration of Egregious Popish Impostures*, a condemnation of the exorcisms performed by Catholic priests in the 1580s.

When he died, Archbishop Harsnett had served three very different monarchs without losing either his life or his living, and had cleverly employed whatever survival tactics were required on the day.

* **Chigwell School** is a co-educational independent school and was founded in 1629 by **Samuel Harsnett.** There are currently around 730 pupils and the school motto is *Aut viam inveniam aut faciam* (Either I shall find a way or I shall make one).

* Shakespeare's *King Lear* (1603–06) is one of his greatest tragedies and many academics agree that he leaned heavily on **Samuel Harsnett's** *Declaration of Egregious Popish Impostures*, from which he takes much of the language used by Edgar when he feigns madness. The play explores the nature of kingship and is based on the various accounts of a semi-legendary ruler of Britain.

* **Little Imp**

In St Margaret's **Woodham Mortimer** is a small brass to **Dorothie Alleine** (1584). She is dressed in pleated Elizabethan costume and her inscription reads:

> *A little imp here buried is,*
> *Her soul to Christ is fled.*

Little Dorothie was only three years old when she died and was obviously held in great affection.

❋ **Shot by his Brother**
A memorial on the north wall of the chancel of St Thomas's **Bradwell-on-Sea** records the sad death of **Cuthbert Macky Shreiber** (1833–1845), son of the Revd Thomas Shreiber. At the age of 12, Cuthbert was accidentally shot by his brother while out hunting.

❋ **The Washington Connection**
In the south porch of **Chelmsford Cathedral** is a stained-glass memorial recalling Anglo-American relations in World War Two:
 To the Glory of God in gratitude for tasks and friendships shared by the people of Essex and the United States Air Force between 1942 and 1945. This porch was enriched and beautified by Essex Friends of the American people in 1953.

❋ The cathedral window also contains the arms of the first President of the United States of America, **George Washington** (1732–99), whose great-great-grandfather, **Lawrence Washington**, was the rector of All Saints' **Purleigh** from 1632–43. In 1643 he was ousted from the parish during the Civil War and in 1657 his son John sailed for America.

❋ In 1892 the 13th-century tower of **Purleigh** church was restored with help from the United States in recognition of the Washington connection. In 1942, Arthur Mee visited Purleigh and 'found a portrait of George Washington and his mother hanging on the wall'.

❋ **No Dissenters!**
A wall monument in the chancel of St Andrew's **Halstead** records that in 1828 the Revd John Manistre, AM, formerly of King's College Cambridge and rector of Stower Provost with Todbere in Dorset bequeathed to the poor of the parish the sum of £80 per annum 'to purchase the best wheaten bread for distribution every Sunday to twenty poor persons who shall frequent this church but not to any dissenter or dissenters whatever'. He died on 10 December 1826.

✳ In the north aisle of St Andrew's **Halstead** is the story of Elizabeth Holmes, spinster, who in 1783 left a legacy of £4,000, of the interest of which £95 was to be given yearly, in £2 portions, to 'decayed housekeepers who have not received parish assistance and the remainder to be given in bread and clothing for the poor'.

✳ **Martha Blewit's Nine Husbands**
A tablet in the church tower of St Augustine of Canterbury **Birdbrook** records the tale of **Martha Blewit** of the Swan Inn (Baythorne End) who was buried on 7 May 1681 having had nine husbands 'consecutively', the ninth (landlord of the Swan) being the one to outlive her. At her funeral the parson chose as his text 'Last of all, the woman died also'.

✳ There is a second tale of marital exuberance in **Birdbrook**. Robert Hogand was 'the husband of seven wives successively', the last of whom he married on 1 January 1739. Between them Martha Blewit and Robert Hogand entered into 16 marriages.

✳ **One Hundred and Ten Ounces of Blood**
Richard Pusey notes in *Essex Rich and Strange* (1987) that in All Saints' **Rickling** an inscription reads:
It was the deceased's advice to the living that noe man should suffer 110 ounces of blood to be taken from him.
Nothing more could be discovered on the subject except that the victim of this blood letting (if such he was) was one Robert Horton, whose remains lie here with those of his wife. Richard Pusey suggests that the amazing '110' should be '10' or even 'No'.

✳ **A Lethal Christmas Pudding**
In St Mary the Virgin **Dedham** is a tablet to **Judith Eyre**, who died in 1747/8 (to take account of the Gregorian calendar then being introduced). The inscription reads:
Judith (Coyte) Eyre, wife of Joseph Eyre, Gent, many years of this parish, who died much lamented in the 35th year of her age – January 25th 1747/8- in consequence of having accidentally swallowed a Pin.

It is said that the pin Judith Eyre swallowed had been accidentally dropped into a Christmas pudding.

❉ Thank God, I have done my Duty!

On the wall of the chapel in St Mary's **Burnham-on-Crouch** is a monument to the man into whose ear the dying Admiral Horatio Nelson (1758–1805) whispered at the Battle of Trafalgar 'Thank God, I have done my duty'. The man was **Dr Alexander John Scott** (1768–1840), curate at Burnham and rector of **Southminster**.

Dr Scott was the personal chaplain of Nelson on HMS *Victory* and appears in the famous painting *The Death of Nelson, 21 October 1805* by Arthur William Devis. He was not a doctor when he took up his appointment, but as Nelson's secretary at the time was also called Scott and to differentiate between the two, Nelson called him Doctor Scott (although he was awarded a Doctorate of Divinity at Cambridge University after Trafalgar). Scott became a great friend of Nelson and went with him on many campaigns. After Nelson died he accompanied the body back to London and stood watch as it lay in state at Greenwich and later attended the funeral procession at St Paul's Cathedral.

In 1807, the 35-year-old Scott married 17-year-old Mary Ryder and took up the curacy at Burnham and rectorship at Southminster, where he persuaded his parishioners to raise funds to help families of those who fell at Trafalgar. He and Mary named one of their daughters Horatia.

❉ Midshipman Nicholson

When the **Wendens Ambo Society** was formed in 1972 one of its first tasks was to preserve the late 19th-century tombstone of **Midshipman William Nicholson** in the churchyard of St Mary the Virgin. Midshipman Nicholson was aged 104 when he died on 15 December 1886. When he was 16 he had been midshipman under Admiral Nelson on the *Vanguard*, the ship which Nelson took to the Mediterranean to recapture Naples from the French. It was on that trip that Nelson was invited to stay at the house of Sir William and Lady Hamilton. At a banquet in the Hamilton's house later that year the attraction between Nelson and Lady Hamilton was first observed.

❈ Lived under Eight Rulers

There are several monuments to the Childs family in St Mary's **Ramsden Bellhouse**, including that to **Anthony Childs**, who died in 1725 aged 81. He had lived under eight rulers – five kings, two queens and the Commonwealth Government – and only just missed George II (who acceded to the throne in 1727).

❈ Lost on the *Titanic*

At the Roman Catholic Church of St Helen's **Chipping Ongar** is found a record and photograph of **Father (Thomas) Roussel Davids Byles**, a priest drowned in the sinking of the *Titanic* in 1912. Thomas Byles (he took the name Thomas at his ordination) was born in Yorkshire in 1870 and converted to Catholicism as a young man. After becoming a priest he was assigned to St Helen's and served as Roman Catholic Rector of Ongar from 1905 until his death. In 1912, Father Byles was asked by his brother, who had moved to New York to run a rubber company, to officiate at his marriage. Father Byles was delighted and embarked on the voyage, purchasing a Second Class ticket on *Titanic* at a cost of £13. He had originally intended to go on another liner, but events conspired to prevent his leaving the parish and his ticket for *Titanic* was bought at the last minute. He boarded the ship at Southampton on 10 April 1912.

Not long after embarkation, Father Byles wrote to his housekeeper in Chipping Ongar, Miss Field, and appeared to be enjoying the voyage. He had teamed up with other clerics and, although he found the noise of the engines disturbing, he was nevertheless looking forward to being reunited with his brother and performing the marriage sacrament.

As the world now knows, *Titanic* struck an iceberg on her maiden transatlantic voyage around 400 miles south of Newfoundland and in less than three hours was lying on the seabed, a giant grave for almost 1,500 passengers and crew. Eyewitnesses later told how Father Byles heard confessions and prayed with the disaster-struck passengers; it was said that he was seen refusing a place in one of the lifeboats. He was one of those drowned and his body, if recovered, was never identified. His brother, on hearing the news, decided to go ahead with his wedding, but it was a sombre affair instead of the joyous family occasion that they had envisaged.

There is a door at St Helen's dedicated to Father Byles by his brothers.

EPITAPHS AND MEMORIALS

❋ The Gipsy Evangelist
A memorial stone to **Rodney (Gipsy) Smith** (1860–1947) in **Epping Forest** reads:

Gipsy Rodney Smith MBE who preached the Gospel of Christ to thousands on five continents for seventy years was born here on 31 March 1860 and called home journeying to America on 4 August 1947.

When only 16, the itinerant Romany was converted to Christianity by William Booth, who persuaded him to join the Salvation Army. In 1877 he became an evangelist with the Christian Mission of London and travelled all over England, preaching in what was called the Gipsey Gospel Wagon Mission. He made over 40 evangelistic trips to America, Australia and South Africa and died aboard the *Queen Mary* while travelling to New York. His ashes were returned to England and special permission was granted by the Lord Mayor of London and Epping Forest Conservator for the memorial stone.

❋ A Very Gallant Gentleman
On the north wall of St Mary the Virgin **Gestingthorpe** is a brass plaque commemorating **Captain Lawrence Edward Grace Oates** (1880–1912). The inscription reads

In memory of a very gallant gentleman. Died March 17, 1912, on the return journey from the South Pole of the Scott Antarctic Expedition.
When all were beset by hardship he, being gravely injured, went out into the blizzard to die in the hope that by so doing he might enable his comrades to reach safety.

When Arthur Mee visited in 1942 he heard tell of 'an old lady, her years running close to the nineties' who walked to the church each week to polish the brass in memory of her son, Captain Oates.

❋ The Village Home
The pioneering Village Home for Orphaned, Neglected or Destitute Girls was opened in **Barkingside** (now part of the Borough of Ilford) by **Thomas John Barnardo** (1845–1905). Although he did not complete his medical training he was known as Dr Barnardo and opened his first home for destitute children in East London (1867). The Village Home (1876–1945) is now part of the Barnardo's Heritage Centre.

A memorial was unveiled to Dr Barnardo in Barkingside on 19 June 1908 and inscriptions on it include a quote from his will:
I hope to die as I have lived, in the humble but assured faith of Jesus Christ as my Saviour, my Master, and my King.
Dr Barnardo also wrote as his own epitaph:
If I had to live over again, I would do exactly the same thing, only better, I hope and wiser, and with fewer mistakes.

✹ At **Barkingside** church is a **Memorial Garden** that was created in 2003 in memory of **HRH Diana, Princess of Wales**, who was President of Barnardo's from 1984 to 1996.

NINE
CUSTOMS AND CURIOSITIES

The nature of a county is often discovered in the way it expresses itself in its customs and traditions. Peculiarly, Essex has often been noted for its witches, perhaps because of the Witchfinder General, but for some reason **Canewdon** used to be called 'the witch country': why is not clear. 'Telling the Bees' is more often associated with the West Country, but it was historically practised all over Essex (and might be still). Bees are said to possess great powers of discernment, so much so that if they are not told of important happenings within the family the entire colony is likely to move elsewhere. In **Stock** during the 1930s, 'Telling the Bees' was essential to keep the bees happy so that they would stay and pollinate the crops. Here are a few more customs and curiosities to be found in Essex.

❈ Gin and Gingerbread

Inevitably many customs in Essex are to do with the sea and fishing. One of the oldest surviving is the **Gin and Gingerbread Ceremony** that signals the start of the annual oyster-dredging season in the first week of September. **The Mayor of Colchester**, dressed in civic robes, sets out from **Brightlingsea** on a traditional barge together with the Chief Executive and the Town Serjeant. They sail to the **Pyefleet Channel** close to **Mersea Island**, where the ancient Proclamation is read, affirming Colchester's rights since 'time immemorial' to the oyster beds. A Loyal Toast is drunk to the Queen with gin, followed by the eating of gingerbread, then the first dredge is made.

Colchester Borough Council's ownership of the fishery dates from a Charter granted by Richard I in 1189 and the current ceremony is thought to have originated some time in the 1540s.

No one is quite sure, however, when gin was first used for the toast, but both gin and gingerbread became both fashionable and widely available in England at the same time, during the 1740s. Gin had been introduced from the Netherlands in the 17th century and by the mid-1700s it was six times more popular than beer.

By tradition, a message is sent to the Queen alerting her to the fact that 'According to ancient Custom and Charter dating back to Norman times…the Colne Oyster Fishery has been opened for the coming season'.

* In 2003 the **Maldon District Council** launched the all-day annual **Oyster and Seafood Festival.** Iced oysters were the dish of the day!

* **The Dene Holes of Thurrock**

The most important groups of **Dene Holes** in England are found only in parts of Essex and Kent, particularly in the **Thurrock** area below **Hangman's Wood** in **Little Thurrock**. There are over 70 pits in a single four-acre piece of woodland. The Dene Holes are shafts going down 50–80ft through sand into the chalk below and are described as 'ancient sinkings…which have proved a mystery to antiquaries from the days of Camden's *Britannia* (1586) to the present'. The narrow perpendicular shafts, between three and four feet in diameter, branch out into chambers or caves. Some have what appear to be footholds.

Their purpose and origin continues to puzzle: they were originally thought to have been created by the Danes (Dane Holes) in the 11th century (for what reason has never become clear), but were later declared 'post-Neolithic' chalk mines, and even secret storehouses for grain in time of war (era unspecified). It has further been suggested that they are the fabled gold mines of **King Cunobelin** of the first century. Later writers have suggested they were hide-outs for smugglers or stores for their contraband, though there is no evidence for any such theories, just as there is nothing to suggest they were used for human habitation at any time. No artefacts have been found that could assist in date-fixing, although the roofs of some of the chambers appear to have been made by bone or horn picks, which could indicate that they were dug in pre-Roman times.

The name Dene is likely to derive from the Anglo-Saxon *den* (a hole or valley) rather than having reference to the Danes.

If the Dene Holes were, in fact, chalk mines (for agricultural use, perhaps, as there are no spoil mounds nearby) it seems strange that anyone would go to so much trouble to 'mine' the chalk when it was more easily obtainable from outcrops in the immediate area.

The history and usage of the Dene Holes continues to intrigue and confuse. In spite of endless investigation and discussion, no conclusive explanation has emerged for their existence.

❋ The Welsh Drovers

In the **Billericay** and **Chelmsford** areas there are still farming families by the names of Evans, Davis, Thomas, Williams, Jones and others associated with Wales. They are the descendants of the North Welsh drovers who drove their stock to the Essex grazing lands via Birmingham, Stratford upon Avon and Luton. In Essex the tired animals, dogs and drovers would rest for anything up to three weeks. Animals would rapidly regain condition on the lush Essex pastures and be ready for the final leg of their journey to the London markets. The locals were often alarmed by the 'wild Welshmen', who shouted at the tops of their voices in 'a barbaric tongue'.

If the cattle were destined for the cattle fairs at **Brentwood**, **Harlow** or **Romford** the dogs, which were bred for their extraordinary homing instincts, would be abandoned on market day and told to 'go home'. The dogs, usually collies or corgis, would retrace the inns along the drove, where they were fed and watered before being sent on their way. When the dogs arrived back in the Welsh villages the families knew that the drovers had arrived in Essex.

Droving started in around AD 800 and continued until the middle of the 1800s when trains made the journey unnecessary. In the days of highwaymen and footpads, the drovers used their own tokens instead of currency, after several had been ambushed and relieved of the few possessions and cash they carried with them for the three to four-week trek.

- In the churchyard of All Saints' **Epping Upland** is a headstone to John Jones, 'late of Madryn Isaf in the County of Caernarvon' who died on 21 November 1835, aged 55 years. His profession is proudly stated as 'Drover'.

- The Welsh poet **Edward Morus** (1607–89) from Denbighshire was a drover and died 'while following his calling, and was buried somewhere in Essex'.

- Old drover routes can be traced in such places as Epping's Long Green, Clapgate Lane and Puck Lane.

- Probate inventories in 17th and early 18th-century Essex contain many references to Welsh cattle.

Through the Ash Tree

In the 1920s the old custom of passing a child through an ash tree was still practised in Essex. In 1925 a sick child of **Fairstead** was taken to **Terling** and passed through a young ash tree, specially cleft for the purpose. The ritual was that the child was undressed and the father and mother stood on either side of the tree, passing the child one to the other. The child was then dressed and the tree bound up. As the tree healed, so the child recovered.

The Maldon Mud Race

Known also as the 'hangover cure' race, the 'Mad' **Maldon Mud Race** is the only event of its kind in Britain and consists of around 250 competitors scrambling 500 yards across the muddy bed of the River **Blackwater** and back at low tide. The race takes place in late December or early January and crowds of anything up to 10,000 cheer on the competitors as they line up at Promenade Park and then struggle through the freezing cold mud, many in fancy dress. There is a prize for the first male and first female across the finish line and another for the last. Competitors come from all over the world, including Germany, Finland, America and New Zealand. The 2009 winner was first-timer Stuart Putt from **Boreham**, who completed the course in 3 minutes 49 seconds. The winner of the ladies' trophy was another first-timer, Vicki Sharman of **West Hanningfield**.

The race is currently run by **The Lions Club of Maldon** and **The Rotary Club of Maldon** and raises money for charity.

❋ A Story 'to make my lady readers laugh'!

Probably the best-known custom in Essex is that of the **Dunmow Flitch** (a salted and cured side of bacon). Its origins are uncertain but it is at least as old as Chaucer's *Canterbury Tales* (1386) where it is mentioned in *The Wife of Bath's Prologue*:

> *Never for them the flitch of bacon though*
> *That some have won in Essex at Dunmow!*

There are several versions of the story, but one is that some time after the **Dunmow Priory of St Mary** was established in the 12th century Robert Fitzwalter, when Lord of the Manor, called at the Priory with his wife. They were disguised as paupers and begged the Prior for his blessing on the first anniversary of their marriage. The Prior was impressed by this display of marital fidelity and as reward for such devotion presented them with a flitch of bacon. Lord Robert threw off his disguise and vowed to endow the Priory with lands on the condition that just such a flitch should be given to any couple who made a solemn oath that they had not repented of their marriage for a whole year. The Prior agreed and so the custom of the Dunmow Flitch began. Couples who claimed the flitch had to undergo a mock trial. Kneeling on two hard pointed stones, the man had to take an oath before the Prior, the monks and the townspeople that he had not quarrelled or had any dispute with his wife within the year. If they were successful the pair would be enthroned in the Prior's chair and paraded round the town.

The custom of the flitch prospered during the 15th century but fell into decline after the Dissolution of the Monasteries. It was revived in the 18th century and awarded by the Lord of the Manor until 1751, when the happy couple was Thomas and Ann Shakeshaft of **Wethersfield**. Their 'trial' was said to have attracted thousands of spectators and accounts of it appeared in journals and magazines. In place of the Prior was a 'judge' and townspeople made up a 'jury'. A counsel for the claimants was also appointed. The flitch was donated by a local benefactor or businessman. Daniel Defoe made mention of it in *Tour through the Eastern Counties*

(1724) but said that he would 'make the ladies laugh at the famous old story of the Flitch of Bacon'.

Songs and rhymes were composed about the flitch and drawings appeared in various broadsheets showing one or other aspect of the ceremony. Even a play *The Flitch of Bacon* was written and performed at the Theatre Royal, Drury Lane, in 1814.

The custom of the flitch survives into the 21st century and is held every four years. In 2008 four couples successfully 'claimed the bacon'.

❋ At **Little Dunmow** the **Flitch of Bacon** public house has a flitch of bacon hanging on the opposite side of the road.

❋ **An Ancient Labyrinth**

The **turf-cut maze** at **Saffron Walden** is the largest publicly-owned turf-cut maze in England and the largest turf labyrinth of such antiquity to survive in Europe. The date of its original cutting is unknown, but it must be at least 17th century as records show that in 1699, 15 shillings was paid to have the maze recut. It was recut in 1828, 1841 and 1859. In 1911, the chalk path was laid with bricks set on edge. In 1979 the brick path was relaid with bricks, this time laid into the ground on their sides.

If any religious or mystical legends were ever associated with this maze they are now lost, but at one time many more such mazes existed across Europe. They were seen as pathways to self-discovery and metaphors for life. Those using flat turf-cut mazes were observed by others to see whether or not they cheated by stepping over the chalk lines. Ancient civilisations believed that the maze was a map of the spiritual journey from the underworld to the surface and its design was sacred. Since the Saffron Walden concentric maze is one of only eight such labyrinths surviving in England, it is of considerable importance.

The maze is circular, with 17 circuits, and is enclosed by a bank and ditch with a mound in the centre. An ash tree once grew on the mound but was destroyed during a Guy Fawkes celebration in 1823. The pathway itself is almost a mile in length (1,500 metres), although its diameter is only 130ft (30.5 metres).

❊ The maze is on the east side of the Common, an ancient meadow over which the people of **Saffron Walden** once had grazing rights. It was historically used for such events as tournaments.

❊ **Saffron Walden** has a second maze in the **Bridge End Garden**. This yew maze was originally planted in 1839 but during the 1980s it was discovered to be so overgrown that a decision was made to replant it. Its design is similar to the original and there is a viewing platform in the centre.

❊ **East London Cabbies' Outing**
Over 50 years ago cab driver **Charles 'Charlie' Albert Flemwell** (died 1996) became Mayor of the London Borough of Newham and in 1952 organised the first **East London Cabbies' Outing** to **Maldon**. Disabled, Down's syndrome and autistic children from the East End of London were (and still are) collected by the balloon-festooned taxis and driven to the first stop, the George and Dragon pub in **Mountnessing**. Then they continue the journey to the **Plume Secondary School**, where the children, carers and taxi drivers are welcomed to Maldon. In the afternoon the convoy wends its way to Promenade Park, where various entertainments are on offer, including face painting, clowns, horse and cart rides and a prize for the best-dressed cab.

❊ When Charlie Flemwell died his son Ken, also an East London taxi driver, kept the custom going in his father's honour. The cabbies give up their day's work to give the children a day out.

❊ **Throwing the Kitchel!**
A **Harwich** tradition known as **Throwing the Kitchel** is believed to have been enacted in mediaeval times and is now part of the annual mayoral ceremony held on the third Thursday in May. The kitchels (or sweet buns) are thrown from the Guildhall window with cries of 'Catch a kitchel, if you can!'.

Until 1949 the Mayor's Day was held in December and coincided with the much older tradition of children being taken to see their godparents at Christmas time to ask for their blessing. In return they would be given a kitchel (a triangular piece of Christmas cake). A similar word *kichel* turns up in Chaucer's *Canterbury Tales* (1386) where it is referred to as a *Goddes kichel* (or sometimes *kechyl*).

Some have interpreted *kitchel* as being derived from *catch-all*, since part of the tradition is that the kitchels are thrown in the air for children to catch. Another thought is that it is a derivative of *kit*, which is an old word for 'a gang or band assembled for a mischievous purpose'.

In *A Glossary of the Essex Dialect* (1880), Richard Stephen Charnock gives *kitch* as meaning 'to catch'.

It is likely that Throwing the Kitchel is a combination of words and customs handed down over many generations. The only other place where a similar custom survives is at Coventry, where Godcakes (small mincemeat turnovers) were traditionally given to godchildren on Twelfth Night.

❋ **Spiritual Home of the Morris Dancers**

Thaxted is considered by Morris Dancers across the country to be their 'spiritual home'. The Morris Ring, founded in 1934, meets annually in Thaxted and in 2008 there were special celebrations for the 500th anniversary of Morris Dancing and the 75th Thaxted Morris meeting.

In common with most folkloric traditions the precise origins of Morris Dancing are obscure, but it is likely that the present form took shape in the Elizabethan era. There was something of a revival in Morris dancing in 1911 when Cecil Sharp, a collector of folk song and dance, founded the English Folk Dance Society, which embraced the Morris Dancers. There are Morris Men at **Blackmore**, **Colchester**, **Chingford** and **Harwich**. The Bullnose Morris Dancers meet in **Vange**, the Mayflower Morris Men at **Billericay**, the Dark Horse Morris at **Maldon** and Morris in the Maze at **Saffron Walden**.

❋ At the patronal festival of St John the Baptist **Danbury**, Morris dancers take part in the celebrations, held as close as possible to Midsummer's Eve.

❋ **The Nine Days Wonder**

One of the most famous Morris Men was William Kempe (1560–1603), who was an actor in William Shakespeare's troupe. He is best remembered for performing a Morris dance from London to Norwich (around 100 miles) in 1600, passing through **Romford**, **Chelmsford** and **Braintree**, where his companion fell into a muddy pothole up to his waist. The dance was later chronicled as *Kempe's Nine Days Wonder*. To earn enough to pay his way he sold garters and, at **Widford**, he was met by Sir Thomas Mildmay, of **Moulsham Hall**, who bought some of the garters as Kempe danced by. At **Chelmsford** he was so exhausted that he had to lock himself in his room and 'pacify the people from the window with words instead of deeds'. He was grateful, though, for 'the good cheer and kindly welcome I had at Chelmsford', but found it impossible to explain that he would rather 'refrain from drinke and be temperate in my dyet' than be entertained with copious refreshment. At **Ilford** he again had to give the crowds the slip as they offered him beer and he was afraid that it would 'draine my litte wit drye'.

❈ The Lepers' Stone

Countryside writer C. Henry Warren in his book *Essex* (1950) refers to a **Lepers' Stone** at the Shortgrove end of **Newport**, which was blown down in a great storm towards the end of the 18th century. The stone had a cavity into which coins were laid by those in the mediaeval Leper Hospital (now gone) in return for food placed there by those on the outside. After the stone blew over it became buried 'to the consternation of the inhabitants, who regarded the event as an omen of disaster – a proof of the regard with which the stone was held in the common memory'.

❈ The Compasses

One of Essex's most enduring mysteries is why three pubs, called the Compasses (**Littley Green**), the Square and Compasses (**Fuller Street**) and the Compasses (**Great Totham**), should be in a straight line 10 miles long. Another three are on another line dissecting the first line through the centre. Several theories have been put forward to explain the significance and many geometrical facts employed to analyse their precise location. Some like to think there is a connection with the Knights Templar, who had a preceptory at **Cressing Temple**.

An explanation for the pubs' names might be that since Essex is bereft of stone, and historically relied on wood for building houses and churches, a large number of carpenters would have been required. Inns were meeting places of various craftsmen and, before universal literacy, the symbol for carpenters was the compass. Thus it is no surprise to find a large number of hostelries with compasses in their name. In addition to the above there is a Compasses Motel at **Chelmsford**, an Axe and Compasses at both **Arkesden** and **Aythorpe Roding**, a Three Compasses at **West Hanningfield** and a Compasses Inn at **Pattiswick**.

❋ City Limits
There are still around 20 **Coal and Wine Tax Posts** in Essex, most of which were erected under the London Coal and Wine Duties Continuance Act of 1861. The posts (or stones) marked the boundaries, approximately 20 miles from Central London, at which duties on coal and wine had to be paid to the Corporation, which exercised the right to measure commodities entering the City. One of the best known is at **Theydon Bois** and stands opposite a house called The Boundary. Another is at Coppice Row, **Epping**, close to the Wake Arms.

❋ Dog Hair Sandwich
In the 19th century there was a strong belief in magic cures of all kinds, such as this cure for whooping cough which hails from **Wickham Bishops** – 'take a hair from the tail of a stray dog and put it between two slices of bread and butter and give to the child to eat'. The author of this snippet did not record whether the cure worked.

❋ *Contra Bonos Mores*
Between 1780 and 1850 it was possible for a man to put his wife up for sale in a public market. In Essex one of the most famous occasions on which this took place was in 1823 in **Chipping Ongar** when a Mr Feake led his wife into the market place on a halter and, according to *The Times* (31 December 1823), 'there exposed her for sale'. The practice was called ***Contra bonos mores*** (contrary to good or public morals) and was illegal. It seems to have happened nonetheless. For many years it was the only means of dissolving a marriage for those without recourse to the law and was known as the 'poor man's divorce'. Sometimes the occasion was preceded by a public

announcement and conducted by an auctioneer. The practice of the woman being led by a halter round her neck was to signify that she was the property of her husband and the purchaser was, thereafter, considered to be the woman's new husband.

The most famous account of a wife being sold was fictional. Thomas Hardy's novel *The Mayor of Casterbridge* (1886) opens with the sale of a wife by the central character, which act haunts him and eventually destroys him.

In the case of Mr Feake, *The Times* recorded that the woman was soon purchased by a young man, a blacksmith of **High Ongar**, at the price of ten shillings. 'Her person was by no means unpleasing, and she appeared to be about twenty-five years of age' continued the report. However, 'the collector of the tolls actually demanded and received from the purchaser the customary charge of one penny, which is always paid upon live-stock sold therein per head'!

✣ Another case of wife-selling occurred in 1830 when a workhouse master was issued with a summons and came before **Epping** magistrates for having led a woman, 'dressed only in a long shift', on a halter from the George Inn to the market place. She was sold for 'half a crown' (two shillings and sixpence) and the man was charged with 'selling goods and chattels without a licence'. However, the case was dismissed not because of any immorality or illegality, but because the magistrate did not consider a wife 'goods or chattels'.

✣ **St George's Joust**

A novel way of celebrating England's Patron Saint takes place at the 800-year old **Cressing Temple Barns** and is known as **St George's Joust**. Falconry displays, jousting and performances by re-enactment groups turn the clock back to mediaeval days, with knights leaping horse to horse and the Black Knight greeted with jeers from the crowds.

Cressing Temple is an atmospheric setting for a celebration of the nation's Patron Saint as the **Knights Templar** had a preceptory here in the 12th century, as well as property at **Witham** and **Rivenhall**. They were one of the three orders of chivalry which followed the English Crusaders into the Holy Land and fought alongside other crusading forces in the defence of

Christian settlements in Palestine and Syria. Cressing Temple was founded on land granted by Queen Maud in a charter dated at Evreux in 1136 and confirmed by her husband, King Stephen (1135–54) at the end of his reign. The preceptory was on a site once occupied by the Romans who, in their turn, utilised a place where Iron Age man dwelled. The 2,000-acre estate was the first grant of rural land that the Knights Templar received in England.

Under Edward II the Templars were suppressed and their possessions handed over to the Hospitallers. The estate suffered at the hands of looters in the Peasants' Revolt (1381) when armour, vestments, gold and silver were borne away and books burned. It was dissolved in 1540 and fell into secular hands for the first time.

St George's Joust is set against the backdrop of the two surviving barns. The weatherboarded **Barley Barn** dates from around 1200 and is the earlier of the two. The brick-nogged **Wheat Barn** is less altered and contains enormous timbers considered 'a master-piece of Romanesque carpentry'. They are the oldest surviving timber-framed mediaeval barns in Europe.

St George was martyred at Lydda in Palestine and his cult gained significance for England during the Crusades. The Cressing Joust takes place in April as his feast date is 23 April.

❉ The **Knight Templars House** (in Knight Templars Terrace), **Kelvedon** is a Grade I listed building.

❉ The legend of the **Cressing Horse** takes many forms but sometime in the 1860s, when freshly cut sheaves of corn were being stacked in the Barley Barn, a horse would be walked round and round in a circle on top of the stack to compress it. The horse was left on top of the stack while the men had their break, but when they returned the animal was nowhere to be seen. Having searched the barn they concluded that it had been stolen. However, some months later one of the men was nearby and heard a muffled 'hummer' (an Essex word for a whinny). Before long he discovered the missing horse, which had sustained itself by eating the grain and straw, but a hole had to be cut in the barn wall to get him out. Unfortunately the horse immediately made for the horse pond and drank thirstily, whereupon the grain inside him swelled up and he died almost immediately.

A slightly amended version was that the horse slipped down between the closely packed sheaves and was not found, again leading the men to think it had been stolen. However, some months later the horse was found in the barn 'as fat and as sleek as a mole'. The ending is the same: the horse bolted and made for the pond, whereupon it drank heavily and then died.

✻ St George's Day

St George's Day does not go unnoticed in **Colchester** as it has been publicly marked for over 100 years. Following the Boer Wars in the late 19th century a wave of patriotic fervour swept the country and three-times mayor of Colchester, Alderman Edwin Sanders (who had lost a son in the war), founded the **St George's Day Parade**. In 1899 the first procession of the town council took place, culminating in a service at St Peter's church. In the same year the **Club St George** was instigated to encourage boys to develop self-reliance, with regular summer camps at **Walton**. In the same year Robert Baden-Powell (1857–1941) published *Aids to Scouting* with very similar aims. In 1908, Baden-Powell formed the Boy Scouts and shortly afterwards the **1st Colchester Scouts** troop became one of the first troops. Since St George is also the Patron Saint of Scouting, the Colchester and District Scouts held a parade on St George's Day thereafter and in 2008 celebrated their centenary.

The founder of the Colchester Scouts, Henry Elwes, became good friends with Baden-Powell and invited him to Essex on many occasions to inspect the troop.

✻ The Gleaners' Bell

Essex by Charlotte Craven Mason (1929) recalls the **Gleaners' Bell of Hadleigh**. During harvest, at eight o'clock each morning and again at six in the evening, the church bell was rung by way of a signal for the gleaners to start and finish gleaning. The gleaners, usually women, were from poor families and farmers would allow them to follow the sheaf makers at harvest time, picking up stray pieces of corn which they were allowed to keep without payment. The practice died out in the early years of the 20th century.

❋ Walking Backwards to Love

A writer in *The Essex Literary Journal* for 1838–39 recounts an old Essex custom practised by unmarried women. They used to fasten their stays by a garter to the bedroom wall when going to bed, then walk into bed backwards. If the woman's lover was true, his apparition would walk round the bed. There is no mention of when this practice died out.

❋ The Mesopotamia Election

There was once an area of **Chelmsford** called **Mesopotamia Island** where a strange custom, **The Mesopotamia Election**, took place as recorded in Wright's *History of Essex* (1836). 'So far back as the memory of man runneth' writes Thomas Wright, there was a custom that 'on the death of an Essex member, or when the Great Council had been dissolved', a mock election took place where the 'candidates' paraded on horseback through the streets, each attended by a page. A band accompanied the riders and they assembled close to where the real candidates were gathered. Humorous speeches were delivered to the gratification of the crowds. The 1830 election was remembered as having 'an unusual display of wit and oratory'. The successful 'candidate' had the mixed blessing of being chaired to the river and thrown in, the chair afterwards broken up. This always took place on the island between two bridges over the River Chelmer. Mesopotamia, in modern Iraq, lies between the rivers Tigris and Euphrates, rather as the island lay between the rivers **Chelmer** and **Cam** and periodically flooded.

❋ The Silent Woman

Until the end of the 19th century there was an inn at **Widford** called the **Silent Woman.** In *Essex Rich and Strange* (1987), Richard Pusey writes that it once had a sign with a half-length portrait of Henry VIII and 'the other showed a headless woman dressed in a costume of old'. The inscription above her read *Fort Bon*, an untutored version of the French for 'Very Good'. A number of inns were named the Silent Woman, the Good Woman, or the Quiet Woman, and the women were all depicted headless. In the case of the Widford woman it was supposed that, since Henry VIII was involved, the woman might be his decapitated queen, Anne Boleyn.

The most likely explanation is a macabre one that was a favourite among innkeepers of the 18th century, whose male customers thought that the ideal woman was a quiet or silent one, and that was only likely to happen if the woman had no head. There is a Quiet Woman in Yorkshire which includes a verse on the inn sign:

> *Here is a woman who has lost her head.*
> *She's quiet now – because, do'ye see, she's dead!*

A one-time landlord of Widford's Silent Woman was, no doubt, lauded for his sense of humour!

❋ Proper Cog'shall

In *Essex* (1950) C. Henry Warren wrote of the richness of Essex country humour and thought that nowhere was it better illustrated than in **Coggeshall**. A 'Cog'shall job' is an idea that is so preposterous 'that it assumes the nature of a joke, even of a fantasy'. To illustrate, Mr Warren gave the example of a man finding that his ladder was not long enough, so he removed the bottom rung and fastened it to the top. That, he says, is a Coggeshall job.

Then there is the man who has to rise early but, finding he has only one match to light the candle, strikes it the previous night to make sure it is a good one.

Alison Barnes, in *Essex Eccentrics* (1975), adds a few more and relates the legend that the people of Coggeshall once tried to fish the moon out of the River Blackwater with hay rakes, thinking it was a ball of gold.

The Brewer Dictionary of Phrase and Fable (1870) records that a Coggeshall job is when the Coggeshall folk wanted to divert the current of a stream, they fixed hurdles in the bed of it for the purpose. And then again – 'another tale is that a mad dog bit a wheelbarrow, and the people, fearing it would go mad, chained it up in a shed'.

Then there was the time the **Coggeshall Town Band** was rehearsing when a friend ran in and told the bandsmen how lovely the music sounded from the street. Immediately they put down their instruments and trooped out to listen.

Anyone who exposes himself to ridicule is referred to as 'proper Cog'shall'.

* **Cinque Port**
Brightlingsea is the only **Cinque Port** outside Kent and Sussex and each year a 'Deputy' is chosen by the Freemen of Brightlingsea to be the Mayor of Sandwich's representative. They would, in the past, have been responsible for maintaining law and order. The 'Deputy' attends an historic ceremony in the Guildhall at Sandwich each June and the Mayor of Sandwich pays an official visit to Brightlingsea, when there is a colourful procession through the town. The 'Choosing Day', or election, is held on the first Monday in December at All Saints' Church. The Freemen gather and any parishioner who has been resident for a year and a day can be put forward to be 'Recognised' and declared a Freeman.

* **The Sign of the Wells**
The fashion of visiting spa centres began in Europe during the 16th century but it was not until the 1700s that interest developed in the supposed healing properties of spa water in England. **Woodford Wells** (now in the London Borough of Redbridge) is one place that recalls the once-popular custom of 'taking the water' or seeking cures through medicinal or healing waters. The two wells are named on a survey map of 1757 as **New Wells** and **Old Wells**. Following experiments on the Woodford well water in 1711 by Dr Benjamin Allen, the Woodford Well became known for its 'purging wells', the water of which was considered to be a cure for many ills. For most of the 18th century, day-trippers from London came looking for 'rest and recuperation', but by the 1820s the craze had abated.

* The **Horse and Well** (called the Horse and Groom Inn in the 1770s) at **Woodford Wells** was first registered in around 1784 and stood at the edge of a green, now built on. In 1722 Samuel Goldsmith, innkeeper of **Woodford Row**, had applied for a licence to erect a coaching house and stabling beside his own house, known as 'The Sign of the Wells', which was the forerunner of the present building.

* Other spas were established at **Dovercourt**, **Hockley** and **Witham**.

* At **Dovercourt** in 1845 a former East Indian merchant named John Bagshaw found a chalybeate (iron bearing) spring on his land. He opened

a spa with a pump room, museum and library to encourage the gentry to 'take the waters'.

❋ The spa at **Hockley** was built in 1843 but the fashion in spas was already on the wane. The pump house and hotel flourished only briefly. There is still a **Spa Road** and **Spa Hotel** to recall the heyday of the Hockley Spa.

❋ The **Witham** Spa was discovered in 1737 by Dr Taverner, who with a developed sense of commerce managed to persuade people to visit Witham, as the effervescence of the water made it impossible to bottle. Witham was the only town in Essex that had any real pretensions to the spas of Tunbridge Wells or Bath. The enterprise is commemorated in **Spa Place**, **Spa Road** and **Little Spa**.

❋ **The Wormingford Dragon**

In the church of St Andrew **Wormingford** is a 1950s stained-glass window that portrays a vivid green dragon devouring a village maiden – only her legs are visible, dangling from the creature's mouth – with St George riding to the rescue (but too late, it seems). The double window was donated by Maria Maud, wife of D.H. Boggis-Rolfe, 'in thankfulness for those who returned from the War of 1939–1945'.

There are several legends associated with the **Wormingford Dragon**, the first of them concerning Sir Bertram de Hayes (or Sir George Marney of Layer de la Haye, it varies) who at the start of the 15th century saw a dragon making its way up the River Stour, devouring people as it went. He reached for his axe and cut down a tree, which fell on the dragon and killed it. Where the dragon came from no one knows and many of the stories include a figure not unlike St George who kills the dragon with a lance.

The second account concerns an escaped crocodile that was presented by Saladin to the Crusading King Richard the Lionheart. The king brought the crocodile to the menagerie in the Tower of London (founded early in the 13th century) from where it escaped, finding its way to Essex. After being chased by villagers the crocodile apparently took fright and disappeared in a pond at **Wormingford Hall**, never to be heard of again.

Whether the creature was a dragon or a crocodile, it lives on in legend both in Wormingford and **Bures Hamlet**, where there are similar tales of a local dragon. The origin of the Wormingford beast might derive from the old word *worm* meaning dragon or reptile and is taken to explain why the village changed its name in mediaeval times.

In 1405 a monk named John of Trokelowe is reputed to have written of the Bures dragon that it was 'vast in body with a crushed head, teeth like a saw, and a tail extending to enormous length'! Although it was shot at by arrows they bounced off his skin. A 19th-century translation of this account can be found in the church.

There is even a story (said to date from 1449) that two dragons, or crocodiles, were seen fighting on the banks of the Stour – one green and one black. The black one triumphed and the place where the fight took place was named Sharpfight Meadow (now called Shalford Meadow).

❈ In the south porch of St Michael's **Fobbing** a 16th-century spandrel has a carving of a man forcing open a dragon's mouth with, it would seem, the intention of placing his head inside.

❈ The Herongate Dragon

Trusted servant of Richard III **Sir James Tyrrell** (1450–1502), of **East Horndon**, was another who is reputed to have slain a dragon. Sir James, who lived at Heron Hall, was asked to track down a serpent-like creature that had escaped from a ship in the Thames and was terrorising the local population of **Herongate**. Sir James was successful in his efforts but died soon afterwards (although he was, in fact, executed for treason by Henry VII). He is rather more famous for having confessed to the murder of the two Princes in the Tower.

Sir James's son, also called James, was said to have gone looking for his father and to have trodden on a bone of the slain creature. He contracted gangrene and had to have his leg amputated. A stained-glass picture of a one-legged man is thought to have once been in the old Herongate church.

❈ King Harold Day

Each October **King Harold Day** is held in Abbey Gardens **Waltham Abbey**. Harold was the last Saxon King, having seized the throne when Edward the

Confessor died in 1066. He died at the Battle of Hastings in the first year of his reign. King Harold Day celebrates pre-Norman England with displays of archery, re-enactments and demonstrations of ancient crafts. Some traditionalists still rue the imposition of the 'Norman yoke'.

❋ The Great Russian Myth

In August 1914 the people of Essex were duped by **The Great Russian Myth**, perpetrated mainly by the press. Following Britain's entry into World War One a rumour was spread that convoys of trains containing a vast Russian Army were travelling in secret from Scotland and would pass through Essex on their way to the south coast to assist the Allied effort on the Western Front. It was genuinely believed by many in **Colchester** that several trains had passed through the North Station, some of them loaded with Russian cavalry, whose jet black horses had plainly been seen! The rumours were officially denied by the government's Press Bureau a few weeks later.

❋ The Beast of Brentwood

The **Essex Big Cat Research Project** continues to record sightings of large cat-like animals in the Essex countryside. King-sized feline footprints were found in concrete at **East Mersea** in January 1996 and in March 2008 a resident of **Colchester** reported seeing a large, unidentifiable animal in Turner Road. A creature described as 'a tawny puma' was seen running across **Galleywood Common**. Other sightings have been made at **Billericay**, **Margaretting**, **Ongar** and **Maldon**.

In October 2006 several people reported seeing a black cat 'the size of a puma' in Weald Country Park, **Brentwood**, and quickly christened it **the Beast of Brentwood**. Police took the reports seriously enough to warn residents to keep their pets inside and to report any possible sightings.

In 2005 a survey by the British Big Cats Society listed Essex as having 50 big cat sightings and said that the numbers were increasing annually.

❋ In April 2008, the *Essex County Standard* reported that 'alligators, poisonous snakes and white-faced monkeys are just some of the weird and wonderful creatures living among us in Essex'. However, they were not in the wild but registered under the Dangerous and Wild Animals Act 1976, brought in to counter the fashion for unusual, dangerous or exotic pets and prevent them from being released illegally into the countryside. Unfortunately it is believed that some animals were let loose before the Act became law and these have survived and bred in the Essex countryside.

✺ The Hanging Buns

For over 100 years there has been an unusual custom at the **Bell Inn** at **Horndon-on-the-Hill** of hanging hot cross buns on the ceiling of the saloon bar. It was started by Jack Turnell, who became the new landlord of the Bell on Good Friday 1901. He marked the occasion by hanging a bun from the bar ceiling. The tradition continues and the oldest person available is given the honour of hanging the bun. During World War Two the ritual continued but a concrete bun was hung instead of the real thing, due to the shortage of food.

One of the Inn's rooms is called **The Anne Boleyn Suite** in honour of the one-time Queen Consort of Henry VIII.

✺ An Absence of Cholera

On Pound Green **Earls Colne** stands the Cholera Pump, erected in 1853 by the generosity of Mrs Mary Gee of Colne House. Mrs Gee had built Colne House in 1840, laying out its extensive grounds, and rebuilt or renovated several other cottages in the parish. In the 1850s the threat of cholera spurred Mrs Gee on to provide the pump so that everyone should have access to fresh water. Unfortunately the water proved undrinkable and the pump was never used. The pump, which carries the inscription *In thankful commemoration of the absence of Cholera*, remains as a monument to good intent and generosity of spirit.

✺ Last Train Home

In 2009 the **Chappel Cider Festival** celebrated its 10th year and the **Chappel Beer Festival** marks its 23rd year. Both are held at the **East Anglian Railway Museum** at the **Chappel and Wakes Colne Railway Station**, one of the advantages being that additional evening services on the **Marks Tey**-Sudbury Branch Line allow those attending the festivals to return home by train.

✸ Sleepy Postmaster!

Halfway up the wall of the old Post Office at **Faulkbourne** seems an odd place for a trap door, but this one had a special purpose. In the days of horse-drawn mail coaches the first post was delivered at four o'clock in the morning, which was too early for the village postmaster. Rather than go down to receive the mail he had the local builder construct a shutter in his bedroom wall, next to his bed, at exactly the right height for the coachman to deliver the post. He was, therefore, not obliged to leave his bed at all and could go back to sleep until a more civilised hour!

MISCELLANY

Essex is twinned with **Jiangsu** (the People's Republic of China), **Picardy** (France), **Thuringia** (Germany) and **Henrico County** (Virginia).

* In 2008 the **Essex-Jiangsu Cultural Festival** was held over nine months to celebrate the 20-year link with Jiangsu Province in China, making it the largest international arts festival ever held in Essex. Events included an exhibition of 43 terracotta figures from the 2,000-year-old collection of the Han Dynasty (only the second time the figurines have been seen outside China and their first visit to Britain), the Nanjing Acrobats, the Yangzhou Puppet Company and Little Red Flowers Performance Troupe.

* In 2009 the **Essex-Jiangsu Festival** was celebrated in **Colchester** and included Chinese dragon dances, a lantern procession, Chinese firecrackers and a Lion Dance. Ribbon and fan dances, plus martial arts displays also took place, culminating in a firework finale in the Castle Park formal gardens.

* The **Chelmsford Theatre Association** was formed in 1957 to campaign for the creation of a professional theatre in **Chelmsford**. In 1962 the Borough Council built the Assembly Rooms (Fairfield Road), now the 505-seater **Civic Theatre**. The smaller **Cramphorn Theatre** provides an innovative programme of film screenings.

* The **Colchester Repertory Company** was formed in 1937 offering weekly productions at the Albert Hall in **Colchester**. In 1968 the search began for a site for a new theatre and the **Mercury Theatre** was opened in 1972.

It is now home to the highly acclaimed **Mercury Theatre Company**, which was formed in 1998 by **Dee Evans** (chief executive) and **Gregory Floy** (artistic director). Alongside the productions in the main house there is a comprehensive range of community and schools work performed in the **Mercury Studio**.

* The Blue Boar Hotel in **Maldon** claims to be the oldest hotel in East Anglia.

* **Saffron Walden** Museum, completed in 1835, is one of the oldest purpose-built museum buildings in England.

* Contrary to popular belief, Basildon Bond notepaper was not named after the Essex town of **Basildon**. In 1911 the directors of a London-based stationery manufacturer, Millington and Sons, were staying at a country house in Berkshire. They were choosing a name for their new rag writing paper and took the name of the house, Basildon Park.

* The surname '**Christmas**' is relatively rare and was originally given to a person born at Christmas (Christ's mass or festival). It is believed to originate from one man who lived in Yorkshire in the 13th century, but for some reason there has been a significant 'cluster' of Christmases in Essex throughout the centuries. The first recorded spelling of the name is in 1185, that of **Roger Cristemesse** in the *Rotuli Dominus* (Essex Rolls).

* A Christmas Field is found at **Castle Hedingham**.

* There is a burial entry in the parish records at **Dedham** for 'Father Christmas' on 30 May 1564.

* **Chipping Ongar** has more than 100 listed buildings and was one of the first Conservation Areas designated by Essex County Council.

* The smallest council house in Britain is a thatched 17th-century cottage in **Rayleigh**. It is thought to have been built by Dutch settlers in the 1670s and is available to rent at £75 a week on the condition that the occupiers

agree to open it to the public once a week. It is administered by a trust through **Rochford Council**. The cottage has only one bedroom, a living room with a kitchen and a small bathroom.

* One of the first concrete houses erected in England was Down Hall, **Hatfield Broad Oak**. It replaced a much older property that had once been maintained by the Hatfield Priory and was owned at one time by Matthew Prior (1664–1721), poet and diplomat, who lived there in 1719 and intended to effect major reconstruction 'regretting that it was timber rather than stone or brick'. Few of Matthew Prior's plans came to fruition and by 1873 it was in a dilapidated state. Sir Henry Selwin-Ibbetson decided to replace it with a house of poured concrete in Italianate style, but keeping the avenue of hornbeams planted by Matthew Prior.

* According to local legend, there is an underground tunnel linking **Barkingside** police station with the magistrate's court over the road.

* **Manningtree** is England's smallest town, covering just 22 acres at low tide (and considerably less at high tide!). The parish boundary has, however, changed over the years and is presently entwined with those of **Mistley** and **Lawford**. A plaque and parish boundary marker, dated 1871, is found at the corner of Mill Lane and Brook Street and marks the spot where Lawford and Manningtree met. The marker stone was originally built into the wall of a cottage in Mill Lane, which straddled the parish boundary, but when it was demolished in the 1970s, the stone was preserved in one of the brick walls of the new development.

* Essex, with 225 institutes and 9,500 members, is the largest federation within the **National Federation of Women's Institutes** (the 'WI').

* In Essex, the WI is not confined to women and efforts have been made to invite husbands to conferences.

* The **Ugley WI** changed its name to 'The Women's Institute of Ugley' but it remains registered as 'Ugley Women's Institute' with the Charity

Commission. (Ugley was first recorded in 1041 as *Uggele* and probably means a woodland clearing belonging to Ugga.)

❋ In 2009 a new group was formed, to be known as the **Colchester WIGs** (Women's Institute Girls).

❋ In Turner's *Herbal* it is stated that there is more **mistletoe** in Essex than in any other county. **William Turner** (1508–1568) was a distinguished ornithologist and botanist.

❋ **Layer Marney Tower** is Britain's tallest Tudor gatehouse. It has been called 'one of the amazing sights of Essex' and Pevsner wrote 'these gatehouses were the ambition of the age'. The towers were to form the entrance of a grand complex envisaged by Sir Henry Marney (1456/7–1523). He intended to build a magnificent mansion for his descendants on the place where his ancestors had lived since the Norman Conquest. Unfortunately for Sir Henry he had no descendants: he died with the house barely started and his son died two years later without an heir. Sir Henry was knighted for his part in routing the Pretender to the throne, Perkin Warbeck, in the 1490s.

❋ The **Essex Wildlife Trust** manages more than 7,000 acres of land in Essex and has seven visitor centres.

❋ **Butlin's Holiday Camp** at **Clacton-on-Sea** was the second such camp to be opened by Billy Butlin when he bought the West Clacton estate early in 1936. He also opened a funfair a few months later, on 11 June. Before long hundreds of chalets were added to the original miniature golf and boating lakes of the old West Clacton complex, and later a Viennese ballroom and indoor swimming pool.

The Clacton Holiday Camp opened in the same week that the Government made it compulsory for employees to be given a week's paid holiday. The average weekly wage then was £3 10s.

During World War Two it was designated a Prisoner of War camp, but was never used as such. It closed its door to holidaymakers in 1983.

* **Cliff Richard** made his first professional debut at Butlin's Holiday Camp, **Clacton-on-Sea**.

* At just 3ft 8in tall and weighing 4st 1lb, **Lewis Spooner** of **Tiptree** claimed to be England's smallest man. In July 1949 the *Essex County Telegraph* announced that 75-year-old Mr Spooner had lately retired from the Anchor Press, having spent his youth travelling the country with fairs and circuses.

* **Go Bananas** outside **Colchester** is the largest indoor adventure play centre in the south-east of England. It includes a Spaceball designed by NASA astronauts.

* The 1,200-acre **Abberton Reservoir** is the largest body of fresh water in Essex. It was completed in 1941, has a 12-mile circumference and contains 25,000 megalitres. Water is pumped into it from the Chelmer, Blackwater and Stour rivers. It was used by the Royal Air Force for practice flights for the breaching of the Mohne and Eder dams during World War Two (RAF's 617 Squadron, the 'Dam Busters'). In his autobiography, *Enemy Coast Ahead* (published posthumously in 1946), the leader of the raid, Wing Commander Guy Penrose Gibson, VC, DFC, DSO (1918–44), referred to it as the Colchester Lake. The last practice flight at Abberton was on the night of 14 May 1943 and the actual attacks on the German dams were made on 16 May. The Visitor Centre is at **Layer de la Haye**.

* The **Hanningfield Reservoir** provides water for 1.5 million people in Essex and has a maximum depth of 55ft (16.76m). It was built in 1957 and cost approximately £6 million. Part of the flooded area covers the ancient hamlet of Peasdown. To the south of Hanningfield Reservoir is a 100-acre **Nature Reserve**.

* The largest village green in Essex is at **Great Bentley**.

* **Lakeside Shopping Centre** at **West Thurrock** was one of England's first out-of-town shopping centres. It occupies more than 1.3 million square

feet of retail floor space with over 320 shops. There are 13,000 free car-parking spaces.

❋ The former public convenience in Coach Lane, **Maldon**, was built in Edwardian times and for many years was used as the town's **Tourist Information Centre**. When it was offered for sale in 2008 the mock Tudor building still contained some of its original internal glazed bricks. The surveyor said that 'the architects and engineers of the Edwardian period, like their forebears in Victorian days, were encouraged by local authorities to construct public conveniences of high standard'. However, when the TIC closed in 2007 the staff moved with all speed to their new quarters in Maldon's shopping arcade!

❋ In the 1930s the garden designer and architect **Oliver Hill** (1887–1968) conceived the **Frinton Park Estate**, an example of modernist architecture that was intended as a showcase for modern design. What is now the Round House was the first building (the Show House in 1934) and although the whole (very ambitious) project was never fully completed there are some 30 or so Oliver Hill houses remaining which demonstrate his original, far-thinking designs. Hill was at first attracted to the Arts and Crafts movement but was later converted to modernism. The Park Estate layout was intended to deter London day-trippers from cluttering the place with vulgarities such as a bandstand 'and the smell of cigarettes on asphalt'. Unfortunately Hill fell out with the developers, but Frinton's modernist houses are the largest such group left in England.

❋ The iconic and much-loved manually-operated wooden level crossing gates at **Frinton-on-Sea** were the subject of a bitter three-year long preservation campaign, organised by the **Frinton Gates Preservation Society**, but in April 2009 they were removed by Network Rail 'in the dead of night', hours before a final protest demonstration was planned. The gates had guarded the entrance to Frinton since the railways arrived in the late 19th century and appear on the Town Council's official crest. Protestors branded Network Rail 'cowardly'.

- The **Brentwood Museum** claims to be the only one situated in a graveyard. The collection of social and domestic objects dates from the 1840s to the 1950s and is housed in a 19th-century cottage, Cemetery Lodge, once home to the local sexton.

- Although the original structure cannot easily been seen (due to rebuilding early in the 20th century), the **Monks' Bridge** at **Coggeshall** is the oldest surviving brick bridge in Britain. The Coggeshall bricks date from around 1225. For reasons as yet unexplained, England appears to have lost its brick and tile-making skills when the Romans left in AD 450 and was slow to regain the art. The Cistercian monks (the monastery was founded in 1142) diverted the River **Blackwater** into a new channel to create a large millpond and fishponds. The bridge is a survivor of the planned water management carried out during the mediaeval heyday of the monastery.

- The 13th-century Grange Barn at **Coggeshall** is the oldest surviving timber-framed barn in Europe. It was originally part of Coggeshall's Cistercian monastery.

- In *Kelly's Directory* (1937) it was recorded that 'the Essex men are mostly employed in husbandry and stock feeding, and only a few in manufactures of silk, etc. at **Braintree** and **Halstead**; there is a silk mill at **Chelmsford**. The lace industry is carried on at the cottage homes of **Coggeshall**, where the delicate textile, usually called **Tambour lace**, is made by hand'.

- Another type of cloth – famed throughout mediaeval Europe – was the **Coggeshall White**.

- Opposite **Ramsey** church is a drinking fountain and horse trough, given to the parish by Mr R.C. Abdy of **Michaelstowe Hall** to replace a pond previously on the site. The long, bath-like trough has cast-iron legs that are shaped to look like horse's hooves.

- **Foresters House** (dated around 1450) is the oldest house in **Harwich**. From 1800 to 1941 it was an ale house called the Foresters Arms, but known locally as the Old Drum and Monkey. It was seriously damaged by incendiaries in World War Two but was restored in 1953 by Winifred Cooper, MBE, President of **The Harwich Society**. It remained her home for nearly 50 years and is now the Society headquarters.

* A signpost at **Upminster Tithe Barn Museum of Nostalgia** (now in the London Borough of Havering) is believed to be the only one of its kind in Essex. The post, known originally as a 'fingerpost', was made at the Wedlake ironworks at **Hornchurch** in the late 19th century. It once stood at the junction of Beredens Lane and Warley Road, **Great Warley**, and was saved from the scrap heap in 1977.

* Original halo (or annulus) signpost finials are becoming ever rarer, but there is one at **Herongate** on the A128 at the junction of the Brentwood, Tilbury and Billericay roads. The text reads 'Essex County Council' and it was made at the **Maldon Iron Works** in the 1920s. There is a similar one at **Felsted**, which carries the name of the parish and 'ECC' (Essex County Council).

* At **Great Warley** there is an unusual half-moon signpost on the B186 bearing the name of the parish.

* The **Great Essex Road** follows a Roman road from London to Harwich and formed part of the original **A12** (as far as Colchester). The starting point was at London's Cornhill. It became the A12 in 1922.

* There are many Roman roads in Essex but the **Via Devana** is one of the most famous: it led from Colchester to Chester. **Stane Street** led from Colchester to St Albans (Hertfordshire). Stane Street traversed **Icknield Street** (not to be confused with the Icknield Way) at **Marks Tey**.

* At 125ft (38m) below ground the **Secret Nuclear Bunker** at **Kelvedon Hatch** (Brentwood) is the biggest and deepest in Essex. It was built between 1952–53 during the Cold War and around 40,000 tons of concrete were used in its construction. It has three storeys and housed

more than 110 tons of equipment. Being only 20 miles from central London, it was designed to accommodate 600 members of the devolved government and military personnel had a nuclear war broken out. The temperature remains at a constant 60°F. Its existence was a secret even to those living in nearby villages, being hidden behind a small rural bungalow. It was decommissioned in 1992 and is now a museum.

* In 2008 **Colchester United Football Club**, known as the Us, moved to the new £14-million all-seater **Weston Homes Community Stadium** at Cuckoo Farm after 71 years at their former ground, **Layer Road**. Formed in 1937, they briefly shared Layer Road with the now defunct **Colchester Town Football Club**, who had used the ground since 1910. The new stadium had been talked about for almost 35 years but work started early in 2008 with completion in time for the start of the 2008–09 season.

   On 18 March Layer Road hosted its final midweek game under lights when the Us took on Hull City, and on 26 April there was a capacity crowd of 6,300 to witness the final match (Colchester United 0 – Stoke City 1) after around one hundred years of football at the ground. The *East Anglian Daily Times* reported it as a landmark occasion, 'a sea of colour and a cacophony of noise'. Supporters turned out in their favourite old blue and white shirts 'armed with flags and banners, and 16,000 balloons were distributed before kick-off'.

* In July 2008 an auction of all the fixtures and fittings was held at **Layer Road** and most of the 516 lots were sold, clearing the ground in preparation for its sale for housing development. The stadium clock was the subject of intense bidding and was sold for £1,600. A spokesman for the Us said that the clock was iconic to the ground 'and has been here for quite a few years. The bidding went on for ages and there was a round of applause when it finished'.

* One of the great milestones in the history of the Us occurred when they beat Don Revie's Leeds United 3–2 in the fifth round of the 1971 FA Cup.

MISCELLANY

* **Colchester United Ladies** football team won promotion to the Football Association's Women's Premier League Southern Division in 2006–07.

* 2006–07 was the Centennial Season for **Southend United FC**. The club was founded in 1906 at the Blue Boar Pub, which still stands close to the Blues' current ground at Roots Hall.

* In 2007 the **Bulmer Brick and Tile Company** supplied nearly 28,000 bricks for the £5.8-billion restoration project at St Pancras Station, London. The bricks were used in the refurbishment of the station's famous arches and are made from the same type of specially washed clay that was used in the original Victorian architecture. The Gothic revival arches are a dominant feature of the station's design and, because the original bricklayers had shaped their own bricks to fit, the replacement bricks had to be specially made.

    There has been a brickyard at the current site occupied by the Bulmer Brick Company since the mid-15th century. The original bricks for the building of St Pancras 150 years ago were also sourced from a brick yard in **Bulmer** not far from the present one.

* During the 18th and 19th century the word 'swank' was peculiar to the inns and drinking holes of **Bocking** and referred to the dregs at the bottom of the tankard, pot or cup. According to the precise quantity it was called either a large or a little swank.

* The cinema at **Harwich** was the first purpose-built cinema (1911) in the country. It closed in 1956 but was reopened in 1981 having been restored by the **Harwich Electric Palace Trust**.

* **Burnham on Crouch** was one of the first towns in England to have a cinema. The Electric Kinema was opened in 1910 in an old public hall. In 1930, however, a rival establishment opened, the purpose-built Princes Cinema, and shortly afterwards the Electric Kinema was demolished. A special feature of the Princes Cinema was that in the 1930s no one was sure that the 'movies' would take off, so a stage was incorporated into the

design, just in case! The Princes was renamed the Rio in the 1960s and continues to this day.

* The 14th-century Green Man public house in **Howe Street** (Great Waltham) claims to be the oldest pub in Essex and still has an old step once used for mounting a horse. One strange tale associated with the Green Man is that in December 1877 William Goren stayed at the Green Man, but during the night sleepwalked onto a glass roof. He fell through it and died soon afterwards.

* The anchovy paste **Patum Peperium** (also known as Gentleman's Relish) is made at **Elsenham**. It was created in 1828 by John Osborn. Mention of the paste is made in Nancy Mitford's novel *Love in a Cold Climate* (1949) when Linda Radlett asks for Gentleman's Relish but is told that it is kept strictly for Uncle Matthew, and is not supposed to be good for children.

* Saint FM 94.7 independent radio station is the largest community radio station in the country. It covers the **Maldon** district and **Colchester** and reaches parts of Kent and Holland. Saint FM has around 100 volunteers and is based at **Burnham on Crouch**.

* Frinton claims to be the last town in England to be attacked by the Luftwaffe at the end of World War Two.

* The motto on the **Chelmsford** District Council armorial bearings is *Many Minds One Heart*.

* The villagers of **Good Easter** hold the world record for the longest daisy chain, made on 27 May 1985. It measured 6,980ft 7in (2.12km).

* The National Federation of Young Farmers Clubs consists of 659 clubs and 48 local federations in England and Wales, 10 of which are based in Essex.

* **Steeple Bumpstead** was one of the first villages to have its own policeman. William Rattigan was appointed the village policeman in

1840 and was the first such appointment after county policing was introduced into Essex.

* The Manor House at **Little Chesterford** is the earliest surviving domestic building in Essex. It was built of stone in around 1200 and in 1320 a timber-framed aisled hall was added. It is believed to be the longest inhabited private house in Essex and Pevsner calls it 'that rare survival, an early 13th-century manor house'.

* The Victorian **railway viaduct** at **Chappel** crosses the Colne valley and it is estimated that between five and six million bricks were used in its construction. The piers were left hollow to save money and reduce the weight. The 32 arches have a span of 30ft and a maximum height of over 75ft. It is half a mile long and 600 men worked on its construction. One of its most unusual features is that it is on a gradient and the Sudbury end is 9ft 6in higher than the **Marks Tey** end. The first passenger train crossed it on 2 July 1849 and it is still in use today. After Battersea Power Station it is the largest brick-built structure in England.

* **Chappel** is so called because it was originally a chapelry of **Great Tey**, but became a parish in 1533. It was originally called Pontisbright.

* The *Essex Chronicle* was founded in 1724 and cost 2½ old pence a copy.

* The eastern half of Essex has one of the lowest rainfalls in Britain. Tendring District, and **St Osyth** in particular, is the driest place in Britain (with rainfall averaging less than 20 inches a year). The low rainfall is given as one of the reasons why the Essex County Cricket Club sited their ground in **Chelmsford**.

* The **Bardfield Cage** on Bridge Street **Great Bardfield** is a 19th-century lock-up and can still be seen (at certain times of the year). It was used to house those disturbing the peace, by whatever means. The lock-up would have had an attendant employed to feed and look after the needs of prisoners while they were incarcerated.

- The **Bank of England's print works** opened at **Debden** (near **Chigwell**) in February 1956 to print banknotes and at one time employed over 2,000 people. Its contract ended in 2002 and it was taken over by the De La Rue Company. Debden is a suburb of **Loughton** built by London County Council between 1947 and 1952 to house Londoners whose homes were destroyed in World War Two.

- **Chelmsford Prison** was the location for 'HM Slade Prison' in the BBC television series *Porridge* starring Ronnie Barker.

- **Southend** is the biggest town in Essex with an urban area population of 325,000.

- **Bobbingworth** is also known as **Bovinger** and, although the two names are interchangeable, they are shown on maps as separate places. Norman Scarfe says Bobbingworth 'is usually called Bovinger' and Arthur Mee writes 'thus [Bobbingworth] is written on the map, but Bovinger it appears on the peace memorial, and thus its people speak of it'.

- During World War One, nut shells were needed to make the 'charcoal' for the poison gas masks and respirators. No fewer than eight tons of chestnuts were collected by the school children of **Colchester** in the town and neighbourhood.

- In June 1917 a new siren was installed at the Borough Electricity Station in **Colchester**. It was called a 'Bellona' and sounded the alarm when an air raid was imminent and then sounded 'Danger past' when the hostile craft had gone. The siren had to be sounded every day at a fixed time to make sure it was working properly and it was quickly nicknamed Dora (Defence of the Realm Act).

- On 22 June 1948 the **SS *Empire Windrush*** docked at **Tilbury**, having sailed from Jamaica carrying servicemen and women returning from the Caribbean at the end of World War Two. On board were also around 600 immigrants, the first to take advantage of a subsidised berth on offer from the British Government. Anyone who could pay the fare of £28 was considered and no papers or visas were needed, since most people living in the Caribbean at that time had British passports. Many came from the West Indies and intended to come to England for a few years only, but most of them stayed to become part of the first generation of multicultural Britain.

※ In 2008, after 75 years of greyhound racing, the **Walthamstow Stadium** closed its gates for the last time on 16 August when the last-ever race was run. Known as the Stow (or Stowaway), the stadium has been called 'the Art Deco jewel in northeast London's dowdy crown'. The aviator, Amy Johnson (1904–1941), attended the opening night as Guest of Honour, having just completed the fastest-ever solo flight from England to Cape Town, South Africa (1932).

※ The **Walthamstow Dog Track** was used as one of the locations for the film *Snatch* (2000), by writer-director Guy Ritchie. It was set in London's criminal underworld and starred Brad Pitt as the 'pikey' Irish traveller, Mickey O'Neill.

※ International footballer **David Beckham** had his first job at the Walthamstow Dog Track as a teenager, collecting glasses from the restaurant. David Beckham was born in **Leytonstone** and as a boy played regularly in Ridgeway Park, **Chingford**.

※ In a survey carried out by BBC Radio 4's *More or Less* programme in 2008, **Manningtree** emerged as having one of the largest ratios of pubs-per-resident in the country (1 pub for every 180 residents). **Chelmsford**, a similar survey concluded, had one pub for every 385 people. Both are in the top 25 of pubs-per-resident charts!

※ **Fyfield** Hall contains oak roof timbers that were felled in 1167–85. It is believed to be the oldest continually inhabited timber-framed house in Britain.

※ **Crittall Windows** is one of Essex's most famous companies and was responsible for the creation of an entire self-contained village and works.

An ironmonger's son, Francis Berrington Crittall (died 1878) started the business in **Braintree** in 1849, which was carried on by his son, Francis Henry Crittall. Francis Berrington began experimenting with a light metal window frame after his mother injured herself trying to open a heavy wooden window and in 1884 the company began the manufacture of the first metal frames. They were first used at the Public Record Office and then in the Houses of Parliament. The business took off when, on a visit to India, he discovered a new market for the frames, which did not expand in tropical heat and were not destroyed by white ants.

The third generation to run the company was **Valentine George Crittall** (1884–1961), born in Braintree and created **Baron Braintree** in 1948. He was elected Member of Parliament for the **Maldon** Division in 1923 and in 1924 was Private Secretary to the Minister for Air.

During World War One, Crittall was turned over to munitions production. When the war ended the company produced a standard metal window for a governmental post-war housing scheme. During World War Two they again turned to munitions production.

* In 1925 the Crittalls acquired **Boars Tye Farm** and the following year the **Silver End Model Village** project was started. Between 1926 and 1932, over 470 houses were built together with shops, a village hall, a hotel, two churches, a school and a factory employing disabled ex-servicemen. It remains a typical example of the Modern movement of architecture; flat-roofed with metal windows and painted white. Pevsner thought it to be one of the earliest instances in England of Modernism. The exponents of the movement sought to break all stylistic and historic links with the past, seeking a style that reflected the post-war mood. The use of metal windows was an integral part of the modernistic rejection of all ornamental and historical allusion.

* The factory village at **East Tilbury** was built by the **Bata Shoe Company** in similar mode to Silver End. The company was founded in 1894 by Czechoslovakian shoemaker Thomas Bata. Work on the village began in 1932 and was based on the company's houses in Czechoslovakia. Rousing marching music was played to arriving and departing employees and

strict timekeeping was rigidly enforced. Thomas Bata's philosophy was 'work collectively, live individually'. The Czechoslovak Modernist architect Vladimir Karfik (1901–85) was involved in realising the ideal of the 'Garden City' principle and was the first to build pre-fabricated buildings outside his native country.

❋ Great Leighs – Sporting History
When the **Great Leighs Racecourse** opened for business in April 2008 it was the first racecourse in Essex since the **Galleywood Racecourse** closed in 1935. It was also the first new British racecourse for 81 years. Although the course was only partially completed, sporting history was made at 1.14pm on 20 April when the first-ever race was run at Great Leighs.

The track is on a 430-acre site, formerly the **Essex Showground**, and its launch was originally planned for 2006. However, less than nine months after it opened the racecourse went into administration. The British Horseracing Authority rejected a renewal of its temporary licence and it remains to be seen what happens to Essex's latest sporting venture.

- ❋ The earliest reference to **Galleywood Racecourse**, which closed in 1935, dates from 1770 when George III granted the 'Queens' Plate' to the track's main event.

- ❋ The **Galleywood** was the only racecourse in the country to go around a church, that of St Michael and All Angels. The racecourse was there first, however, the church being built in 1873 by a wealthy brewer, Arthur Pryor (1816–1904) of **Writtle**. Before 1874 the ecclesiastical parish of **Galleywood Common** was part of **Great Baddow**, **West Hanningfield** and **Moulsham Hamlet**. Some of the railings from the old racecourse can still be seen on the common.

- ❋ At **Tolleshunt D'Arcy** can be seen one of the few remaining original maypoles in the country. It is topped by an ornate weather-vane. Maypoles are used in the traditional celebration of May Day (1 May), which heralded the arrival of summer.

✳ During the Commonwealth Government (1649–1660) the Puritans banned maypoles, considering them the 'last remnants of vile heathenism round which people in holiday times used to dance, quite ignorant of its original intent'. At the Restoration a 134ft high maypole was erected in celebration beside the church of St Mary-le-Strand, where it stood for 50 years until Sir Isaac Newton (1642–1727) bought it and removed it to **Wanstead**. There it was given to the Revd James Pound, Rector of Wanstead and an enthusiastic astronomer. The Royal Society lent him a telescope (then the largest in the world) and Sir Isaac Newton provided him with the maypole on which to mount it. A rhyme was written in honour of the maypole, beginning

Once I adorned the Strand
But now I have found
My way to Pound
On Baron Newton's Land.

✳ The **Meridian Line** crosses Sun Street **Waltham Abbey** (in front of the Meridian Coffee Shop), where two plaques are set into the pavement. It then passes on into the ancient Abbey grounds, where it is marked by the Meridian Gateway.

✳ **Ice houses** were introduced from France in the 17th century and were used on country estates to store food and ice until the invention of refrigerators. They were shaped like igloos, with domed roofs, and were invariably approached via a short tunnel. Inside ice was tightly packed to make them as airtight as possible. Ice houses were useful for preserving food, but the ice itself was also used in the summer for drinks and at dinner parties. An ice house once stood at Stubbers Adventure Centre **Upminster** and, although it has now gone, the site is identified. Another stood at The Hyde **Ingatestone**, but was demolished in 1965, and another at Black Hall Gardens, **Bobbingworth**. At **Great Braxted** the Du Cane family had one built with no entrance tunnel and only a round hole for access. Peter Du Cane is said to have offered £100 to anyone on the estate who would live in the ice house for a year without shaving or washing, but with food, drink and tobacco provided. One man took the bet and won his £100 and ever afterwards the ice house was known as the Hermit's Cave.

❋ Founded in 1893 by Essex County Council, **Writtle College** moved to its present site in 1940 and is one of the oldest red-brick colleges in the United Kingdom. Pevsner describes it as 'mildly Neo-Georgian'. Known formerly as Writtle Agricultural College and before that the Essex Institute of Agriculture, Writtle College is now affiliated to the **University of Essex**.

❋ In 2008 **Writtle College** won Silver at the Chelsea Flower Show with the slogan 'Driest county – floral bounty' (a reference to Essex being one of the driest counties in England).

❋ Arthur Mee recorded that **Writtle** has two greens and on St John's Green 'the dwellers in olden days paid a tax known as **Green Silver**, a halfpenny a year for the privilege of looking out on the green'.

❋ The ancient oak at **Great Yeldham** is the oldest tree in Essex. The Yeldham Oak, although now dead, is thought to have been on the small green for over 1,000 years. Due to its great age the tree, over 30ft in circumference, is encased in iron bands to support it. A younger replacement oak also stands on the green, planted by the Parish Council in 1863.

❋ One of the best known TV chefs, **Jamie Oliver** grew up in **Clavering** where his parents Trevor and Sally Oliver run the Cricketers public house. Trevor trained at the **Southend Catering College** and then worked in London and Switzerland before returning to Essex and managing the Prince of Wales at **South Ockendon**. The couple came to Clavering in 1976.

❋ **BBC Radio Essex** was launched on Bonfire Night 1986 and was formally opened by Marchesa Maria Marconi (widow of Guglielmo Marconi) six days later, on 11 November. It covers a population of 1.5 million and broadcasts from studios in **Chelmsford** with offices at **Colchester**, **Southend** and **Thurrock**.

* For the past 23 years, the **Essex Country Show** has been held in September at Barleylands, **Billericay**. Attractions include vintage steam engines, working heavy horses, a craft marquee, the Sheep Show, vintage cars, 50 rural demonstrations and over 150 trade stands.

* The **Guild of Essex Craftsmen** is a voluntary non-profit making organisation founded in 1964 to promote and support local handmade crafts.

* **William Penn** (1644–1718), founder and Absolute Proprietor of the Province of Pennsylvania in the English North American Colony (later the United States of America), was educated at **Chigwell School**. William Penn became a Quaker (the Religious Society of Friends) in 1667 and in 1681 obtained a grant of land in America in settlement of a debt owed by Charles II to his father, Admiral Sir William Penn of **Walthamstow**. There he established the Colony of Pennsylvania as a refuge for persecuted Quakers and other Nonconformists, calling it a 'holy experiment'. One of the school's four day houses is named Penn.

* In 1965 **Canvey Island** was chosen to be the first place in the country where all the domestic gas appliances were converted to use natural gas.

* Gunpowder was produced in the **Waltham Abbey** area from at least the 17th century. First mention of it appears in a contract listed in the Calendar of State Papers, which includes correspondence dated 1561 between Marc Antonio Erizzo and John Tamworth of Waltham Abbey, who bought saltpetre and sulphur. In 1662 Thomas Fuller, curate at Waltham Abbey, complained that 'the mills in my parish have blown up five times in seven years but blessed be God, without loss of any man's life'.

    The 'powdermills', as they were known locally, were acquired by the Crown in 1787. Today the **Royal Gunpowder Mills** are open to the public and have re-enactment days relating to mediaeval sieges and the battles of the Civil War.

* The last remaining Royal Gunpowder magazine of its type in the world can be seen at **Purfleet Heritage and Military Centre**.

* The first self-service Tesco supermarket was opened in Essex in an old cinema at **Maldon** in 1956.

* **Colchester Zoo** was started in 1963 and can now claim to be one of Europe's finest zoos. It has over 260 species including elephants, giraffes, tigers and free-flying birds of prey, plus a number of species that are part of a European Endangered Species Breeding Programme. The Patagonian sea lion pool has a 24m underwater viewing tunnel. Colchester Zoo won the East Anglian Tourist Board large visitor attraction in 2006.

* **Epping Forest** is the remnant of the once vast **Forest of Essex**. It covers 6,000 acres spread over a 10-mile crescent stretching from Forest Gate in the south to **Epping** in the north. Its future was secured by the Epping Forest Act (1878) when it was dedicated to the 'use and enjoyment of the people' by Queen Victoria. The Green Ride (**Chingford** to Epping) was created for Queen Victoria's 'triumphal drive' at the opening ceremony in 1882.

* Under the New Town Act of 1946, eight New Towns were created for south-east England. Two of them were **Basildon** and **Harlow**. The need for extra housing came about mainly due to the destruction of much of London during World War Two. The idea was to create self-contained towns in 'congenial surroundings'.

* The name **Basildon** was taken from the Saxon 'Beorhtels Hill', which was the original name of the village at the heart of the development. The Advisory Committee of Greater London Planning was set up in 1949 and plans were drawn up for the new town to accommodate around 50,000

people and include the already well-established urban districts of **Billericay** and **Thurrock** and the parishes of **Laindon**, **Basildon**, **Vange**, **Pitsea** and parts of **Nevendon** and **Wickford**. Basildon was the largest of the eight towns of 7,800 acres.

❋ In 1966 the cosmetic manufacturer **Yardley of London** relocated to **Basildon** from its home of 60 years in East London. Yardley was founded in 1770 by William Yardley, who sold swords, spurs and buckles to the aristocracy. He took over a failing lavender soap business after his son-in-law went bankrupt and turned it into an international cosmetics company.

❋ Two famous ex-Yardley employees are **Dave Gahan** (lead vocalist for the group Depeche Mode) and **Alison Moyet**, who embarked on a solo singing career in 1984.

❋ **Harlow New Town** was, in the 1940s, a rural area and, unlike Basildon, did not contain any existing urban districts or large parishes. Among the smaller parishes incorporated were **Latton**, **Netteswell** and the **Parndons**. The old church of St Mary and St Hugh in Churchgate Street is of great antiquity, its flint walls interspersed with Roman tiles. It was known in the 18th century as St Mary and All Saints' and in the 19th century as St Hugh's.

❋ There were once 32 public houses in **Harlow New Town**, many of them with the names of butterflies and moths including Drinking Moth, Essex Skipper, Purple Emperor, Small Copper, White Admiral and Painted Lady (now called the Jean Harlow).

❋ The **Ford Motor Company** arrived in **Dagenham** in 1929 and the factory opened two years later. Although car production ceased there in 2002, Ford of Dagenham employed many thousands of people over the years. One of Ford's most popular cars, the Cortina, was manufactured at Dagenham. The plant now designs and builds Ford diesel engines. The **Ford Tractor Plant** was opened at **Basildon** in 1964.

MISCELLANY

* The **New Hall Vineyards** of **Purleigh** is one of the oldest and largest English wine producers in England. Established in 1969 by the Greenwood family the site has proved ideal for a vineyard. The vines are planted between 12m and 24m above sea level and produce an above-average crop, usually providing in excess of 250,000 bottles of wine each year.

* There are five other vineyards in Essex at **Great Bardfield** (Bardfield Vineyard), **Boxted** (Carter's and Nevards and Coggeshall Vineyards), **East Mersea** (Mersea Vineyard) and **Great Sampford** (Sandyford Vineyard).

* In 2008, **Sandyford Vineyard** at **Great Sampford** had two of its wines selected by Tesco's local sourcing schemes – the Sandyford Clover Hill white (which won the East Anglian Wine Growers' Association wine of the year in 2005) and Special Reserve Red.

* The **British Vitamin Products Company** was founded in **Chelmsford** in the 19th century but changed its name to **Britvic** in 1971. It began producing fruit juices in 1938 and is now one of the leading soft drinks companies in Great Britain and the Republic of Ireland.

* On 1 April 1839 the newly erected but not completely finished **Hythe Bridge** (Colchester) fell into the River Colne. When the Mayor was told he thought it was a joke, declaring 'It's April the first!' However, it was true and the townspeople were not best pleased that £1,000 had been spent on the collapsed bridge.

* Essex has one of the highest numbers of recorded moated sites of any county. A report compiled in 1978 by the Moated Sites Research Group showed that of a total of 5,307 sites in Britain, 548 were in Essex. Some of them were constructed as long ago as the 13th and 14th centuries and were dug for a variety of reasons, including drainage (where a house was built on raised land), defence, or as part of a water source or fishpond. One of the earliest surrounded the palace built by King John at **Writtle** in 1211. Those constructed during the Tudor period were usually status symbols.

- One of those who survived the wreck of the *Sea Venture* off Bermuda in 1609 (see Chapter Three, Coastal Essex) was **John Rolfe** (1585–1622). Although Rolfe lost his wife and child, he survived to accompany **Captain Christopher Newport** to America, taking with him a Bermudan variety of 'sweet scented' tobacco seeds. He cultivated them in Virginia to such good effect that it was the economic saviour of the ailing Jamestown, providing tobacco as a successful cash crop. Ironically, James I (after whom the settlement was named) loathed the use of tobacco in any form and even published an anonymous pamphlet in 1604, in which he warned that smoking was 'loathsome to the eye, hateful to the nose, harmful to the brain, dangerous to the lungs'.

- In another quirk of fate, tobacco growing became popular in Essex during the 1660s until shareholders in the Virginian plantations managed to get its cultivation in England prohibited.

- John Rolfe is, perhaps, better remembered as the husband of **Princess Pocahontas** (1595–1617) a native American princess, whose father was Chief of the tribes of the Tidewater region of Virginia. She is reputed to have died on the north shore of the Thames, in Essex (buried in Kent).

- In 1916 an airfield was established at **Stow Maries** to counter the air attacks from German Zeppelins. It was used by the Royal Flying Corps (which amalgamated with the Royal Naval Air Service in 1918 to form the Royal Air Force). When the war ended in 1918 there were around 219 personnel and 16 aircraft at Stow Maries. However, after it was closed that same year some of the buildings, still incomplete, were never finished and the site was returned to agriculture.

    Although it was not recommissioned during World War Two, Stow Maries nonetheless became a target for the Luftwaffe. On one occasion in 1940 it was used as an emergency landing runway for a damaged 242 Squadron Hurricane fighter plane.

    Stow Maries Airfield is remembered on the village sign and a red cross on the steeple of St Mary and St Margaret's parish church is dedicated to the pilots, some of whom are buried in the churchyard.

MISCELLANY

* In the 1950s and 1960s flights to the Channel Islands were operated out of **Southend Airport** by **Channel Airways** (1946–1972), founded by Squadron Leader Reginald John 'Jack' Jones. One of 748 Viscounts that flew out of Southend is on permanent exhibition at the Imperial War Museum in Duxford.

* **London Southend Airport** still has flights to Jersey during May to September, operated by the Flybe service.

* During the 1950s **Aquila Airways** operated commercial seaplane flights out of **Harwich** using Sunderland flying boats. They had routes which included Madeira and Las Palmas, but ceased trading in 1958.

* Aviation history at **Stansted Mountfichet** goes back to World War Two when a runway was built for bombers by the United States Army Air Force (USAAF). The airfield took its name from the nearby village, but in a very short time it was shortened to 'Stansted'. American engineers arrived in July 1942 to mark out the area and begin construction: the area was eventually to cover almost 3,000 acres, making it the largest Ninth Air Force base in East Anglia and turning it almost overnight into an American 'township'.

   By the end of World War Two, Essex had 23 operational military airfields and all but three – **Debden**, **Hornchurch** and **North Weald** – were built after 1939.

* In 1947 Stansted was decommissioned and handed over to the Air Ministry. Civil aviation began and the first-ever summer charter flights commenced. Almost 20 years later the newly-created British Aviation Authority (BAA) took control of the airport. A new terminal was built in 1969 and Stansted grew steadily to become London's third busiest international airport, with around 22 million passengers passing through annually. Future expansion of the airport is highly controversial as BAA seeks to raise the passenger cap to 35 million, the cap on flights to 264,000 and gain permission for a second runway.

❋ Between 1985 and 1991 the current **Terminal Building** at Stansted was built. It cost £400 million and was designed by **Norman Foster** (born 1935, now Lord Foster of Thames Bank) of Foster Associates and opened by HM the Queen in March 1991. The huge skylight, which lets in natural light, was a radical step forward in airport design. It features a 'floating' roof, supported by a space frame of inverted pyramid-shaped trusses.

❋ Under the Long Term car park at **Stansted Airport** lies a very rich Roman burial and beneath the main runway are the remains of a Late Iron Age settlement.

❋ On 31 March 2009 the newly-elected President of the United States **Barack Obama** and his wife Michelle arrived at **Stansted Airport** on Air Force One to attend the G20 Summit in Dockland's ExCel Centre, East London. They were flown from Stansted by helicopter to the US ambassador's London residence. The following day Essex TV chef **Jamie Oliver** and a team of former apprentice chefs from *Fifteen London* cooked a 'Best of British' meal for the Downing Street Dinner attended by leaders of the G20 group of nations. Some of the wild mushrooms used in the menu were foraged from woodlands around England, including **Epping Forest**.

BIBLIOGRAPHY

Barnes, Alison *Essex Eccentrics* (1975)
Cox, J. Charles *The Little Guides: Essex* (1952)
Domesday Book: A Survey of the Counties of England compiled by direction of King William I (Editor John Morris) (1983)
Hough, John *Essex Churches* (1983)
Hunter, John *The Essex Landscape* (1999)
Johnson, Derek *Essex Curiosities* (1973)
Manning, S.A. *Portrait of Essex* (1977)
Mee, Arthur *The King's England: Essex* (1942)
Pusey, Richard *Essex, Rich and Strange* (1987)
Scarfe, Norman *Essex: A Shell Guide* (1968)
Sealey, Paul R. *The Boudiccan Revolt Against Rome* (1997)
Simper, Robert *The Barge Coast of Suffolk, Essex and Kent* (2007)
Smedley, Norman *Life and Tradition in Suffolk and North-East Essex* (1976)
Yearsley, Ian *Islands of Essex* (2000)

Also works by **Hervey Benham**, **Samuel Bensusan**, **C. Henry Warren** and **Thomas Wright**